G U I D E B O O K

TOURING KYIV

GUIDEBOOK

BALTIJA DRYK

KYIV 2003

ISBN 966-96041-7-6

Publisher **"Baltija Dryk"**
Chief Editor **Ruta Malikenaite**
Authors and Draftsmen **Virginijus Strolia,**
Mikhail Kal'nitskiy

Text Authors **Mikhail Kal'nitskiy**
(culture-historical part)
Alisa Grigoruk (practical part)
Editor **Alisa Grigoruk**
Art edition **Elena Zheleznyak,**
Julia Mitchenko, Vitaliy Mitchenko
Design and makeup **Stanislav Stefanovich**
Director of Advertisment: **Dmitriy Belokon**
Photographer **Victor Khmara**
Axonometric **Alexander Sedak**
Reviewer **Dmitriy Malakov**
(culture-historical part)

Translation to English and German
Dmitriy Pugach
The Cards on the flyleaves
GNPP "Kartografiya"

There have been used illustrated materials of the
state archives funds: Kyiv, Pshenichny ZGA KFFD,
RGIA (St.Petersburg), the Methodic Fund NIITIAG.
The Collections: **M.Kal'nitskiy,**
Yu.Mosenzhnik, M.Rybakov
The publishers extend special acknowledgments
to **Dmitriy Vortman** for the important consulta-
tions during the work on the book.

© 2002 "Baltija Dryk", Kyiv
The certificate of the inclusion of the publishers,
producers and dealers to the State
Publisher Register: Series DK, # 643 of
10.23.2001, issuer by Ukraine State
Committee of the Information Policy,
Television and Broadcasting.
51/2, A.Barbus St., Kyiv, Ukraine, 03150
Phone / Fax: +380 44 5021047
e-mail: baltija@ukr.net

© Guidebook "Touring Kyiv" ™

The Advertiser is responsible for the
advertising materials.
The Editors did their best to include in the Guidebook the most correct data for June 2003, but with
time the phone numbers, prices, working hours
and so on may change.

TABLE OF CONTENTS

- *safety and health*
- *post and telephone*
- *money*
- *to Kyiv by car*
- *traveling by air*

- *to Kyiv by bus*
- *to Kyiv by train*
- *city transport*
- *drinks*
- *national cuisine*

- *in the open air*
- *in Pirogovo*

- *along the Dnieper*
- *Hydropark*
- *at night*
- *cinema*
- *to the theatre*
- *theatre for children*

- *circus*
- *zoo*

We are pleased to present to you the capital of Ukraine - Kyiv.

The world has other cities that are older, bigger, richer, smarter and more comfortable. But Kyiv is beautiful and unique in its own way. The city's natural landscape with the boundless expanses of the Dnieper is in itself remarkably picturesque. The architectural ambience of the city has been built up over fifteen centuries of construction. Set amidst the natural landscape, the city's architectural masterpieces create a unique impression. Many historic monuments are preserved in Kyiv. These memorials remind us of the outstanding Kyivans who made their city famous throughout all the continents.

Kyiv's location was preordained by nature itself for a unique settlement. The city arose on the frontier between the forest and forest-steppe zones, in a place where trade between tribes was lively. The city is situated on the river Dnieper - one of the most important navigation arteries in Europe, part of the ancient trade route "from the Varangians to the Greeks." It is also the place where the Desna flows into the Dnieper. The landscape consists of a series of elevations intersected by streams and ravines, which create secure natural fortifications.

The legend about the founding of Kyiv tells: "And there were three brothers: one known as Kiy, the second - Scheck, and the third - Khoriv; and their sister was Lybid. Kiy settled on the mountain that is now the

The founders of Kyiv according to the chronicles: Kiy, Shchek, Khoriv and their sister Lybid. Sculptors A.Kushch and others

Borichev Slope; Scheck settled on the mountain now known as Shchekavitsa; and Khoriv lived on the mountain now known as Khorevitsa. They built a town, and they called it Kyiv after the oldest brother. The forest round the town was big and there were a lot of animals. Those men were wise and clever, and their people were called the Polians." This is the starting point of the history of the city on the Dnieper-Slavutych - the acknowledged spiritual centre of Rus, Ukraine and the eastern Slavs.

Unfortunately, Kyiv's virtues constantly attracted the predatory attention of invaders. It is difficult to name any other European capital that has been conquered and destroyed so often. But after every defeat, Kyiv rose even more beautiful - like a Phoenix from the ashes.

Today Kyiv is the capital of Ukraine, a sovereign state belonging to the UN and the Council of Europe. Kyiv has a population of more then 2.6 million people. It occupies an area of 827 square kilometres. Every day Kyiv receives numerous visitors, eager to see its shrines and architectural ensembles, museums and parks, theatres and stadiums. Whether the chestnuts are in bloom or the lindens are fragrant, whether the trees are painted in autumn colours or snow covers the roofs and hills - the city on the Dnieper is always beautiful and ready to greet you hospitably.

Kyiv in Spring

"THE MOTHER OF RUSSIAN CITIES"

People were living on the territory of present-day Kyiv as far back as the late Paleolithic epoch, 20 thousand years ago. In the ensuing centuries, in the times of so-called Tripolye Culture, in the Scythian period, and during the great movement of peoples, a whole series of settlements appeared on the ridge of hills above the Dnieper. At the turn of the 6th century, these formed the city. Kiy and his successors ruled here until the 9th century. But in 882 the Varangian Prince Oleg arrived from Novgorod, occupied the city, and made it the centre of a large state joining the Kyiv and Novgorod lands. At first the Kyivans were polytheistic and worshipped idols. The wooden statues of the pagan temples rose

Kirilovskaya site

over peasant's houses (the first stone houses appeared only in the middle of the 10th century). But the influence of Christianity grew as a result of regular contacts with the Byzantium Empire. From the chronicles we learn that Saint Elijah's Church existed as far back as 944.

KIRILOVSKAYA SITE

The Kirilovskaya site is the oldest known site of settlement on the territory of Kyiv. Vikentiy Khvoyka, an architect, discovered it in 1893. He carried out excavations in the area of Kirilovskaya St. (now 59-61, Frunze St.). A cultural stratum was discovered at the bottom of a hill, at a depth of 20 meters. It consisted of the remains of wooden dwellings, mammoth bones and stone tools. People were living there between 20,000 and 15,000 B.C. They lived by hunting mammoths, which they chased and drove over the edge of a cliff. Ancient and intricate

V.Khvoyka

Mammoth tusks, Kirilovskaya site

decoration is visible on some of the tusks. There would probably have been many more valuable finds, but the local residents pillaged the excavation. They thought that the carved mammoth bones could cure fever.

"FROM THE VARANGIANS TO THE GREEKS"

Around the turn of the 10th century, a transport and commercial route was formed along the rivers and lakes of Eastern Europe, linking the lands of the Varangians (Scandinavians) and the Greeks (Byzantium). It passed along the Neva, Volkhov, Dvina and Dnieper rivers. It was sometimes necessary to drag the

ships overland from river to river. Kyiv was one of the most important points on the route "from the Varangians to the Greeks."

PROPHETIC OLEG

The Scandinavian commander Oleg (Helgi) was a confidante of the Varangian Prince Rurik, the ruler of Novgorod. After Rurik died leaving an infant son Igor, Oleg became regent and assumed supreme power for life. In 882, he gained control over Kyiv after killing the local rulers Askold and Dir (see 81). His words about Kyiv became proverbial: "Here will be the mother of Rus cities." The chronicles tell the legend of the prince's death, which later

A postage stamp commemorating the 100th anniversary of the discovery of the Tripoliye Culture

CHRONICLE

15,000 - 20,000 B.C. - Kirilovskaya Paleolithic Site.

Approx. 3000 B.C. - Ancient settlement at Kudriavets - a site from the epoch of the Tripoliye culture; this is the oldest known fortification on the territory of Kyiv.

Approx. 500 B.C. - Khotov Scythian settlement near Kyiv; this was the most northerly Scythian settlement.

2nd cent. B.C. - 1st cent. A.D. - Memorials of the Zarubnetsk Ante-Slavonian culture.

482 A.D. - Conventional date of the founding of Kyiv by the Polianian Prince Kiy.

provided the basis for A.Pushkin's ballad "The Song of Prophetic Oleg." Oleg was warned in a prophecy that his death would come from his favourite horse. The prince decided never to ride him again. Eventually the horse died. When Oleg was shown the remains of the horse, he laughed at the prophecy and put his foot on the horse's skull. A snake emerged from the skull and bit Oleg, killing him. He was buried on the Shchekavitsa Hill (see 62).

Illustration to A.Pushkin's ballad "The Song of Prophetic Oleg".
V.Vasnetsov

"KYIV LETTER"

Discovered in an ancient synagogue in Egypt, this letter is now kept at Cambridge University. It is written on parchment in Hebrew. In it the Jewish community of Kyiv ask their fellow Jews for help in the case of Jacob Ben Hanukke. Jacob had acted as guarantor for his brother when he borrowed money from a gentile. When the brother was robbed and killed, his creditors seized Jacob. The community paid part of the debt. Jacob had to pay the rest with money collected from other benefactors.

The Kyiv Letter is the oldest known document that mentions Kyiv. It is evidence of the antiquity of the city's Jewish community, which appeared at the time when

The Kyiv Letter

the Kyiv lands bordered on the Khazar kingdom, which adopted Judaism as its state religion (9th-10th cent.).

PRINCESS OLGA'S REVENGE ON THE DREVLIANIANS

The tribe of Drevlianians (who inhabited the forests north-west of Kyiv) killed Prince Igor Rurikovich when he came to them asking double the usual tribute. The naive Drevlianians decided to offer their prince as a husband for Igor's widow Olga. The chronicles tell how the fierce Olga took revenge. She had one embassy buried alive. She burnt another in a bathhouse. Finally, she laid siege to Iskorosten, the Drevlianians' capital. After a long siege, she finally agreed to accept a symbolic tribute: three pigeons and three sparrows from each yard. When she was given what she asked for, she ordered her men to tie smouldering ropes to the birds and release them. The birds returned to their yards, and the

wooden city caught fire. Later Princess Olga visited Tsargrad (Byzantium) and was christened there. Her grandson, Vladimir Sviatoslavovich, converted Russ to Christianity. Both Olga and Vladimir were canonized.

A YOUTH WITH A BRIDLE

In the year 968, while Prince Sviatoslav was off on a military campaign with his troops, a tribe of warlike Pechenegs besieged Kyiv. The Pechenegs surrounded the city preventing anyone from escaping to call in reinforcements. But one boy found a way to communicate with the prince's forces. He took a bridle, sneaked up to the enemy ranks and asked in the Pecheneg language: "Has anybody seen my horse?" The resourceful youth was allowed through. When he came to the river, he rushed into the water and eventually reached his people. The Pechenegs were soon repelled.

"I AM COMING AGAINST YOU"

Olga's son, Kyiv Prince Sviatoslav Igorevich liked military campaigns. His contemporaries left a description of his appearance that bears a strong resemblance to the future Zaporozhye Cossacks: a long moustache, a shaven head with a single lock of hair, an earring. When planning a campaign

Princess Olga

against his neighbours, the warlike prince would send a threatening massage to them: "I am coming against you." He won victories over the Khazars, Viatiches and Danube Bulgars. But the Pechenegs killed Sviatoslav. Their chief set his skull in gold and made it into cup.

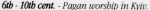

Oleg on the throne of Kyiv. Fragment from the Radzivillan chronicle

CAPITAL CITY

The choice of faith by Prince Vladimir

The flourishing of Kyiv as the capital of Kyivan Rus is linked to the names of the great princes Vladimir Sviatoslavovich and his son Yaroslav the Wise. Prince Vladimir introduced Orthodox Christianity in Rus, initiated school education, reformed the army, and established the system of vassal princedoms dependent on the Kyiv throne. Yaroslav carried out grandiose construction projects in Kyiv and created the first Legal Code ("Russian Truth"). He founded the first library, and promoted the arts and crafts. In those days, the monarchs of many European countries considered it an honour to become related to the Kyiv princes by marriage. The later rulers Vladimir Monomakh and Mstislav the Great consolidated the supremacy of Kyiv in Kyivan Rus. During their rule, the state occupied a great stretch of territory from Lake Ladoga and Lake Onega to the Black Sea, from the Carpathians to the rivers Volga, Oka and Don. The capital city, Kyiv, was a stronghold with numerous stone cathedrals and towers, and large areas of wooden dwellings. Historians estimate that the population of Kyiv was 50,000-100,000. Eventually, however, other cities grew stronger, and Rus disintegrated into separate princedoms, among which Kyiv was comparatively small. On several occasions, rival princes attacked and pillaged Kyiv (the fiercest attack was by Prince Andrey Bogolubsky of Vladimir-Suzdal). The Mongol conquest was a fatal blow for Kyiv. In 1240 Batu Khan captured the ancient city. Thousands of people died, and many holy places were destroyed. Its former greatness lost, by the 14th century Kyiv was reduced to an outlying district of the Grand Duchy of Lithuania, which annexed the Kyiv princedom to its possessions.

THE CHOICE OF FAITH BY PRINCE VLADIMIR

When Vladimir Sviatoslavovich resolved to abandon paganism for monotheism, he summoned representatives of the main monotheistic religions to his court. The prince questioned each of them about their faith. Listening to the Moslem representative, Vladimir was pleased to learn that Islam allowed polygamy (he had 800 concubines himself), but he could not accept the prohibition on alcohol and said: "In Russ drinking is enjoyment, we can not exist without it." The Jewish representative admitted that his tribe had been dispersed all over the Earth for its sins. That did not suit the prince at all. German Catholics also proposed their faith. But the exhortation of the Orthodox priest was most convincing. Vladimir's emissaries visited Constantinople, where they attended an Orthodox service in Saint Sophia's Cathedral. They told the prince: "They took us to the place where they serve their God, and we did not understand where we were - on Earth or in Heaven. Nowhere else is there such beauty!"

THE CHRISTENING OF THE KYIVANS

The Christening of Russ. Fragment. V.Vasnetsov.

Prince Vladimir carried out his decision to be christened in a peculiar way. He took his fleet to the Byzantine city of Khersones in Crimea. Threatening a long siege, he forced the city to surrender. Then he announced to the Byzantine Emperors Constantine and Basil that he had decided to be christened and that he required their sister Anna to become his wife. After he was christened in Khersones, he built a cathedral there. Then he returned to Kyiv, where he christened his 12 sons at the mouth of the Pochayna River. He cast down the old idols, and ordered all his subjects to be christened. The mass

Mongol on foot

CHRONICLE
980 - 1015 - Rule of Vladimir Sviatoslavovich.
988 - Chronicle date for the christening of the Kyivans.
1019 - 1054 - Rule of Yaroslav the Wise.
1037 - Chronicle article on the building of "the City of Yaroslav", St.Sophia Cathedral and the Golden Gate.
1051 - Foundation of Pechersk Monastery.

of people gathered on the bank of the Dnieper. N.Karamzin wrote: "Vladimir appeared there accompanied by a council of Greek priests. At his signal, a huge number of people stepped into the water. The adults stood in the river up to their chest and neck. Parents were holding their children in their arms. Priests said prayers and sang praises to the Almighty."

KYIV GRIVNAS

The modern name for the Ukrainian currency "grivna" dates back to Old Russian griv-

The Athletes. V.Vasnetsov

nas. It comes from the word "griva," which means neck. In ancient times, nobles wore gold and silver rings round their necks. Such jewellery or pieces of it served as a means of payment. Eventually, the name grivna came to be used for the kind of monetary units used in major commercial transactions. Bulky pieces of cut silver of a definite form and weight were used for this purpose. Kyiv grivnas were hexagonal

A Kyiv grivna

in form and weighed 161-164 grams. This kind of money was in use from the 11th-15th centuries.

GEORGIYEVSKY LANE, IRININSKAYA STREET

Many of the Kyiv Princes were known by two names: their Slavonic name and an orthodox one that they assumed when they were christened. Yaroslav the Wise took the name Georgiy. His wife, the Swedish Princess Ingigerda, took the Orthodox name Irina. During the construction of "the City of Yaroslav" (see 32), the stone Georgiyevskaya and Irininskaya cathedrals were built in honour of the patron saints of the prince and princess. Both buildings were destroyed during Batu Khan's conquest. A new cathedral was built in place of the Georgiyevskaya cathedral in the 18th century. In the mid-19th century, a memorial in the form of a column of old bricks was erected over the foundations of the Irininskaya cathedral. These structures were destroyed in the 1930s. Now the names of Georgievskiy Lane and Irininskaya Street, which are located in the upper city, are the only reminders of these lost structures.

HEROES OF RUSSIAN EPICS

The Bylinas were works of oral folk poetry in Rus. The plots and characters were developed over the ages. Among the favourite characters of the epic Bylinas were the Kyivan knights Il'ya

Yaroslav the Wise and Irina-Ingigerda

Muromets, Dobrynia Nikitich, Aliosha Popovich and others. We see them at the court of Prince Vladimir of Kyiv (who is given the epithet "Beautiful Sun" in the Bylinas), in battles against the enemies of Rus, in wise discussions and amusing escapades. Many of these folk characters had real prototypes. For example, the remains of Il'ya Muromets are preserved in the Near Caves at Kyiv Pechersk Lavra (see 91).

CONQUEST OF KYIV BY BATU KHAN

The siege of the Kyiv fortifications by the Mongol-Tatars lasted several weeks. An enormous army surrounded the city. According to a chronicler: "You could not hear anything because of the creak of their carts, the roar of their camels, and the neighing of their horses. And the land of Rus was filled with the enemy." Finally the horde's siege engines destroyed the fortifications near the Lyadskiy Gate (situated at the present-day Maydan Nezalezhnosti). The invaders were not able to take

Mounted Mongol

control over the whole city at once, but the walls of the old Desiatinnaya Cathedral, the Kyivans' last stronghold, fell on 6 December, 1240 (see 30).

1113 - 1125 - Rule of Vladimir Monomakh.
1125 - 1132 - Rule of Mstislav the Great.
1155 - 1157 - Rule of Yuri Dolgoruky.
1169 - Prince Andrey Bogolubsky's attack on Kyiv.
1240 - Capture of the city by Batu Khan's horde.
1362 - Annexation of Kyiv to Lithuania
by Prince Olgerd.

Helmet.
12th - 13th
centuries.

THE HETMAN ERA

When Kyiv was part of Lithuania, the Crimean Tatars dominated Ukraine's vast southern expanses. They carried out devastating raids on Ukrainian territory - sometimes coming as far as Kyiv. But gradually a force was formed to protect the southern frontier. These daring troops were the Cossacks. The Cossack movement developed and spread through the whole of Ukraine. The Cossack chieftains were called hetmans. Formally, according to the "Magdeburg Right," the citizens of Kyiv were not subject to the authority of the Hetmans. But the most prominent hetmans

A Zaporizhzhyan Cossack

- such as Piotr Konashevich-Sagaydachny, Bogdan Khmel'nitsky and Ivan Mazepa - exercised an enormous influence over the life of Kyiv. Sagaydachny supported the Kyiv community ("Bratchiki") and school, and helped to restore the city's Orthodox metropolitanate during the period of the church union. As leader of the Ukrainian people in the war of independence, Khmel'nitsky liberated Kyiv from Polish rule. Mazepa was a patron of learning and a builder of churches. Many of the figures of the Hetman era received their education at the Kyiv-Mogila College and Academy (page 58). Many Cossacks lived in the city. But under the influence of the Russian Tsars, Ukraine's autonomy was restricted in every possible way. The last Hetman was Kyril Razumovsky. In 1764, Catherine II abolished the Hetmanship altogether. During the Hetman Era, Kyiv had a population of 10,000-20,000.

The Kyiv coat of arms of 1672

THE "MAGDEBURG RIGHT"

In the 15th century, the Lithuanian authorities granted Kyiv this old European code of municipal self-government. The residents of the city - the burghers - were granted a certain degree of independence from the central government in resolving property and judicial issues. The magistrates, headed by the "void," managed the life of the city. The crafts were managed by the guilds. For centuries kings, hetmans and tsars had to reckon with Kyiv's liberties. But as time passed, the city elite reduced the "Magdeburg Right" to a cover for privileges and abuse of power. In 1834, Kyiv lost it forever. The "Magdeburg Right" column is a monument to this page of Kyiv's history (see 54).

THE PEREYASLAV AGREEMENT

After concluding that it was impossible for Ukraine to free itself from the Poles on its own, Bogdan Khmelnitsky decided to ask for help from the Muscovite Tsar. In Pereyaslav in 1654, Cossack leaders swore allegiance to Tsar Alexey Mikhaylovich in return for an oral promise from the Tsar's ambassador Buturlin that Russia would respect the autonomy of Ukraine. The population of Kyiv was required to swear allegiance to Moscow. The Kyivans went to churches to take the oath, although not as willingly as the Soviet historians would have it.

Bogdan Khmelnitsky

THE USHAKOV PLAN

Up till the end of the 18th century, Kyiv was a frontier town on the right bank of the Dnieper. Much attention was paid to its fortifications. In 1695, a detailed plan of Kyiv was drawn up for defensive purposes under the direction of Ivan Ushakov, colonel of the local garrison. It has survived to this day. Although the plan does not observe scale and the graphics are very primitive, it is a priceless source of information about Kyiv in those times.

Podol

CHRONICLE

15th century - Kyiv was granted the Magdeburg Right.

1482 - Khan Mengly-Gyrei sacks Kyiv.

1569 - Lublin Union, Kyiv falls under Polish rule.

1614-1622 - Hetmanship of Piotr Konashevich-Sagaydachny.

1648-1657 - Hetmanship of Bogdan Khmel'nitsky.

1654 - Kyivans swear loyalty to Tsar Alexey Mikhaylovich.

IVAN MAZEPA'S COAT OF ARMS

Hetman Ivan Mazepa was famous as a patron of arts, giving generous donations for the support of culture, and for construction of churches and monasteries. Mazepa was extremely active in Kyiv. Here he built the Nikolsky and Bogoyavlensky Cathedrals (which have not been preserved), an academic building in Podol, a monumental wall with towers round the Kyiv-Pechersk Lavra, and the Vsekhsviatskaya church above the Economic Gate of the Lavra.

Mazepa was extremely jealous of his reputation. And wherever possible he placed his coat of arms - the so-called

Ivan Mazepa "kurch"
(silver forks crossed over a bar with bent ends, with stars and a crescent against a red background). This sign was visible on the facade of cathedrals and in their interior, on glass and silver covers, and on paintings. But later, when Mazepa was anathematised, all examples of the "kurch" were searched out and destroyed.

UKRAINIAN BAROQUE

The exquisite baroque style dominated European culture between the end of the 16th and the middle of the 18th centuries. In Ukraine, it acquired some unique features. The general European baroque tendencies coming from Poland were united with national motifs in an original way. Many of the shrines that were built resembled the local wooden churches. They were composed of three-, five- and eight-edged units (the usual shape for wooden churches because of the limited length of logs). The fronts were decorated with bright ornaments. In the interior you could find original woodcarving. A lot of baroque buildings were erected under Mazepa, giving rise to the term - "Mazepa baroque."

Ukrainian baroque. Voenno-Nikolsky Cathedral. 18th century

NATALIA DOLGORUKOVA

The former cenobite of the Florovsky monastery Nectaria, whose secular name was Natalia Dolgorukova (Dolgorukaya), is buried in Kyiv-Pechersk Laura. The daughter of the famous Field Marshal Boris Sheremetiev,

she was a beauty in her youth. She married Prince Ivan Dolgorukov, who was then the favourite of Tsar Peter II. But the Tsar soon died, and during the rule of the new queen Anna Ioanovna, Dolgorukov fell into disgrace, was exiled and eventually executed. Dolgorukova remained faithful to her husband in his disgrace and went into exile with him. After his death, the widow entered the Kyiv Monastery, to which she left a considerable part of her fortune (see 150).

KYIV'S FIRST BANK

The Empress Catherine II was the first Russian ruler to introduce banknotes - known as assignations - in the Empire. This was very convenient, since

The assignation bank. Drawn in 1812

bad roads made the shipment of large sums of coinage a serious problem. "Banking assignation offices" appeared in many towns. The Kyiv office was situated in Podol. But the first bank in the city did not last for long - from 1781 to 1788. The empress was not able to use the printing press effectively. Too many assignations were issued, the exchange rate against coins fell dramatically, and the "assignation offices" were hastily closed.

667, 1686 - *Poland de-facto and de-jure recognizes the rule of the Tsar of Moscow over Kyiv.*
1687-1709 - *Hetmanship of Ivan Mazepa.*
1695 - *First detailed plan of Kyiv.*
1781-1788 - *Activity of the first bank office.*
1782 - *The image of the Archangel Michael is chosen as the coat of arms of the city.*

The "Kurch"

THE CENTRE OF THE SOUTH-WESTERN TERRITORY OF THE EMPIRE

Roman-Catholic church in Kyiv.
1846. Taras Shevchenko

From the times of the Empress Catherine II, when the vast lands of right-bank Ukraine were transferred from Poland to the Russian Empire, Kyiv ceased to be a frontier outpost. Tsar Pavel I drew up the new borders of Kyiv Province, now wholly situated on the right bank (the left bank belonged to Chernigov Province). Under Emperor Nikolay I, the city became the stronghold of autocracy in the Southwestern territories (Kyiv, Podol and Volyn provinces). This was the home of bureaucracy, censors and gendarmes. At the same time, the freedom-loving Ukrainian spirit found an outlet in secret and legal organizations like the Brotherhood of Cyril and Methodius (whose members included Taras Shevchenko), "Gromada" (meaning Community) and the "Ukrainian Club." The industrial boom drove the city's rapid growth at the turn of the 20th century. On the eve of the First World War, the population of Kyiv exceeded 600,000.

HEROES OF THE YEAR 1812 AND DECEMBRISTS IN KYIV

Kyiv was not directly involved in the war with Napoleon, but the biographies of some participants in the events of the year 1812 are linked to our city. Alexey Tormasov, Mikhail Golenishchev-Kutuzov and Mikhail Miloradovich were military governors of Kyiv. The romantic hero of the Battle of Borodino, Alexey Touchkov IV and the "cavalry-woman" Nadezhda Durova were born in Kyiv. The valiant general Nikolay Rayevsky served here. His daughter Maria married the Decembrist Sergey Volkonsky. Other well-known Decembrists served in the city: Sergey Trubetskoi, Vasiliy Davidov and Yakov Andriyevich.

M.Volkonskaya

FIRST NEWSPAPERS

The information bulletin "Kyiv Announcements" started appearing in 1836. The first private liberal newspaper "Kyiv Telegraph" appeared in 1859. According to the writer N.Leskov, at first this publication committed some absurd misprints. For example: "It was printed: all Kyivans are onanists; it should have read: all Kyivans are optimists." The conservative newspaper "Kyivan" appeared in 1864. The first Ukrainian daily "Rada" appeared in 1906. Incidentally, it has become fashionable recently to revive such old newspaper titles.

The first Kyiv newspapers

CULTURAL UNIONS

From the times of Nikolay I, official propaganda hammered into the public the guiding principle: "Orthodoxy, autocracy, national character." Those who were unwilling to accept such a formal ideology (with its strong taste of Great Russian chauvinism) found a way of escape in the form of cultural societies and unions. Between 1882 and 1907, the monthly "Kyiv Antiquity" was published. The paper's editorial office was a meeting place for liberal intellectuals with a feeling for Ukraine's glorious past. The Kyiv literary and artistic society was active from 1895 to 1905. Between 1908 and 1912, the Ukrainian Club met under the chairmanship of the composer N.Lysenko. Sooner or later, however, these unions all incurred the displeasure of the regime and were closed down.

THE "SUGAR CAPITAL"

Sugar beet began to be grown in the South-western territory in the first half of the 19th century (one of the initiators of the business was Count A.Bobrinsky). In the second half of the century, dozens of sugar-mills were represented in Kyiv. The board of the

CHRONICLE

1793 - Transfer of right-bank Ukraine from Poland to the Russian Empire.

1834 - Liquidation of the Magdeburg Right in Kyiv.

1845-1847 - Activity of the Brotherhood of Cyril and Methodius.

1853 - Opening of the first permanent bridge over the Dnieper and the monument to Saint Vladimir.

1870 - Beginning of railway communication in Kyiv.

1888 - Celebration of 900th anniversary of the christening of Rus; opening of the Bogdan Khmel'nitsky monument.

All-Russian Society of Sugar Manufacturers was also based in Kyiv. Kyiv was recognized as the "sugar capital," and this contributed significantly to its development.

CHARITY

Rich philanthropists supported most of the establishments that served the poorest Kyivans free of charge. The services of sugar producer Nikolay Tereshchenko (who established the hospital for labourers, and subsidized schools and orphanages) were commemorated during his lifetime when one of the Kyiv's streets was named Tereshchenkovskaya in his honour. The clan of "sugar kings," the Brodskys, built the Jewish Hospital (now the Regional Hospital), the Bacteriological Institute and the Children's Hospital. Industrialists Iona Zaytsev and Izrail Babushkin established free surgical hospitals. Commercial counsellor Mikhail Degtyarev bequeathed millions of rubles in cash and real estate to the city for construction and support of

L.Brodsky

a refuge for the sick, elderly and orphans - the Degtyarevskaya Hospice on the street now named Degtyarevskaya.

KYIV ENGINEERS

The ideas of technical progress were broadly developed. The world-renowned railroad engineer Alexander Borodin developed the newest models of railway engines. In 1878, he installed electric lamps in the Kyiv railway works. In 1880, he installed one of the first telephones in the city between two floors of his house at 17, Tereshchenkovskaya St. Military engineer and industrialist Amand Struve designed a railway bridge across the Dnieper river (see 163), developed the municipal water mains, and in 1892 organized Kyiv's electric tram system - the first in the Russian Empire, and the second in Europe (after Berlin). Adolph Abragamson had two engineering diplomas - one Russian and one German. His contemporaries named him the "squared engineer." Kyiv is obliged to him for the country's first funicular railway.

"CONSTRUCTION FEVER"

Economic growth led to population increase. This made it profitable to invest in construction of private houses with

apartments for the owners to rent out. Sometimes such investment turned into "construction fever" - due in large

A.Struve   A.Borodin

part to a well-planned system of mortgage credits. This was what happened around the turn of the 20th century. The laws of the market regulated the "fever attacks": if supply of apartments exceeded demand for any length of time, there was a period of recession until the next surge of population growth. Almost all the old buildings in the city with four or more floors were the consequences of "construction fever."

EXHIBITIONS ON CHEREPANOVA MOUNTAIN

Exhibitions at which different establishments and firms presented their achievements were organized regularly in Kyiv. The exhibitions of 1897 and 1913 were especially successful. Both were held on the slopes of Cherepanova

Participants in the first All-Russian Olympiada

Mountain, where today the National "Olympics" Sports Complex is located (see 131). Among the actions that ran concurrently with the All-Russian exhibition of 1913 was the first All-Russian Olympiad.

The center of Kyiv at the beginning of the 20th century

T.Shevchenko

1892 - The city's first tram system.
1897 - The city's first car.
1908 - Creation of the "Ukrainian club" - a union of national intellectuals headed by composer N. Lysenko.
1910 - First flight by aviator Sergey Utochkin over Kyiv.
1911 - Murder of prime minister Piotr Stolypin in Kyiv.
1913 - All-Russian industry exhibition.
1913 - The first All-Russian Olympiad in Kyiv.

15

KALEIDOSCOPE OF REGIMES

The most complicated and contradictory period in the city's history was the time of the Revolution and Civil War of 1917-1920. According to different estimates, power in Kyiv changed hands 14-18 times. The city was an arena for bloody fighting, involving the Ukrainian leaders of different political orientations, pro-Moscow Bolsheviks, White Guardists, and German and Polish occupants. Kyiv was for some time the capital of an independent Ukrainian state, but eventually the Soviets took power - seriously and for the long term.

A postcard from the time of the Civil War

THE TELEGRAM OF DEPUTY BUBLIKOV

Kyivans received the news from railway men that the Tsar had fallen. During the February Revolution, railway engineer Alexander Bublikov, a member

State Symbol of the UPR (project)

ment in Ukrainian history. With the beginning of military operations against Bolshevik Russia in January 1918, the UCC issued its fourth Universal.

"We, the Ukrainian Central Council, inform all the citizens of Ukraine: from now on the Ukrainian People's Republic has become an independent, free and sovereign state of Ukrainian people. We want to live in friendship and consent with all neighbouring states: Russia, Poland, Austria, Romania, Turkey and others. We want to live in friendship and accord, but none of them should interfere in the life of the independent Ukrainian Republic. Power in it will belong to the people of Ukraine alone..."

Former Pedagogic Museum - the seat of the Central Council

of the State Council, was delegated to the Ministry of Communications. While chaos reigned in the official telegraph channels, Bublikov informed the management of all the railroads, which used special communications cables. The news of the fall of the monarchy spread through Kyiv from the Administration of the Southwest Railway in moments.

FROM THE IV UNIVERSAL OF THE CENTRAL COUNCIL

The Ukrainian Central Council (UCC), created in March 1918, became the first national parlia-

THE JANUARY REBELLION AND THE BOMBARDMENT OF KYIV

The leftist forces reacted to the Central Council's efforts to create an independent state by starting an insurrection. In January 1918, the Bolsheviks incited a rebellion at the Arsenal Plant, in the railway shops and among the workers of Podol. The street fighting lasted several days and ended with the victory of the Ukrainian units. But meanwhile, armed units of the Soviet Republic under Mikhail Muravyov were strengthening their positions on the left bank. His forces began to bombard Kyiv with long-range artillery.

Rebellion of the Arsenal workers in Kyiv V.Kasiyan, 1939

State Symbol of UkSSR of 1919

CHRONICLE

March 1917 - *The liquidation of the monarchy in Russia reported.*
1917 -1918 - *Ukrainian Central Council (UCC) holds power.*
November 1917 - *Armed rebellion against the Russian Provisional Government in Kyiv. III Universal of the UCC proclaims the Ukrainian People's Republic (UPR).*
January 1918 - *The first Ukrainian banknotes issued.*
January 1918 - *IV Universal of UCC proclaims Ukraine independent.*
February 1918 - *Kyiv captured by the Bolsheviks.*
March 1918 - *Beginning of the German occupation of Kyiv, restoration of UPR.*

Hetman P.Skoropadsky.

Innocent people were killed, monuments were destroyed. Eventually, the Bolsheviks occupied Kyiv. Muravyov showed Kyivans the meaning of Red Terror.

WAS M.GRUSHEVSKY PRESIDENT OF UKRAINE OR NOT?

Sometimes one reads that the history professor Mikhail Grushevsky was Ukraine's first president. But that is a misunderstanding. For the whole period of the Ukrainian People's Republic the position of president did not exist. The position was not mentioned in the first Ukrainian Constitution, passed on 29 April, 1918. M.Grushevsky was the Head of the Ukrainian Central Council.

SECRETARIES, MINISTERS, COMMISSARS

The first sovereign government of Ukraine was the General Secretariat established by the Central Council. Agitating against it, the Bolsheviks claimed that it was a bourgeois government in

The monument to M.Grushevsky.
Sculptor V.Chepelik, 1998

which only generals took part. The Bolsheviks themselves called their government the Council of People's Commissars. The Ukrainian government had to change its signboard. It became the Council of People's Ministers.

"FUENTE OVEHUNA"

In 1919 the play "Fuente Ovehuna" (Sheep Spring) by the Spanish dramatist Lope de Vega was staged at Kyiv's Solovtsov Theatre. At the play's climax was a peasant insurrection against an unjust lord. Kyiv was Soviet at the time. The revolutionary play was performed by the best actors and staged by the talented producer K.Mardzhanov. It stirred great emotions in the audience, some of whom watched the play before going into battle. The theatre had never encountered such a delighted audience response before.

"TORTURE BY FEAR"

The White Guards led by A.Denikin occupied Kyiv in autumn 1919. They stood by as Jews were massacred. The massacres took place at night. Hidden in their homes, the doomed people cried terribly -

they could not protect themselves. Many people could not endure hearing the horrible crying. Even the White ideologist Vasily Shulgin had to admit that it was "torture by fear."

ONE-DAY MONEY

Whenever power changed hands in Kyiv, new banknotes were issued, and the old money became just paper. Kyivans had to quickly get used to the new currencies. Sometimes people would hold on to the banknotes of different regimes - Bolshevik, Petlura, and Denikin - just in case. Some banknotes were given nicknames. For example, the 1,000 ruble bills with the image of the State Council issued by the Provisional Government were called "dumkas." Small-denomination banknotes worth 20 and 40 rubles were known as "kerenkas." The Denikin 1000-ruble banknotes with their

A.Denikin

The General Secretary of the UPR

Ukrainian money from 1917 - 1920

image of the Tsar-Bell were called "bells." Some of the Ukrainian banknotes were called "eggs with onion" because of their colouring. The Bolshevik banknotes were called "sovznaks."

THEIR WAY BEGAN IN KYIV

The people mentioned below are among the brightest stars in the sky of the 20th century. Destiny decreed that at the end of their life, they were far away from Kyiv. But this city was the starting point - the place where they were born, studied or started out on their independent career. This list demonstrates how generously Kyiv has given its talents to humanity.

Konstantin Grigoriyevich PAUSTOVSKY (1892-1968). Writer. Studied in Kyiv. Published his first stories in the magazines "Lights" and "Knight." See 112-114, 118

Isaac Emmanuilovych BABEL (1894-1940). Writer. Studied in Kyiv. Published his first short story in the magazine "Lights." See 113, 122, 124

Igor Ivanovych SIKORSKI (1889-1972). Aircraft designer. Studied in Kyiv. Created his first aircraft here. See 39, 140

Alexander Nikolayevich VERTINSKY (1889-1957). Artist, poet, performer of his own songs. Was born and studied in Kyiv, made his debut on the Kyiv stage, was published for the first time in the magazine "Kyiv Week." See 109, 132

Militsa KORYUS (1909-1980). Singer. Film star. Studied in Kyiv, became a professional singer here.

Viktor Platonovich NEKRASOV (1911-1987). Writer. Was born in Kyiv, received his architect's diploma here, lived and worked in Kyiv until his forced emigration. See 31, 104

Reinhold Moritsevich GLIERE (1875-1956). Composer, conductor, teacher. Was born and studied in Kyiv, director of the Kyiv Conservatory. See 103, 124, 130

Alexander Porfirievich ARKHIPENKO (1887-1964). Sculptor, painter. Was born and studied in Kyiv. See 44, 128

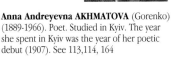

Anna Andreyevna AKHMATOVA (Gorenko) (1889-1966). Poet. Studied in Kyiv. The year she spent in Kyiv was the year of her poetic debut (1907). See 113,114, 164

Mikhail Afanasiyevich BULGAKOV (1881-1940). Writer. Born and studied in Kyiv. In 1913 he married Tatiana Lappa in the Church of Nikola the Kind in Podol. See 44, 50, 55, 62, 112, 118

Golda MEIR (Mabovich) (1898-1978). Israeli stateswoman. Was born in the family of a Kyiv carpenter. See 130

Kazimir Severinovich MALEVICH (1878-1935). Painter. Teacher. Was born and studied in Kyiv.

Otto Yuliyevich SCHMIDT (1891-1956). Mathematician, geophysicist, arctic researcher, public figure. Studied in Kyiv, began his independent scientific activity here. See 118, 124

Lev Isaacovich SHESTOV (Shvartsman) (1866-1938). Philosopher. Was born in Kyiv. See 57, 118

Vladimir Samoylovych HOROWITZ (1903-1989). Pianist. Was born and studied in Kyiv, gave his first concerts here. See 103, 117

Sergey Pavlovych KOROLEV (1907-1966). Constructor of rockets. Studied in Kyiv, first took part in construction of flying machines here. See 105, 140

Il'ya Grigoriyevich EHRENBURG (1891-1967). Writer, public figure. Was born in Kyiv. See 122

Alla Konstantinovna TARASOVA (1898-1973). Actress. Was born and studied in Kyiv. Made her debut here on the stage of the theatrical school. See 80

Nikolay Aleksandrovich BERDIAYEV (1874-1948). Philosopher. Was born and studied in Kyiv. See 118, 129, 142

Sergey (Serge) Mikhaylovich LIFAR (1905-1986). Ballet dancer, choreographer. Was born and studied in Kyiv. See 105

UNDER THE POWER OF THE "SOVIETS"

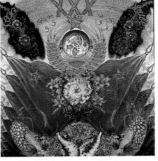

The 30th Anniversary of the USSR.
1947. K.Bilokur

Just after the Civil War the Ukrainian capital was transferred to Kharkov. Only in 1934 Kyiv became the main city of the republic. Its global transformation in the socialist manner continued year after year. Church domes were replaced with industrial buildings - the creations of the five year plans, administrative buildings with the hammer and sickle on the facades, co-operative housing projects. The Second World War interrupted the process, taking hundreds of thousands of lives and leaving Kyiv in ruins. But after the liberation of Kyiv, the "building of communism" continued. Stalinist splendour was followed by Khrushchev's ascetism and then the gigantomania of the Brezhnev epoch. However, even under this enforced mask, Kyiv was able to preserve romantic reminiscences that are apparent to the interested and careful gaze.

THE RENAMING OF THE STREETS

There is no simpler and more radical way to inform the public about changes than a mass renaming of streets. The Soviet regime was especially active in this respect. Back in February 1919, after the Red's took over the city the press announced that at least forty streets would be renamed. Later the number increased. Sometimes they were given the names of living leaders or unorthodox Marxists. Then those that proved disagreeable had to be removed and replaced with signs with new names. Thus Trotsky St. became Artioma St., then Bera Borokhova St. - and finally Shota Rustaveli St. The record is held by Olesia Gonchara St.: it was renamed twice in tsarist times, and 5 times after the revolution.

MILITANT ATHEISM

The communist ideologists were not happy with the role of Kyiv over many centuries as the spiritual base of the domestic Orthodox faith. A fierce struggle against the religion was unleashed everywhere. In a high profile trial, in 1929 the monk Yevladiy Chekhun was tried on a trumped-up criminal charge. The monk ended up in prison,

and a campaign of "indignant letters of working people" was organized that resulted in the closure of the Lavra, the Florovsky Monastery and other Kyiv cloisters. A sign reading "Monks are the deadly enemies of working people" was hung up on the Uspenskiy Cathedral in

Execution of war criminals on Kreshchatik, 1946

the Lavra. A few years later, they began to destroy cathedrals without paying any attention to their cultural value or the feelings of believers.

THE GREAT PATRIOTIC WAR

"Kyiv was bombed, and we were told that the war had begun" - these are the words of a folk song. At dawn on 22 June 1941 our city entered a tragic epoch.

Each day brought new victims. The blunders of the leaders and the crimes of the barbarians condemned Kyivans to sorrow and misery. But every day brought feats of courage; ordinary people became heroes, enduring harsh trials of their physical and spiritual strength. Those years divided the history of the 20th century into two periods: "before the war" and "after the war."

CHRONICLE

1922 - The inclusion of the Ukrainian Soviet Socialist Republic (UkSSR) in the USSR.

1927 - The annexing of left bank territories to Kyiv.

1932 - The foundation of the Kyiv Region.

1934 - The transfer of the capital of the UkSSR from Kharkov to Kyiv.

July - August 1941 - the heroic defense of Kyiv in the Great Patriotic War.

1941 - 1943 - Nazi occupation.

Medal "For Defense of Kyiv"

"THE SIXTIES GENERATION"

After Nikita Khrushchev condemned Stalin's despotism at the XX Congress of the Communist Party of the Soviet Union (1956), many people hoped for improvements in social life. People became braver. They started to

Air raid warning, 1941.
1972. S.Kaplan

speak aloud about matters they had previously not dared to think about : bogus official dogmas, the criminal destruction of the best people of their time, the squeezing out of the Ukrainian language and the neglect of cultural traditions. But the Communist regime still did not want the whole truth exposed. The fates of Kyiv's "generation of the sixties" developed in different ways: the poet Vasiliy Stus was tortured in camps; the artist Alla Gorskaya died under mysterious circumstances; the historian Mikhail Braychevskiy was excluded from the academic world and denied the possibility to publish his works; the writer Victor

Nekrasov had to immigrate. However, many of them showed real courage defending the honour of their generation in the years of stagnation.

KYIV GUESTS

The capital of the Ukrainian Soviet Socialist Republic received many high-ranking foreign guests: presidents, prime-ministers, members of royal families. Among them are Charles de Gaule, Josef Bros Tito, Karl XVI Gustav King of Sweden, Richard Nixon, Salvador Aliende, Fidel Castro, Indira Gandhi.

DYNAMO KYIV

For many years the footballers of Kyiv Dynamo were consid-

Pavilion of the Exhibition Center. 1980

ered the favourites of the city. The team was founded in 1927. In the first USSR Championship in the Spring of 1936, the

Kyivans won the silver medal. In 1961 Dynamo became the first non-Moscow club to win the USSR Championship. Later on the team became the undisputed leader of Soviet football, winning the USSR Championships and the USSR Cup many times. But the team achieved its most spectacular success in European tournaments. In 1975 Dynamo became the first Soviet team to win the European Cup Winners' Cup and the UEFA Super Cup - the prize for the best club of the continent. In 1986 the Kyivans won the Cup Winners' Cup for the second time. Oleg Blokhin became the team's best striker and its most famous player. Valeriy Lobanovskiy became the most titled trainer.

JUBILEE OF THE CITY

The date given for the foundation of Kyiv - the year 482 - is only approximate. For several reasons it was convenient to celebrate the jubilee in 1982. The 1500th anniversary was celebrated with great pomp. A special medal was established, the monument to the founders of the city was unveiled (see 163), the Golden Gate was reconstructed and so on. This is where the tradition originated of celebrating Kyiv Day at the end of May with a festival on the Andreyevsky Spusk, which Kyivans have continued.

November 6, 1943 - Liberation of Kyiv by the units of the 1st Ukrainian Front.
1960 - Opening of the first Metro line.
1965 - Presentation of the "Golden Star" medal to the Hero-City Kyiv.
1980 - Olympic football tournament in Kyiv.
1982 - The 1500th anniversary celebration.
1986 - Chernobyl Atomic Power Station accident, in spite of deteriorating radioactive conditions the 1 May festival takes place.
1988 - Celebration of the 1000th Anniversary of the Christening of Rus.
1990 - Raising of the national flag in front of the Kyiv City Council building.

Art exhibition on Andreyevsky Spusk

21

MODERN KYIV

The year 1991 was a turning point in the history of Kyiv and of all Ukraine. After the unsuccessful hardline coup in Moscow, the Verkhovnaya Rada of the Ukrainian Soviet Socialist Republic adopted the Act of Independence of Ukraine, after which this city was transformed from the servant of an allied country into the capital of a sovereign European state. The years that followed brought a multitude of events, ambiguous and contradictory. The abolition of the one-party system, free elections - as well as cynical policy, scandals and "black PR." The liberalization of the economy - and the dramatic material differentiation of society, meager pensions, and the arbitrariness

Near the Great Patriotic War Museum

of officials. Broad access to information that was previously prohibited - and the decline of morals, a shower of dirt and violence in the press and on the TV screen. The lifting of ideological barriers to culture and art - and the creation of even higher financial barriers. The restoration of lost relics - and the feverish execution of ambitious construction projects. All that has happened in the last 10 years has still to be thoroughly reconsidered. But the people are gradually getting used to living in an independent country, taking care of themselves and relying on their

own strengths. In the meantime, historians of Kyiv have filled in a multitude of gaps in the biography of their city, and

Kreshchatik at night

now more and more people draw delight and profit from getting acquainted with the places of interest of the capital of Ukraine.

In a Kyiv park

Postcard dedicated to the celebration of 10 years of Independence of Ukraine. Publishing house "Baltija Dryk."

CHRONICLE

August 24, 1991 - *Declaration of the independence of Ukraine.*
December 1, 1991 - *All-Ukraine referendum expresses support for independence. First presidential elections in Ukraine.*
1992 - *The adoption of new state symbols.*
1995 - *Archangel Michael again becomes the symbol of Kyiv.*
June 26, 1996 - *Introduction of the current Constitution of Ukraine.*
1996 - *Introduction of the national currency - the hryvnia.*
1997-2000 - *Reconstruction of the Mikhailovskiy Gold-Domed Monastery.*
1998-2000 - *Reconstruction of the Uspenskiy Cathedral in the Kyiv-Pechersk Lavra.*
January 1999 - *Adoption of the law "About the Capital of Ukraine - the Hero-City Kyiv."*
May 1999 - *First election of the city mayor.*
August 2001 - *Celebration of 10 years of Ukraine's independence.*

SIGHTSEEING

SEVEN WONDERS OF KYIV

GARDENS AND PARKS ABOVE THE DNIEPER

The most pleasant place in the city. Stretching along the green slopes above the Dnieper are the Vladimirskaya Hill (see 43), the Kreshchaty Park (see 66), the City Garden (see 67), the Mariinsky Park (see 67), the Askold's Grave Park (see 81), the Park of Eternal Glory (see 80), and the Botanical Gardens (see 144).

"THE HOUSE WITH CHIMERAS"

The most unusual house. The creation of the irrepressible fantasy of Vladislav Gorodetsky, architect, romantic and passionate hunter, who splashed out on the front of the building a whole world stemming from his creative imagination (see 71).

SOPHIA CATHEDRAL

The greatest and most famous of the old cathedrals of Eastern Europe, a world-famous master-piece of architecture, with frescos and mosaic art (see 36-37).

KIYV-PECH-ERSK LAVRA

One of Europe's holiest repositories of Orthodox relics. An architectural and artistic complex and museum are here united with the resting place of the imperishable remains of the Saints in the Near and Far Caves, where pilgrims have worshipped for hundreds of years (see 82-93).

VLADIMIR CATHEDRAL

The most outstanding complex of sacral art of the late 19th century. The paintings in the cathedral are the work of such great artists as V.Vasnetsov, M.Nesterov, M.Vrubel and others. They exerted considerable influence upon domestic and European art (see 124).

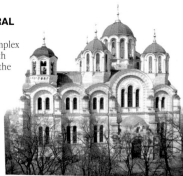

KHRESHCHATIK ENSEMBLE

The most grandiose architectural ensemble of the Soviet era. After it was destroyed in the war, the central street arose like a triumphant chord of beauty and optimism (see 99-106).

ANDREYEVSKY SPUSK

The most picturesque street. Astonishing landscape, the incomparable Andreyevskaya Church, the original Castle of Richard the Lion Heart, Bulgakov's reliquiae and a lively market for souvenirs and art works (see 45-50).

Fresco in St. Sofia's Cathedral

25

ARCHITECTURAL GLOSSARY

Apse - a semicircular (sometimes polygonal) projection in the wall of Christian Church buildings.

Arcade - the chain of arcs, similar in shape and size, leaning on the pillars or columns.

Caryatid

Attic - 1)the wall over the cornice or the storey crowning the building;
2) the room under a steep roof; it may serve as a residence.

Baroque - the architectural style of 16 - 17 centuries remarkable for its decorative splendour and complexity of form.

Bas-relief - a sculptural (low relief) image on a flat surface.

Byzantium Style - stylistic manner of domestic architecture of the middle of 19 - the beginning of 20 century using motifs of ancient Byzantium architectural style; remarkable for its monumentality and structural massiveness.

Caryatid - a column in the form of a woman's figure supporting the projecting parts of a building.

**Classicism,
the Classical Style** - the architectural style of 17 - the beginning of 19 centuries, developing the traditions of the antiquity and remarkable for its simplicity, harmony and restraint of form.

Cornice - the horizontal lug crowning the walls of the building and supporting the roof.

Console - a projection in the wall for the supporting of various parts of the building (cor-

nice, balcony etc.) or the installation of decorations on it.

Constructivism - the architectural style of 1920 - 1930s remarkable for its strivings toward simple and functionally justifiable forms.

Counterfort - the vertical lug in the wall, strengthening it and making it stable.

Decor - the art decoration of the building.

Empire - architectural style of the beginning of 19 century, closing the development of classicism.

Entablature - the upper horizontal part of the building leaning on the columns.

Ercer - a semicircular or polygonal projection in the wall, with

A fragment of the decor

windows, usually taking in several stories and enlarging the interior space.

Frieze - decorative horizontal band of sculpture between the architrave and cornice.

Gallery - 1) the long narrow covered passage joining two separated parts of the building; 2) the long narrow covered corridor or the balcony around the facade of the building; 3) an open gallery in a church in the form of a balcony.

Gothic - the architectural style of the 12 - 16 centuries remarkable for its pronounced lofty aspirations, use of pointed arches and vaults, and abundance of sculptural decorations.

Pediment

High relief - sculptured images which stand out from a flat surface with a depth of more than half their volume.

Maskaron - the relief detail of the decor in the shape of a mask.

Modern - the architectural style of the end of 19 - the beginning of 20 century remarkable for its original decor, free planning and using of new building materials.

Narthex - the entrance room at the west side of a Christian church.

Pediment - the completion (usually triangular) of the building facade, portico or the colonnade confined by the two pitches of roof on the sides and the cornice at the bottom.

Portico - a porch roof supported by columns at regular intervals.

Propylaeum - columns placed in front of the entrance of a building or other territory and positioned symmetrically in relation to the direction of movement.

Pylon - a support in the form of a massive column.

Renaissance - the architectural style of the 19 - the beginning of 20 centuries imitating the monumental buildings of the Renaissance Epoch (14 -16 centuries).

Rotunda - a circular edifice (building, pavilion, hall) usually surrounded by columns and crowned with a dome.

Socle - the lower part of the exterior wall of the building lying directly on the foundation and projecting outwards in comparison with the upper part.

A moulded decoration in "Renaissance Style"

THE UPPER
CITY

THE UPPER CITY

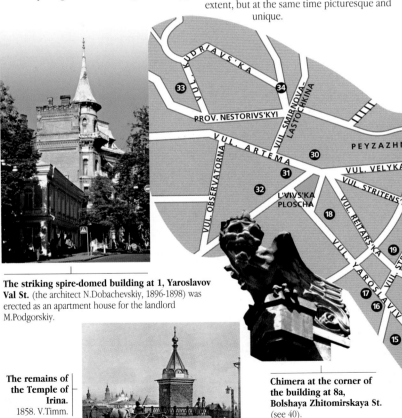

In ancient times Kyiv was the political, economic and spiritual centre of Kyivan Rus. It consisted of the fortified hill area - the Upper City, and the crafts and trade area at the foot of the hill in Podol. It was in the Upper City that the first site of ancient settlement in Kyiv was established fifteen centuries ago. Later the princes ruled over the lands of ancient Rus from here. Vladimir the Saint, Yaroslav the Wise, Vladimir Monomakh and other rulers contributed to the flourishing of the city.

Marvellous churches and palaces towered in the Upper City. This was a place of enlightenment, art and crafts. Embassies came here from far afield to find brides for their kings. When the Mongol hordes ravaged the city, it was the upper part that suffered the most. For a long time it was left in ruins. Not many buildings survived, and only a few of those have been preserved to the present time to testify to the former grandeur. Subsequent generations have given the Upper City a new appearance - old-fashioned to some extent, but at the same time picturesque and unique.

Fragment of the front of the building at 31/16, Reytarskaya St.

The striking spire-domed building at 1, Yaroslavov Val St. (the architect N.Dobachevskiy, 1896-1898) was erected as an apartment house for the landlord M.Podgorskiy.

The remains of the Temple of Irina. 1858. V.Timm.

Chimera at the corner of the building at 8a, Bolshaya Zhitomirskaya St. (see 40).

Anna Yaroslavna - the daughter of Yaroslav the Wise - married king Henry I and became the Queen of France.

The memorial sign on the building of the Academy of Arts and Architecture (20 Smirnova-Lastochkina St.) to mark the founding of the Academy of Arts of Ukraine in 1917.

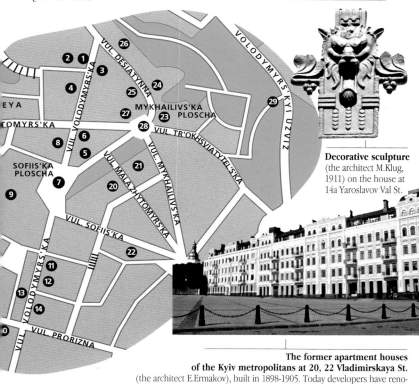

Decorative sculpture (the architect M.Klug, 1911) on the house at 14a Yaroslavov Val St.

The former apartment houses of the Kyiv metropolitans at 20, 22 Vladimirskaya St. (the architect E.Ermakov), built in 1898-1905. Today developers have renovated the buildings and added an attic story.

KYIV DETINETS

The National Museum of Ukrainian History.
1936-1937. Architect I.Karakis

The oldest part of Kyiv is located around the vicinity of the beginning section of Vladimirskaya St. The place where the city was concentrated before the rule of Vladimir Sviatoslavovich has been turned into an archaeological reserve around the National Museum of Ukrainian History. Among the well-known archaeologists who worked here were Vikentiy Khvoyka, Dmitry Mileyev, Mikhail Karger, Stefaniya Kiliyevich, Viktor Kharlamov, Piotr Tolochko and others. Thanks to their research, we can picture for ourselves what old Kyiv was like. Up until the 10th century ramparts bound the town. Their outline can be seen on the territory of the reserve. Prince Vladimir expanded the city to an area of 10 hectare and created a new system of fortification. Historians often call this the city of Vladimir Detinets. This name was used for the old city fortification - the place where they could hide ("det") old people, women and children in case of danger.

DESIATINNAYA CATHEDRAL 1

An elevated stone perimeter marks the place where the first stone church in Rus - the Temple of the Mother of God - was built in 989 - 996. Master builders were summoned from Byzantium for the construction.

The lime

On the day of the ceremonial consecration of the cathedral, Prince Vladimir promised to give a tithe of one tenth of his income ("desiatina") for its needs. That is the origin of the other name of the cathedral. Prince Vladimir was buried here in 1015. The building also housed the first school in Rus. It was destroyed during the invasion of Kyiv by Batu Khan. The last defenders of the city took shelter here. They were buried alive under the collapsed walls of the church. A stone cross is

dedicated to the courageous Kyivans. There is currently some talk about the possibility of restoring the Desiatinnaya Cathedral, but specialists believe that there is not enough scientific data available to do so.

From the Historical Museum

LIME TREE

Near the place where the Desiatinnaya Cathedral stood grows an ancient lime-tree (now its powerful trunk is supported with a prop, but the tree still blossoms every year). Some botanists think that the mighty lime-tree is 800 years old, meaning that it was a contemporary of the first Russian stone church.

NATIONAL MUSEUM OF UKRAINIAN HISTORY 2

2, Vladimirskaya St.
☎ 228–65–45
Ⓜ Zolotiye Vorota
Day off – Wednesday

The "classical style" museum building was originally meant for an art school. The History Museum has been located here since 1944. The exhibits represent all periods from ancient times to the present day.

The displays have been renovated in recent years. In contrast to the ideological stereotypes of the totalitarian period, the glorious and tragic past of the independent Ukrainian state.

PAGAN TEMPLE

In a shallow pit to the right of the entrance of the museum, an oval platform with four ledges has been restored. The archaeologist V.Khvoyka uncovered it during excavations in 1907-1908. He identified the find as the remains of a pagan temple where the old Slavonic people made sacrifices to their idols. He came to this conclusion on the basis of the animal bones and skulls, and the layers of coals and ashes that were found there. The "stone idols" placed along the front of the museum also date back to pagan times. Actually these are not Kyiv idols, but museum

Desiatinnaya Church (reconstruction)

exhibits brought from the burial mounds of the south Ukrainian steppes.

REMAINS OF THE PRINCES' PALACES

The memorial stone to the first school

On the way to the observation platform behind the History Museum, you can see the uncovered remains of the base of a stone building - a palace from the first half of the 10th century that is called the "Prince's yard in the city" in the chronicles. It is the oldest known stone building in Kyiv, and dates to the times of the rule of Olga and Sviatoslav. The palaces of the later rulers were situated in "the city of Vladimir." Some masonry in the roadway on the other side of Desiatinny Lane marks the location of the so-called West Palace from the first half of the 10th century. If you go to the beginning of the lane and turn left onto Vladimirskaya Street, you can see traces of another palace of the

The Trubetskoi House

same period - the South Palace. A picture of the building as it is imagined to have looked is depicted on the memorial sign. Apparently one of the palaces was the prince's residence, and the other was the parade hall where the prince held banquets with his guards and attendants. The glorious knights from the old Russian epic stories gathered there. Here, according to a poem by A.Pushkin, Vladimir gave his daughter in marriage to the brave knight Ruslan. Nowadays, a house is situated on the site of the old South

Palace at 4 Vladimirskaya St. The well-known writer Victor Nekrasov was born here in 1911.

THE LAND-SCAPE ALLEY

In the 1980s, the verge of the Old Kyiv Hill between Detinets and Lvovskaya Square was transformed into a promenade (designed by the architects A. Miletskiy and others, and the archeologist P. Tolochko). From here you can admire the picturesque landscape of the old hills, the Dnieper and Zadniprovye. A special staircase leads up to the spur of the Old Kyiv Hill - Detinka (this peculiar topographic name probably comes from the nearby Detinets). Near the National Museum of Ukrainian History, the alley leads to a spacious viewing platform. Here there is a symbolic stone with an inscription: "Where the Russian land came from."

THE TRUBETSKOI MANSION   3
3, Vladimirskaya St.

This two-story classical building with a mezzanine dating from the first half of the 19th century is sometimes called "the Trubetskoi House," as it was bought in 1867 by Princess Elizabeth Trubetskaya. The mansion has long drawn the attention of archaeologists. Under the Trubetskoi House were found the remains of a pagan

The memorial on the site of the prince's palace

place of worship dating from the X century and the foundation of a big stone rotunda from the 12th century, which is believed

to have been the prince's reception hall. Now the house is home to a department of the Institute of Archaeology of the National Academy of Sciences of Ukraine.

THE CENTRAL TELEGRAPH BUILDING   4
10, Vladimirskaya St.

This building was designed for the Nobility and Peasant Land Banks, which regulated the supply and demand for land plots, buying them up from members of the nobility and selling to wealthy peasants. On the balcony railings there are images of warriors' heads.

The Central Telegraph building. 1910-1911 Architect A.Kobelev

The architect was paying tribute to the antiquity of the place. Unfortunately, you cannot say the same about the next building - the super-modern office building at 12 Vladimirskaya St. In the middle of the street in front of these buildings, the foundation of the entry-gate of "The city of Vladimir" is set in red quartzite. Another archaeological monument can be found in the yard of 9 Vladimirskaya St. - here the foundation of the Fedorovskiy Monastery Church was discovered. This church was founded in 1129 by the Kyiv Prince Mstislav (whose Christian name was Fedor) - the son of Prince Vladimir Monomakh and the English princess Gida.

"THE OUT-OF-TOWN FIELD"

A t the turn of the 11th century, the neighbourhood beyond the limits of "Vladimir's Town" was a largely undeveloped area known as "the out-of-town field." But under Yaroslav the Wise, the area quickly began to be built up. The prince created a new perimeter of the city fortifications - "Yaroslav's Town," which encompassed an area six times greater than that of "Vladimir's Town." The monumental St.Sofia's Cathedral, stone churches and residential houses were built here. The remains of the ancient fortifications were levelled in the 19th century.

Caryatid

THE PRESENCES   5
15, Vladimirskaya St.

The citadel of Kyiv's bureaucrats was located in a spacious building built in 1854-1857 by the architects M.Ikonnikov, K.Skarzhinskiy and I.Shtrom. This was the seat of the so-called "Presences" - the official gubernatorial establishments. The officials needed more and more space, and the building was repeatedly enlarged and extended. In the Soviet period, the former "Presences" became the seat of the internal affairs and judicial bodies. From 1919 to 1937, Vladimirskaya Street was named after the writer V.Korolenko, and the house was known by its address "15, Korolenko St." They used to say at the time: "15, Korolenko Street is the highest building in Kyiv - you can see Siberia out of its windows!"

STAROKYIVSKIY FIREHOUSE   6
13, Vladimirskaya St.
☎ 212–65–19
Ⓜ Zolotiye Vorota
Days off – Saturday, Sunday

The building adjoining "The Presences" at the intersection of Vladimirskaya and Bolshaya Zhitomirskaya streets (built by the architect M.Ikonnikov in the 1850s) was designed for the Starokyivskiy District fire department. The fire tower, which is surmounted by a metal mast, has survived to the present day. Long before the invention of the telephone, a look-out kept watch on the tower, and in case of fire hung out special balloons or crosses (at night lights were used instead). There was a special combination of symbols for every district of Kyiv. If suspicious smoke was seen anywhere in the city, the "code" of the area was displayed on the tower, and all the fire squads rushed in that direction. This building now contains the firemen's museum.

THE MONUMENT TO BOGDAN KHMEL'NITSKIY   7
Sofiyskaya Square

This is one of the most famous monuments in the city - a distinctive emblem of Kyiv. The artist and sculptor Mikhail Mykeshin designed this monument. He planned to embody in his creation the idea of the "sole and indivisible" Russian Empire,

St.Sofia... Above and past it raged all the turmoil, which devastated its native land; the outer part of its architecture testifies to a succession of centuries, against the assault of which it stood, as an unbreakable rock among sea waves! - But from its mysterious depths, the palpitating darkness of its arches, still breathes the sacred antiquity of the fatherland of the days of the Yaroslav!

Andrey Muraviov. "St.Sofia"

Starokyivskiy fire tower

and proposed to decorate the pedestal of the monument with the figures of the triumphant Slavs united with Russia and the bodies of their prostrate enemies. The latter were to be represented by a Jesuit, a Polish noble and a Jew who were being trampled under the horse's

Sofiyskaya square. The monument to B.Khmel'nitsky

hoofs. Although the local authorities were opposed to this design, fearing that such a monument would spark ethnic conflicts, it was approved by the Tsar. But the grand idea was blocked by a prosaic obstacle: the construction of the monument was to be financed from public donations, and the amount collected was three times less than was needed for the design according to Mykeshin's estimate. The money was barely enough to cast the statue of the Hetman on horseback, bring it to Kyiv and place it on a temporary brick pedestal in the centre of the square in 1881. The affair drew out for another seven years, until eventually the architect Vladimir Nikolayev designed a modest but expressive-looking mound-shaped pedestal. The treasury provided the money required. The ceremonial unveiling of the monument took place in June 1888, during the festivities dedicated to the celebration of the 900th anniversary of the Christening of Rus.

THE FORMER CHARNETSKY HOTEL 8
16, Vladimirskaya St.

The building that currently houses the Uzbek embassy was built by the architect V.Nikolayev as a private hotel for Franz Charnetsky in 1879. The famous artists Mikhail Vrubel and Mikhail Nesterov lived here. The building was later used as a comprehensive school for some time. Among its graduates

was the talented film director Larissa Shepitko in 1955. The building was later given to a ministry. The Ukrainian poet and human rights activist Vasil Stus worked in the information department in the basement until his arrest in January 1972.

GOOD WORK

In 1898 construction began on a revenue house for the Kyiv metropolitans at 20, Vladimirskaya St. Here there was a stonewall enclosing a courtyard. It was in the way and had to be torn down. The contractor thought that his workers would quickly deal with it, but this turned out not to be the case. The 18th century wall turned out to be so solid; they couldn't break it with crowbars. It was not possible to use explosives because all the precautionary measures needed would be too expensive. The contractor eventually had to send for experienced stone dressers from a labradorite quarry. A team of professionals came with special equipment to break monolithic rock. Only then did the wall give way. When the first piece came off, there was such a resounding crack that books fell off the shelves in a nearby house.

M.Mykeshin

The design for the B.Khmel'nitsky monument

Zaborovsky Brama

THE NATIONAL RESERVE "ST.SOFIA'S CATHEDRAL" 9

24, Vladimirskaya St.
☎ 228–67–06
Ⓜ Zolotiye Vorota
Day off – Thursday

According to legend, St.Sofia's Cathedral was built on the spot where Yaroslav the Wise won a decisive victory over the nomadic Pechenegs. In the 17th century, a monastery was established in the Cathedral's precincts. It existed till 1786, after which it became the residence of Kyiv's metropolitans. In 1934 the site was turned into a state architectural and historic reserve - now known as the National Reserve - St.Sofia's Cathedral.

ST.SOFIA'S CATHEDRAL ❶

In 1990 it was included on the UNESCO world heritage list. Now it is used as museum (see 36-37).

ST.SOFIA'S BELL TOWER ❷

The main entrance to the Cathedral's courtyard is located in the base of the majestic 76-meter bell tower. It was erected at the end of the 17th century, and was subsequently rebuilt several times. The walls of the tower are abundantly decorated with ornamental details, prominent among which are, on the front of the third level of the tower, relief portraits of the Apostle Andrew and Prince Vladimir (on the side of the square), and of the Apostle Timothy and

Archangel Raphael (on the side of the Cathedral). On the second level there is an 800-pood bell, which was cast in the 18th century.

THE METROPOLITAN'S RESIDENCE ❸ "ZABOROVSKIY BRAMA" ❹

To the west of St.Sofia's Cathedral stands a two-story ceremonial baroque palace. For over 200 years it served as the residence of the Kyiv metropoli-

Plan of the National Reserve St.Sofia's Cathedral

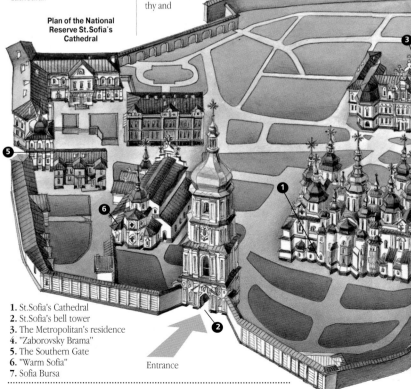

1. St.Sofia's Cathedral
2. St.Sofia's bell tower
3. The Metropolitan's residence
4. "Zaborovsky Brama"
5. The Southern Gate
6. "Warm Sofia"
7. Sofia Bursa

Entrance

tans. The entrance arch behind the metropolitan palace is known as the "Zaborovsky Brama." Actually, it can only be seen from the outside, from Georgievskiy lane. The arch was built in 1744-1746 (by the architect I.G.Schedel) at the command of the Kyiv Metropolitan Raphael (Zaborovsky) - an enthusiast for ecclesiastical art and a patron of arts. The "Brama" is decorated in a rich variety of Ukrainian-baroque style ornamental patterns. Here you can see the miter and panagy (symbols of the metropolitan's power) and Zaborovsky coat of arms - a flaming heart framed in palm branches. In the first quarter of the 19th cen-

tury new construction in the lane raised the ground level to such an extent that the low arch had to be blocked up.

THE SOUTHERN GATES ⑤

The wall, surrounding the Sofia estate, was erected in the 18th century. Apart from the "Zaborovsky Brama" it also has

The Metropolitan's palace

The Holy Warrior
11th century fresco
in St.Sofia's Cathedral

the so-called Southern Gates with a tower, mounted by a spear. In an adjacent building lived the outstanding Ukrainian novelist Grigory Kosynka (Strelets), who fell victim of political

repressions in 1934. To the left of the gate is situated the former Sofia's "Hlebnaya" (bakery), built in the 18th century. Later this was the siege of the Consistorian (head body of the local eparchy). The building has been rebuilt several times.

"THE WARM SOFIA" ⑥

To the south of St.Sofia's Cathedral there is a small church known as "The Warm Sofia." Up until the end of the 19th century, the vast cathedral had no heating. For many years, during the winter divine services were held in this church, which was built in the 1720s. Originally this was the dining hall for the Sofia estate with the temple of St.Lazarus. Later it was renamed as the Church of Christ's Nativity. Now the premises house an architectural museum.

SOFIA BURSA ⑦

This two-story building was erected in the middle of the 18th century according to a design by the architect M.Yurasov. It was designed to house the monastic cells. After the Sofia monastery was closed, the building became the home to a church educational establishment - the Bursa (after 1840 - a religious school). Now the building houses the Central State Archive-Museum of Ukraine's Literature and Art - an outstanding collection of documentary and artistic cultural treasures.

ST.SOFIA'S CATHEDRAL

For Yaroslav the Wise, the building of St.Sofia's Cathedral was an act of assertion of the state power of Kyivan Rus. As a sign of the state's status as the successor to the citadel of the Orthodox Church - Byzantium - the cathedral of Kyiv's metropolitans was named after St.Sofia - the major holy place of Constantinople. Ac-

Oranta

cording to the religious interpretation, the Greek word "Sofia" (wisdom) represented the embodiment of the Lord's Wisdom - Jesus Christ. In historical literature we find two dates for the beginning of its construction - 1017 or 1037. The correct date is a subject of argument to this day.

ANCIENT AND PRESENT APPEARANCE

Today the dimensions of the Cathedral may not appear especially impressive. But remember that it was built in the first half of the 11th century, when most of the architectural jewels of Europe did not yet exist. In those days the metropolitan of Kyiv Illarion said of St.Sofia's Cathedral: "The church is wonderful and glorious. There is nothing of the kind in any northern country." During the succeeding violent centuries, the temple was restored after destruction, reconstructed and enlarged. Inside the Cathedral there are models of St.Sofia's Cathedral in its initial and present form. On the eastern front where the plaster has been partially removed, strips of orange and pink masonry from the times of Yaroslav are visible. It is an alternating sequence of layers of big stones with mortar and thin bricks. This method was borrowed from Roman-Byzantine building practice.

MOSAICS AND FRESCOS

The 11th century mosaics in St.Sofia's Cathedral are preserved only partially. But even the parts

Mosaic fragment

that have survived are wonderful pieces of art that rank alongside the mosaics of Ravenna and Venice. Researchers have counted 177 hues. Unknown Byzantine and Kyiv masters composed amazing images and compositions from small glassy bricks called smalt. The most significant mosaic is the image of the Blessed Virgin, Oranta (Praying), in the apse of the altar. Since ancient times this image has been called the "Unbreakable Wall." There is a legend that this image protects the city. In the main dome there is a half-length image of Christ Pantocrator (Almighty) as a threatening judge. Other surviving mosaics include the "Annunciation," "Eucharist" and "Consecrators." Only one out of the four mosaic images of archangels in the dome of St.Sofia's Cathedral

has survived. In 1880 Mikhail Vrubel skilfully restored the other images using paint. The ancient frescoes have also suffered considerably. The unique group fresco

portrait of the family of St.Sofia's Cathedral founder - Yaroslav the Wise - has survived only partially. A fresco with four figures has been preserved on the south wall. These are the portraits of Yaroslav's sons. But some people suggest that we actually see here the portraits of his daughters. This version is attractive because Yaroslav's daughters were well-known personalities in European history: Elisabeth was queen of Norway, Anna was queen of France, and Anastasia was queen of Hungary. Unique fresco compositions survive on the interior walls of the towers with stairs leading to the gallery: "Reception by the Byzantine Emperor" (the image most likely represents the visit of the Kyivan Princess Olga to Constantine Porphyrogenitos), a bear hunt, a mock combat between masked figures, musicians, the Byzantium race track... The reason why there are so many secular themes here is that, originally, the prince and his retainers entered the staircase leading to the gallery through an external door. For this reason, the interior of the towers was not included as part of the shrine and was not considered sacred.

GRAFFITI

If we look attentively at the interior walls of the cathedral, we can see in places numerous scratched inscriptions - graffiti - right over the paintings. If today somebody scratched something like "Vasya was here" on the wall of a church, he would rightly be called a barbarian. But there is some good from this: the contents of about 300 items of graffiti in Sophia Cathedral dating from the 11th-17th centuries is of great academic interest. The autographs of the princes Vladimir Monomakh and Svyatopolk Izyaslavovich were found here.

SOFIA NECROPOLIS

In the time of Kyiv Rus the cathedral was the crypt of the princes. The tomb of Yaroslav the Wise and his wife Irina has been preserved here. It is located in one of the north altars. The white marble sarcophagus weighs about 6 tons and was probably crafted in the 7-8th centuries. It is decorated with carved images of the cross, palm and cypress branches, birds and

The sarcophagus of Yaroslav the Wise

fishes (supposed to be symbols of the departure of the spirit for Heaven and of the silence of the still body), and Greek letters that represent the initials of the slogans "Jesus Christ is victorious" and "The light of Christ enlightens all." In 1930 the tomb was opened up, and the remains were analysed. The separate bones of a male and female skeleton were found. Obvious signs that the male skeleton was lame

Ancient frescos in St.Sofia's Cathedral. 1850s. M.Sazhin

served as evidence that the remains really did belong to Yaroslav the Wise, since historians knew that the prince was lame. The anthropologist and sculptor Mikhail Gerasimov tried to recreate Yaroslav's image based on the skull found in the tomb. His bust is on display in the Cathedral. The burial places of other princes (including Vladimir Monomakh) have not survived to the present day.

Memorial stone to Yaroslav the Wise

MEMORIAL PLACES IN THE "CITY OF YAROSLAV"

Yaroslav the Wise built up the area of the Upper City, surrounding it with earth ramparts. Access to the Upper City was through three gates, known in the annals as the Golden Gate, the Lyadskiy Gate (see 106) and the Jewish Gate (see 44). The ancient fortifications were destroyed long ago. A network of streets now covers the area, with numerous historic and architectural monuments from the last few centuries. Only a few place-names recall the times of Kyivan Rus: the Golden Gate, Yaroslavov Val Street, Malo-Podvalnaya Street, Irininskaya Street...

THE GOLDEN GATE 10
40a, Vladimirskaya St.
☎ 224–70–68
Ⓜ Zolotiye Vorota
Day off – Thursday

This was the main entrance to "Yaroslav's city." Above an enormous arch rose the cross of the Blagoveshenskiy church with its gold-plated dome (maybe that was why it was called the Golden Gate, echoing the Golden Gates of Constantinople and Jerusalem). During the long years of destruction and decay

The Golden Gate

in the Upper City following Batu's conquest, the gate gradually was destroyed. In the middle of the XIX century the old earth ramparts were levelled, and the ruin of the old structure was left in the middle of the square as a monument. But to mark the jubilee celebrations in 1982, a full-size mock-up of the gate was constructed according to a design by the archaeologist S.Vysotsky, the restorer E.Lopushinskaya and the architect N.Kholostenko. The original ruins are hidden within the new structure, as if in a gigantic holster. In 1997 an old work by the

Y.Hasek

sculptor Ivan Kavaleridze depicting Prince Yaroslav the Wise sitting with a model of St.Sofia in his hand was reproduced on a much larger scale near the Western side of the Gate.

THE BUILDING OF THE SECURITY SERVICE OF UKRAINE 11
33, Vladimirskaya St.

The grey walls of the imposing building belonging to the Security Service of Ukraine recall not only the sinister KGB of the totalitarian period, but also the Gestapo which was based here during the fascist occupation. This building was built in 1913 for the Regional Zemskaya Uprava - the central office of the local representative bodies of Kiev Province. The metropolitan architect V.Shuko drew up the plans. Olga Stolypina - the widow of the Russian prime minister murdered in Kyiv - laid the symbolic foundation stone. After the revolution the building was converted into

Inside the Golden Gate

the Palace of Labour - the city's trade union centre. In 1934-1939, it was the seat of the Central Committee of Ukrainian Bolsheviks.

BERETTI MANSION 12
35, Vladimirskaya St.
Closed to visitors

The Kyiv architect A.Beretti designed this building for himself in 1848. In 1927-1934, its walls housed the history section of the Ukrainian Academy of Sciences headed by Mikhail Grushevsky. Now the building houses the SBU waiting room, with the inscription on the front: "Visitor are admitted 24 hours a day" (the satirist Mikhail Zhvanetsky once joked about that "But when do they let them out?").

THE FORMER HOTEL PRAGUE 13
36, Vladimirskaya St.

The first three floors of the hotel were built in 1880-1882 according to a design by the architect A.Shile. In 1912-1913, on the order of the Czech public figure Vyacheslav Vondrak, three more

The former restaurant Leipzig

floors and a roof-terrace for a summer-restaurant were added. This was the hotel Prague. During World War I, when many Czech and Slovak subjects of the Austro-Hungarian Empire refused to fight against their Slav brothers and surrendered to the Russians, the Prague was a centre of attraction for Vondrak's compatriots. One of them was the writer Yaroslav Hasek, who lived in the hotel in 1916-1918. In the spring of 1917, he published his story-pamphlet "The Good Soldier Swejk in Captivity." The protagonist, whom Hasek had invented in peaceful times, was here plunged into the events of the world war for the first time. With this story written in Kyiv, the Czech writer started work on the novel "The Adventures of the Good Soldier Swejk."

The Good Soldier Swejk.
S.Kovalenkov

THE FORMER RESTAURANT LEIPZIG 14

39, Vladimirskaya St.

This building was erected in 1900-1901 according to a design by the architect K.Shiman. It is interesting

to note that the person who ordered the project - Piotr Grigorovich-Barsky, a dealer in hunting arms - intending to build the most sumptuous building in the city miscalculated his finances and went bankrupt. One of his creditors bought the building and finished the construction. At the beginning of the 20th century this was the cafe-confectionery Marquise. Middle-aged Kyivans remember the German restaurant Leipzig, which was located here.

THE ACTOR'S HOUSE (KARAIME KENASA) 15

7, Yaroslavov Val St.

The architect V.Gorodetsky, 1898-1902 built this building in eastern Moorish style for the local Karaim community. The tobacco magnate Solomon Kogen financed the construction. The building was designed as a house of prayer - or Kenasa (meaning "the gathering") - for the Karaim. The Karaim are a people of Turkish descent whose religion is close to Judaism, though they do not recognize the Talmud. In Soviet times, the Kenasa was used for festivities, now it is the Actor's House.

THE HOUSE OF DOCTOR YANOVSKY 16

13b, Yaroslavov Val St.

A memorial plate marks a modest building in a yard. This was the home of Doctor Feofil Yanovsky, a

general practitioner who worked tirelessly for the public good. He was a prominent scientist, and the first Ukrainian doctor to be made an academician. He never refused to help the suffering, took no payment from the poor, and sometimes

The Actor's House

gave his own money to those in need. The whole city mourned on the day of the doctor's funeral in 1928. Yanovsky was a devout Christian, and in addition to Orthodox clergy, a Roman Catholic priest and a rabbi took part in the mourning.

THE SIKORSKI HOUSE 17

15, Yaroslavov Val St.

This residence set in spacious grounds belonged to the well-known Kyiv psychiatrist Ivan Sikorski. At the back of the yard is the building where his son Igor Sikorski - the internationally renowned aeronautical engineer - spent his childhood and youth. It was here that he first tested his aircraft designs. This site is now occupied by a new building, 15b, which was the home of the academician Viktor Glushkov - a scientist who contributed much to the development of cybernetics and computer design.

I.Sikorski

Fragment of the front of the restaurant Leipzig

DRAMATIC INSTITUTE 18
40, Yaroslavov Val St.

This building was built in 1905-1907 by the architects P.Gollandsky, P.Aleshin for specialized elementary schools. Patron Nikolay Tereshchenko bequeathed the means for its foundation and the initials "NT" are visible on the front. In places they alternate with the letters "AT" (Alexander Tereshchenko, son of Nikolay, supervised the construction). In 1937-1941, a specialized artillery school was located in the building of the former Tereshchenko specialized schools. Later the building was transferred to the dramatic school, now the Institute of Dramatic Arts named in honour of Ivan Karpenko-Kary, a dramatist and leading figure of the Ukrainian stage. Among the alumni are the stars of the Kyiv stage Ada Rogovtseva and Bogdan Stupka.

Caryatid

STRELETSKAYA AND REYTARSKAYA STREETS

The names of these streets take us back 300 years to the time when a Muscovite garrison was stationed in Kyiv. The garrison consisted of streltsy (infantry) and reytary (cavalry). Most of them settled in Podol, where they arrogantly and provocatively violated the rights of the Kyiv burghers. The latter tried their hardest to get the troops moved from Podol to the Upper Town. For example, the burghers offered Kyiv voevode Petr Sheremetiev a substantial bribe, consisting of 100 rubles "in honour" - to have the cavalrymen moved. The voevode

Mascaron

was already rich enough, and he said that he would take the money for building new houses for them in the Upper Town. The Kyivans were so happy they promised him another 100 rubles "in honour," but the punctilious Sheremetiev also spent this money on providing the cavalry men with new homes.

ADDRESS OF UKRAINIAN CLASSICS

On 15, Streletskaya St. there is the old private residence of the noble Kyivan family of the Grigorovych-Barskiys. In 1893-1894 Lesia Ukrayinka lived in this building when she was writing the poem "An Old Tale." Now the Norwegian embassy is located here. At 19, Reytarskaya St., we can see the modest building where the Ukrainian composer and teacher Nikolay Lysenko lived in 1888-1894. Piotr Chaykovsky visited him here and listened to the music to Lysenko' opera "Taras Bulba."

Lesia Ukrayinka

AMBULANCE HOSPITAL 19
22, Reytarskaya St.

The building was built in 1912-1914 for the local ambulance society. The society was funded from tax, municipal grants and donations. The society's cars went out on calls, saving dozens of lives a day. The front is richly decorated in the Florentine Renaissance style. It was designed by the architect Joseph Zektser (later by a tragic coincidence he was to die in this same building after being run over by a tram). The house to the right at 20/24, Reytarskaya St. is in the modern style and dates from

Chimera

the same period (Architect A.Verbytsky). The variety artist Yuri Timoshenko - Tarapunka from the popular satirical duet "Tarapunka and Shtepsel" - lived here.

MONSTERS ON THE FRONTS

The unusual details on some of the facades of the Upper Town are worthy of closer attention. The corner window of the building in the Mauritanian style at 31/16, Reytarskaya St. (architect N.Yaskevich, 1900) is held up by two little dragons. The former residence of Sofia Chokolova, the wife of industrialist, at 32, Bolshaya Zhitomirskaya St. built in the modern style (1911) is called "The House of Snakes." Under the corner window on the right there are two concrete snakes

A house on Reytarskaya Street

intertwined. In 1912 the engineer M.Bobrusov built a revenue house at 8-a, Bolshaya Zhitomirskaya St. using the motifs of Romantic Gothic architecture. One of the most effective details of this building is a sinister chimera sitting on the left corner. The physiognomies of medieval monsters look out at us from the end-walls.

MEMORY OF SCIENTISTS

Some well-known scientific figures lived on Bolshaya Zhitomirskaya Street. Alexander Shargey, who was liable for military service in the Civil War, avoided mobilization by hiding at his stepmother's place in the house at #18. He acquired documents in the name Yuri Kondratuk and under this name went down in the history of space travel. His prophetic ideas about interplanetary flight were even used by the Americans during the development of the Apollo project for landing astronauts on the Moon. The philosopher and priest Sergey Bulgakov lived in the house at #26. The late XIX century residence at #28 is currently occupied by the Botanical Institute. It was previously home to the Microbiology Institute of Microbiology,

D.Zabolotniy

whose first director was Daniil Zabolotniy - an outstanding fighter against plague. In 1928-1929, he was the President of All-Ukrainian Academy of Science. He lived in an apartment adjoining the Institute.

HOUSE OF MIKLUKHO-MAKLAY [20]

17, Malaya Zhitomirskaya St.

This building belonged to Captain Vladimir Miklukho-Maklay - the brother of the well-known traveler and anthropologist. The captain died as a hero in the Battle of Tsushima. His battleship "Admiral Ushakov" was one of the few Russian ships that were able offer resistance to the Japanese fleet.

The doctor's house at 17/2, Bolshaya Zhitomirskaya St.

Ruins of Golden Gate, 1840s.
M.Sazhin

THE LESKOV HOUSE [21]

21, Mikhaylovskaya St.

Additional floors were built onto the old buildings here in the late 1940s. In the second half of 19th century, they belonged to the doctor and society figure Alexey Leskov. His brother, the writer Nikolay Leskov, often came to visit him here.

LITERARY MEMORIAL HOUSE-MUSEUM OF T.SHEVCHENKO [22]

8a, T.Shevchenko lane

☎ 228–35–11

Ⓜ Maydan Nezalezhnosti

Day off – Friday

This lane and the adjoining area were formerly known simply as "Goat Bog" - because of a pool from which goats presumably came to drink.

Kyivans called "Goat Bog" Kozinka. Here on Kozinka, in the modest house of engineer Ivan Zhitnitsky, three friends took up residence in the spring of 1846. They were the writer Alexander Afanasiyev-Chuzhbinsky, the painter Mikhail Sazhin, and the poet and painter Taras Shevchenko. The painters worked all day long, depicting poetical views of Kyiv and ancient monuments. In the evening they returned to the Kozinka for friendly tea drinking. Shevchenko lived here until the beginning of the next year. The house has been preserved. There is an exhibition of the Kobzar's personal things, engravings and pictures, autographs, and rare editions. There is a Taras Shevchenko memorial studio in the attic.

House-museum of T.Shevchenko

THE NEIGHBORHOOD OF MIKHAYLOVKAYA SQUARE

The north-eastern part of the Upper City was separated from the other parts of Old Kyiv plateau by ravines. It was called Mikhaylova Mountain after the Mikhaylovsky Gold-Domed Monastery that was situated there. After the monument to Prince Vladimir was erected, the mountain was called Vladimirskaya. As time passed, the ravines were covered up with earth and the vast Mikhaylovskaya Square was formed. When Kyiv became the capital of Soviet Ukraine in 1934, the authorities decided to unite Mikhaylovskaya and Sofiyskaya squares, creating a gigantic parade ground and governmental centre. This project was abandoned halfway through, although the Mikhaylovsky Gold-Domed Monastery and the bell tower were already destroyed. In recent years, these lost historical monuments were reconstructed.

Mikhaylovskaya Square

MIKHAYLOVSKY GOLD-DOMED MONASTERY 23
(see 146)

THE MINISTRY OF FOREIGN AFFAIRS 24
1, Mikhaylovskaya Square

The massive grey ministry building was built in 1936-1938. At first it was the seat of the Central Committee of the Communist Party of Ukraine, then of regional and city party organizations. The architect I.Langbard, who won the competition for the creation of a governmental centre, built it according to a design. This was the only part of the design that was com-

Memorial plate to V.Simirenko

pleted. An identical building was to have been built in place of the Mikhaylovsky Monastery. In between the two, a 75-meter statue of Lenin would have stood facing the river with his back to the square. The ministry is built almost exactly where the ancient Triokhsviatitelskaya church stood before it was demolished in the 1930s.

THE SIMIRENKO MANSION 25
9, Desiatinnaya St.

The architect V.Nikolayev erected this elegant neo-Greek building in the 1890s. At first it belonged to the entrepreneur Vasiliy Simirenko - a patron of Ukrainian culture and one of the sponsors of the magazine "Kyiv Antiquities."

According to his will, after his death the building became the property of the Ukrainian Scientific Society. Art scholars and archaeologists worked here. Under the Nazis, the mansion was the seat of the Union of Ukrainian Writers (wiped out by the Gestapo in 1942). Now it houses the British Embassy.

BALAKHOVSKY APARTMENT HOUSE 26
8, Desiatinnaya St.

This building was erected in 1914 for the Balakhovsky family of sugar magnates. Daniel Balakhovsky, a music lover; once organized a concert in Kyiv given by his good friend - the composer Alexander Skryabin. In 1919 Skryabin's widow with her mother and three children lived in the mansion. Soviet commissioners quickly became interested in the big and comfortable building. The residents were ordered to leave the premises within 48 hours. They sent a telegram to the head of the Soviet People's Committee V.Ulianov-Lenin: "While a monument to the composer Skryabin is being erected in Moscow, the Soviet authorities are throwing his family out of their house in Kyiv." Nobody knows whether the leader of the

Ministry of Foreign Affairs. Pediment with state symbols

world proletariat ever read this telegram, but the residents of the house were left in peace. Afterwards however this was the residence of Ukraine's party leaders.

THE FORMER TECHNICAL HIGHSCHOOL **27**

2, Bolshaya Zhitomirskaya St.

The architect A.Beretti built this late-classical building in 1858-1861. It was later enlarged. In 1873 it was bought by the Kyiv Technical Highschool - a secondary educational establishment whose graduates could enter technical universities.

The Technical Highschool .
From a post-card from the beginning of the 20th century

The Christening of Rus

Among those educated here were the architects Pavel Aleshin and Yevgeniy Yermakov, Anton Straus, the inventor of drill driven piles, the revolutionary Piotr Zaporozhets, the artist Constantine Kryzhitsky (he was interested in drawing from early childhood and once accidentally handed in to his teacher a copybook with his drawings instead of his math copybook; the teacher approved the boy's talent). After the revolution the building was used as a teaching institution, a musical theatre and now is used as an establishment.

The monument to Princess Olga

THE MONUMENT TO PRINCESS OLGA **28**

In 1911 the Kyiv department of the Emperor's Russian War and History Society proposed to build an alley of statues reflecting the centuries-old past of Kyiv around Mikhaylovskaya and Sofiyskaya squares - "The Historical Way." But only the first step was made: in front of the Real College a monument was erected depicting Princess Olga flanked by Apostle Andrew and the Saints Cyril and Methodius. The young sculptor Ivan Kavaleridze won the competition for the design. The monument was opened in September 1911. The statues were made out of plaster with marble fragments. It was formally considered a model for the future monument, which was to be made from more durable materials. But it was not time that destroyed the monument - it was demolished by the Soviet authorities (for some time the pedestal was occupied by a bust of Taras Shevchenko). But the original monument was replaced in marble in 1995-1996.

VLADIMIRSKAYA MOUNTAIN

The "Vladimirskaya Mountain" park was laid out at the end of the 19th century. This is a popular place for recreation - green, pleasant, with old pavilions and beautiful views visible through gaps in the leaves. After their high-school graduation party many pupils wait for the dawn in the romantic park. The traditional religious procession to mark St.Vladimir's Day on July 15 (28) used to start from here. A pavilion with a panorama entitled "Calvary" was opened at the entrance to the park from Triokhsviatitel'skaya Street in 1902. A circular picture of Jerusalem and the crucifixion of Jesus Christ were created by Austrian artists (unfortunately the panorama was removed in 1934).

THE MONUMENT TO PRINCE VALDIMIR **29**

The first sculptural monument in Kyiv was unveiled in 1853. A.Ton designed it. The majestic

Vladimirskaya Mountain.
1913 I.Izhakevich

statue of the canonized prince with a cross in one hand and the princely crown in the other is set on a brick pedestal covered in cast iron and shaped in the form of a chapel. The pedestal is decorated with an alto-relievo depicting the Christening of the Kyivans. We can also see here in relief the regalia of Order of St.Vladimir (stars and crosses) symbolizing the christening "by fire and sword," as well as the coat of arms of Kyiv - Archangel Michael.

LVOVSKA SQUARE, KUDRIAVETS

The residents of old Kyiv left the "city of Yaroslav" on the road to Halich, Zhitomir and Lvov through the so-called Jewish Gate near the present day Lvovska square. The name of the gate came from the Jewish quarter, which used to be located near here. The gate in this direction later became known as the Lvovskiye Gate. Not far the gate was the fortified north-west rim of the Upper Town - known in the annals as Kopyrev end (this name maybe originates from the name "Kopyr"). Archaeologists uncovered the remains of four Christian churches here. Later on the neighbourhood was known as Kudriavets ("curly" - either because of the foaming water in the nearby streams or because of a leafy hill). The present-day system of streets was formed during the 19th century.

HOUSE OF COMMERCE 30
8, Lvovska Square

Architect V.Yezhov built the high-rise House of Commerce in the 1960-1970s. The incongruity of this skyscraper with its 4-floors of retail space and 24-floors of office space near to the unobtrusive "city of Yaroslav" is obvious.

ARTISTS' HOUSE 31
1/5, Artema St.

This large building with its spacious conference-hall and numerous exhibition rooms was opened in 1978 (architect A.Dobrovolsky). The front is decorated with seven feminine figures. These are not the muses as is often claimed (there should be nine muses). These are the sculptural symbols of the different artistic genres.

FORMER ART SCHOOL 32
2, Vorovskogo St.

Now a teacher training college, in 1902-1920 this building was the Kyiv Art School. A pleiade of talented artists was raised here:

Aristarkh Lentulov, Mane-Kats, Alexander Osmerkin, Anatoly Petritsky, Karp Trokhimenko, Alexander Tyshler, sculptors Alexander Arkhipenko, Ivan Kavaleridze and many others. The teachers included architect Vladimir Nikolaev (the first Head of School), painters Grigory Diachenko, Fedor Krichevsky, Alexander Murashko, Nikolay Pimonenko and sculptor Fedor Balavensky.

PUSHKIN MUSEUM 33
9, Kudriavskaya St.
☎ 212–42–06
Ⓜ Zolotiye Vorota
Day off – Monday

This is one of the newest museums in the city. It opened in this building in 1999. The museum was based on Yakov Berdichevsky's collection of Pushkiniana. The exhibits include several editions published during Pushkin's lifetime, and materials concerning Pushkin's

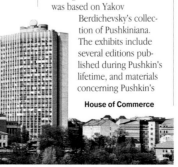
House of Commerce

Artist's House

residence in Kyiv in 1820 and 1821. Architect M.Ikonnikov built the building where the museum is located in 1882. Architect A.Krauss reconstructed it in 1894. The family of Afanasy Bulgakov, a professor at Kyiv Religious Academy, lived here for several years. His oldest son, the future writer Mikhail Bulgakov, went to school from this house. Incidentally, Bulgakov wrote a play about Pushkin.

F.Krichevsky

THE OLDEST BRIDGE 34

As a result of the state vodka monopoly, a liquor warehouse was built at 14, Kudriavskaya St. in 1896. In order to provide easy access to the warehouse, a small bridge-viaduct was thrown across the Voznesensky ravine (engineer V.Bessmertny, 1897). Today it is the oldest bridge in the city.

**ANDREYEVSKY
SPUSK**

ANDREYEVSKY SPUSK

In recent decades the Andreyevsky Spusk has become a cult street for Kyivans and visitors. There are several reasons for this. First, there is the beauty of the street (which was emphasized by the thorough renovation carried out in the 1980s). Second, the increasing interest of society and the authorities in monuments of culture (not only those like Saint Andrew's Church, but also conventional buildings). Third, the lifting of the prohibition on the creative legacy of Mikhail Bulgakov, whose name is inseparably linked to the history of the Andreyevsky Spusk. And finally, the permission for artists to trade their works freely in the street. Today's Andreyevsky Spusk is comparable to Monmartre in Paris for its picturesque sights and abundant artistic life.

"**Pronya Prokopovna and Svirid Golohvastov**" - a statue erected near Saint Andrew's Church (sculptors V.Shchur, V.Sivko, 1999) depicting the heroes of the play by M.Staritskiy "After Two Hares," as played by the actors M.Krynitsyna and O.Borysov.

The Ukrainian writer **Hryhor Tutunnik** lived at 34, Andreyevsky Spusk.

Workdays and holidays in Andreyevsky Spusk

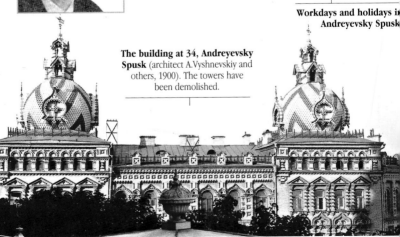

The building at 34, Andreyevsky Spusk (architect A.Vyshnevskiy and others, 1900). The towers have been demolished.

One of the halls of the memorial museum of **Mikhail Bulgakov.** On the wall is a portrait of Afanasiy Bulgakov, the writer's father.

Rare antiquarian books. "The Museum of One Street."

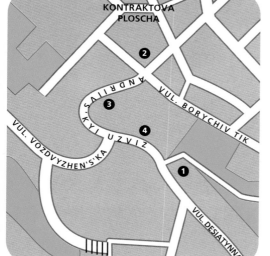

KONTRAKTOVA PLOSCHA

VUL. BORYCHIV TIK

ANDRIYS'KYI UZVIZ

VUL. VOZDVYZHEN'S'KA

VUL. DESIATYNNA

Memorial plate to Mikhail Bulgakov on "The Turbin House."

The Day of Kyiv on the Andreyevsky Spusk.

Storefronts with displays. "The Museum of One Street."

SAINT ANDREW'S CHURCH 1

23, Andreyevsky Spusk
☎ 228–58–61
Ⓜ Zolotiye Vorota
Day off – Thursday

Saint Andrew's Church, an outstanding monument of the 18th century, was declared a museum in 1968.

THE LEGEND ABOUT THE APOSTLE ANDREW

The hill where the church is located was called "Andrew's Hill" after the Apostle Saint Andrew. "The Chronicle of Bygone Times" contains an ancient legend about the Apostle Andrew, who travelled around the world and preached. One day he came to the banks of the Dnieper-Borysthenes River and spent the night there.

F.B.Rastrelli

In the morning he said to his followers: "Do you see these hills? On these hills, God will spread his grace. A town will appear, and God will raise many churches." And having blessed the place, the Apostle placed the cross on the mountain. The tradition binds the construction of the cross with the location of Saint Andrew's Church.

MONOGRAM OF SOVEREIGN

The idea to construct the church originated with the Empress Elizabeth Petrovna. She visited Kyiv in 1744, and with her own hand she laid the first foundation stone of the future church on Andreyevskaya Hill. Now the monogram of the sovereign is inscribed on the frontons of Saint Andrew's Church.

Elizabeth Petrovna

THE AUTHOR OF THE DESIGN

The church was originally designed by the famous architect Johann-Gottfried Schedel. However, the empress eventually handed over the new project to her favourite, the even more famous architect Rastrelli. The chief-architect of the court, Francesco Bartholomew Rastrelli (in Russia he was called Varpholomey Varpholomeyevich), was known for numerous constructions in the baroque style - grandiose palaces and churches in Petersburg, Petergof, Tsarskoe Selo. But the Church of Saint Andrew with its modest proportions is perhaps the most harmonious and picturesque work he left behind.

THE BUILDER OF THE CHURCH

Rastrelli was constantly occupied with construction work in the capital. So the experienced architect Ivan Michurin was dispatched from Moscow to take direct charge of the construction of the Church of Saint Andrew. He coped with the task successfully in spite of many difficulties. Many problems arose due to underground streams in the rock of the hill that threatened to wash away the foundation. The architects had to deepen the foundation. As a result, the temple was placed on strong socle in the form of a two-story building built by Michurin. The roof of this building acts as the terrace near the church.

INTERIOR DECORATION

The elegant interior of the church is close to the rococo style. The carved golden three-tier central icons are magnificent. They were created by a special group of painters. Among the artists who did the work were the leading master of those times Alexei Antropov (one of Antropov's works in the church - the icon "The Last Supper" - was for a long time attributed to... Leonardo da Vinci). Two ancient pictures "The Choice of Faith by Prince Vladimir" and "The Sermon of the Apostle Andrew" are placed separately.

Element of the interior

KEEPER OF THE SANCTUARY

Looking at the present magnificence of the church, it is hard to believe that there were times when it was deserted and unattractive. The Empress Elisabeth planned to take personal care of the church. Therefore the church serves no parish, and there is no bell tower to call the congregation to divine services. But the empress died

A.Muraviov

before the work was finished. After her death, the court took no interest in the Kyiv church.

The church was at last consecrated in 1767. But there was not enough money to maintain it. All that was left was to hope for help from voluntary keepers of the sanctuary. Such a keeper was Andrey Muraviov. He was known for his essays about Christian churches, including those of Kyiv. His efforts made it possible to collect funds for the reconstruction works. After Muraviov died, his remains were interred in the socle building of Saint Andrew's, in the Sergievskaya church developed by Muraviov.

"IT IS BEAUTIFUL"

Kyivans and tourists admire Podol and the Dnieper from the terrace of the church. Mikhail Maksimovich, the first head of Kyiv University, remembered how in 1835 he was standing on the terrace with Gogol. Walking on the terrace, they noticed a Ukrainian girl admiring the landscape. "Why are you looking there?"- asked Nikolay Vasiliovich. "Because it is beautiful" - the girl answered simply.

The Last Supper.
A fragment. The 18th century.
A.Antropov

RESTITUTION OF THE LOST IMAGE

From time to time the temple needed reconstruction. The repair works altered the appearance of the church, and after two centuries the church did not look much like the author's plan. But in 1963 Rastrelli's original drafts were found in Vienna. This made it possible to re-establish the original appearance of the facades. This plan was carried out during the restoration in the 1970s (architect-restorer V.Korneyeva).

Detail of the iconostasis

49

"The Museum of One Street" [2]

2b, Andreyevsky Spusk
☎ 416-03-98
Ⓜ Kontraktovaya Square
Day off – Monday

The museum occupies the lower floor of one of two adjacent modern style buildings (architect K.Shiman, 1910-1915), which belonged to the entrepreneur-tanner Akim Frolov - you can still see the initials A.F. on one of the fronts. "The Museum of One Street" is a small but unique and exciting exposition, prepared with love and humor by enthusiasts. It is hard to conceive what an immense layer of historic and cultural events are directly connected with the short Andreyevsky spusk.

"The Turbin House." Mikhail Bulgakov Museum [3]

13, Andreyevsky Spusk
☎ 416-31-88
Ⓜ Kontraktovaya Square
Day off – Wednesday

From 1906-1919 (off and on) this famous "house of unusual design" was the residence of the son of a Kyiv professor of theology, the future writer Mikhail Bulgakov. His family occupied the flat on the first floor (the ground-floor from the yard). The ground floor (cellar from the yard) was the residence of the landlord-engineer V.Listovnichiy. It is in this apart-ment with cream-colored curtains that the action of the novel "The White Guard" and the play "The Days of the Turbins" takes place. A literary memorial museum was opened in the house to mark the 100th anniversary of the writer (May 15, 1991). On the upper floor there is an exhibition: only the authentic Bulgakov objects have a conventional appearance; all the replicas are made from plaster. The lower floor contains thematic exhibitions. The muse-

"Richard's castle"

um's collection was prepared by Kyiv collectors, Bulgakov scholars and theatrical historians, with the active support of the descendants of Bulgakov and Listovnichiy. The house, built in 1888 (architect N.Gardenin), was thoroughly renovated before the opening of the museum (architect I.Malakova). There is a memorial plate with the writer's portrait at the front of the house. The Soviet officials took a dim view of the "anti-Soviet" Bulgakov, but they had no choice. For a long time already, people could see the inscription "House of Bulgakov" scratched into the wall of the house.

"The Castle of Richard Lionheart" [4]

15, Andreyevsky Spusk

The romantic name in honour of the medieval English king was given to the building by the writer V.Nekrasov. In reality the

Andreyevsky Spusk

owner of this house was the contractor Dmitri Orlov. The building was erected in 1902-1904, and the owner didn't bother to clear the project with the local authorities, which resulted in a scandal. It has been established that the modernized gothic fronts were practically copied from a published design for a Petersburg building by the architect R.Marfeld. But the stunning relief of Andreyevsky spusk softened the effect of this plagiarism. The half-cellar of the building contained a barber's shop and two stores - a grocery and a butcher. The other premises were used as apartments to let. It is known that the Kyiv artists G.Diadchenko, I.Makushenko and F.Balavenskiy liked to stay in the Orlov house. The church historian S.Golubev also lived here. In 1911 Orlov died

The Cat Behemoth.

under mysterious circumstances while building a railroad in the Far East. His widow, who was left with five children, had to sell the house to pay the debts. This is now one of the most popular buildings in Kyiv, it is currently being renovated as a hotel. A nearby metal staircase leads to an observation platform at the top of Uzdykhalnitsa Hill - a spur of the Andreyevskaya Hill.

"The Turbin House"

NO KYIV WITHOUT PODOL

NO KYIV WITHOUT PODOL

Podol is rightly considered to be one of the most popular districts in Kyiv. The refrain of a popular song begins with the words: "No Kyiv without Podol." It is an embodiment of the democratic spirit in our city. Craftsman worked here, businessmen traded here, the "fathers of the city" sat in the Magistrates' Hall here, and they all prayed in the numerous Podol churches. Meanwhile, the houses of prayer of other communities - Polish, Armenian, Greek, German, Tatar, Jewish - were also to be found in Podol. The altruistic enthusiast of the Ukrainian enlightenment Galshka Gulevichevna established the School of the Orthodox Brothers here - the future Kyiv-Mogilanska Academy. Podol is the old craftsmen's settlement - the Potters and Tanners; it is the Brodsky Mill and the old electric power station; it is the 200-year-old water main and solar clock; it is Kyiv's first chemist's shop and the first automobile; it is the first tram line in the Russia Empire; it is the River Fleet, the Contract Fairs and the Zhitniy Market. Podol was destroyed by enemy tribes. Catherine II planned to demolish it. In 1811, a huge fire burned down most of the buildings in Podol. The flood waters of the Dnieper overflowed onto the Podol streets. But this district is immortal.

The memorial plate at the Contract House to mark the concert tour **of Ferenz Liszt** (see 56).

The memorial sign in honour of 100 years of Kyiv's tram system. The first tram line was opened in May 1892. It led through the modern Vladimirskiy Spusk and Podol.

The statue of Samson in the fountain of the same name (see 56).

"The Korobka House" at 20/2, Sagaidachnogo St. (architect L.Stanzani, 1830s) was built for the gold-smith Fedor Korobka. This is one of the best examples of a classical building in Podol.

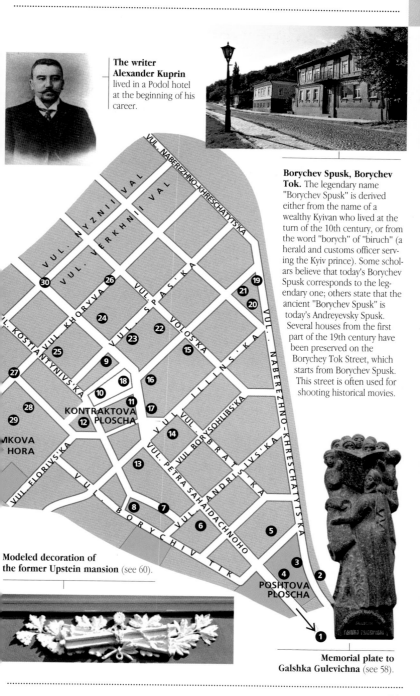

The writer Alexander Kuprin lived in a Podol hotel at the beginning of his career.

Borychev Spusk, Borychev Tok. The legendary name "Borychev Spusk" is derived either from the name of a wealthy Kyivan who lived at the turn of the 10th century, or from the word "borych" of "biruch" (a herald and customs officer serving the Kyiv prince). Some scholars believe that today's Borychev Spusk corresponds to the legendary one; others state that the ancient "Borychev Spusk" is today's Andreyevsky Spusk. Several houses from the first part of the 19th century have been preserved on the Borychey Tok Street, which starts from Borychev Spusk. This street is often used for shooting historical movies.

Modeled decoration of the former Upstein mansion (see 60).

Memorial plate to Galshka Gulevichna (see 58).

"THE MAGDEBURG RIGHT COLUMN" **1**
Naberezhnoye Shosse

This was the first monument in Kyiv. It was erected in 1802 by the architect A.Melensky to honour the confirmation by Tsar Alexander I of the Magdeburg Right for the Kyivans (see 12). The base of the column contained the "Kreshchatiksky source" - a small basin filled with water from underground springs (this water was believed to cure eye diseases). This monument is also called "the monument to the Christening of Rus" as it stands more or less at the same place where Vladimir christened his sons, and also "the lower monument to Prince Vladimir" (there is an inscription at the base of the column "To St.Vladimir - the Enlightener of Russia").

THE RIVERBOAT STATION **2**
Pochtovaya Square

Pochtovaya Square is the gateway to Podol. From ancient times riverboats berthed at its quays. In the 19th century steamboats started to navigate the Dnieper, and a row of quays stretched along the bank near Pochtovaya Square. In 1953-1961 the architects V.Gopkalo, V.Ladny and others, built a new riverboat station at the Square. The building with its mast-like tower resembles a steamboat.

At the end of the 19th century the United Society transported passengers on the Dnieper for Steam Navigation. But there were many private ship-owners too. Competition meant that the price of transportation was reduced to a minimal level. The United Society, for example, charged 20 kopecks for a ticket from Kyiv to Kremenchug, while for the same price the private owners also provided a complimentary bun. When the fall in prices became too disadvantageous, the United Society resorted to radical measures: they rented all the private boats and established fixed prices for tickets.

The Post Station

THE POST STATION **3**
Pochtovaya Square

A mail-coach station was opened in 1865, giving the square its name. The single-story station building has been preserved. Although of modest dimensions, the building took a very long time to build - from 1852 to 1865. The Post Station was a whole complex with stables, coach-halls and service outhouses, but most of them were demolished when the subway station was built. Now the building is used as an exposition hall.

The Magdeburg Right Column

"SHEVCHENKOVA CHURCH" SITE **4**

During the atheistic bacchanalia of 1935, the Church of Christ's Nativity, which formerly stood between the Post Station and today's Sagaydachnogo Street, was levelled. In May of 1861, the coffin with the remains of Taras Shevchenko was kept in this church during its shipment from Petersburg for burial in Kanev. Thousands of people gathered to say farewell to the Great Kobzar. A passer-by asked: "Who is the deceased?" The answer was: "A simple peasant, but with the status of a general." The church was subsequently called "Shevchenkova." Now there is a plan to restore it.

BRODSKY MILL ELEVATOR **5**
13, Borichev Spusk

The biggest flour-milling enterprise in old Kyiv was founded in 1857. In 1870 it became the property of the Brodsky family of sugar manufacturers. In 1892 it became the property of the

The cable railway

joint-stock company subsequently named after Lazar Brodsky. The notorious Stalinist functionary Lazar Kaganovich worked there as a loader, but he was fired for attempting to organize a strike. The mill building was destroyed by fire in 1920. The elevator was preserved - an enor-

The Riverboat Station

mous building built in 1907 with a tower that dominates the square. Now it is used as a book depository.

"THE SOUL PHARMACY"

In the middle of the XIX century on today's Sagaydachnogo Street there was a bookshop with a library called "the cabinet for reading news about Russian literature." The owner, retired captain Pavel Dolzhikov, grandiloquently called his establishment "the Soul Pharmacy." For some reason, a stuffed boar was on display in one of the library's windows. In 1848 Nikolai Gogol visited Kyiv for a few days. Dolzhikov knew about his arrival and dreamed of luring the famous writer into his shop. But during one of his strolls round the city, Gogol came to Podol himself. It was just starting to rain, and he decided to take shelter in the library. But Dolzhikov did not recognize the author and shouted at him: "This is not a tavern! Clear off!" Gogol was taken aback and responded: "Now I know why you have a dummy in your window - it's you yourself." And he went away. Later Dolzhikov almost tore his hair out when he learnt the identity of the person he had been so rude with.

THE BALABUKHA ESTATE 6

27, Sagaydachnogo St.

This residence belonged to the Balabukha family of merchants. They were famous for producing tasty jam and candied peel. It was said that the Balabukhas got the recipe from the court confectioner of Catherine II, who was stuck in Kyiv for a long time when he broke his leg. A one-story building dating from the late XVIII century and an annex on the side of Sagaydachnogo

Street built by the architect L.Stanzani in 1839 have been preserved. In front of the annex there is a small square with a sculpture representing a Zaporizhzhyan Cossack and a Kobzar.

Pokrovskaya church

POKROVSKAYA STREET 7 POKROVSKAYA CHURCH 8

What makes this street unique is the fact that it has retained its direction and a few buildings from the period before the fire of 1811. At that time it was part of Podol's main transportation artery, and the heart of its social and business life. The first floor of house #4 - today the Podol lyceum is situated here - was built in 1799-1801 by the architect A.Yeldezin as the original Contract House (see 56). The Church of Nikola the Kind built by the architect A.Melensky in 1800-1807 stood at 6 Pokrovskaya Street until the 1930s. In 1913 the 22-year-old Mikhail Bulgakov married his first wife, Tatiana Lappa, here. After the church was barbarously demolished, all that remains is the bell tower from the beginning of the 18th century. The classical-style mansion at #5 (1808) initially belonged to the Kyiv jeweler Samson Strelbitsky. At the end of the

The "Widow's House"

19th century, the then owner - merchant and philanthropist Mikhail Degtyarev - maintained an old people's home here. He also founded the "Widow's House" on 1, Pokrovskaya St. Built by the architect V.Nikolaev in 1891, it provided free accommodation for women in need. Now the mansion is the residence of the US ambassador, and the "Widow's House" is home to the National Bank of Ukraine Academy. The street is named after the Pokrovskaya church, built by the architect I.Grigorovich-Barsky in 1766. Its elegant decorations, authentic Ukrainian porches - "ganky" - and traditional division into three parts give the church the characteristic features of the Ukrainian Baroque. In 1824 a warm section with a chapel dedicated to St.John the Warrior was built adjoining the eastern part of the church. Nearby stands the bell tower dating from the first part of the 18th century. A second brick tier was built on later. More than 500 years ago an Armenian church stood on almost the same spot. Archaeologists have investigated its foundations.

The Balabukha Estate

CONTRACT FAIRS

The Contract Fairs were moved from the Volyn village of Dubno to Kyiv in 1797 by the decree of Tsar Pavel I. They were held in Kyiv every year from January 15 to February 1 (old calendar). Not only was it a place for ordinary trade, agreements - called "contracts" - were concluded here between landlords and merchants. This provided a huge boost to the development of Kyiv, which at the time did not see many public events. For the days of the fairs, Kontraktova Square was filled with temporary kiosks. Wealthy people and nobility from the whole Southwest Territory came to the city. At the same time, the Contract Fairs attracted a mass of pickpockets and swindlers to Kyiv. Prices for hotels and trading spots shot up. When property-owners in Podol leased their apartments, they made it a special condition that the tenant should free several rooms for the time of the fair. The tradition of Contract Fairs continued into the 1920s, but with the end of the New Economic Policy it disappeared. Only now are attempts being made to revive it.

The Contract House

CONTRACT HOUSE 9
1, Mezhigorskaya St.

The Fair's headquarters were at the Contract House. At first it was situated at 4, Pokrovskaya St., but in 1817 a new building was put up for it. It was just a part of a project by the architect William Geste that has never been fully realized. At the centre of "the Geste Complex" was to be the seat of the city magistrate, to the left - the post-office, and to the right - the Contract House. The city government of the time could only find the money for one building (proposals recently have been made to complete the ensemble). The Contract House contained the richest shops, stockbrokers' and notaries' offices. Contracts were registered

"Samson" fountain

here. On the second floor there was a concert hall. Well-known artists, such as the singer Angelica Catalani, the violinist Henryk Wieniawski and the pianist Ferenc Liszt (who, by the way, met his future wife Caroline Sayn-Wittgenstein during a concert tour in Kyiv in 1847), gave concerts here during the Contract Fair. At different periods, Alexander Pushkin, Denis Davidov, Nikolai Gogol, Adam Mickiewicz, Honore de Balzac and Taras Shevchenko visited the Contract House. Between fairs the city authorities used the house at their discretion. The building is now home to the Ukrainian Interbank Currency Exchange.

THE "SAMSON" FOUNTAIN 10

This arched brick pavilion, decorated with Corinthian columns, was built in 1749 by the architect Grigorovich-Barsky, above a fountain that was part of Kyivs' first water supply system. To mark the 100th anniversary of the Battle of Poltava in 1809, a naive wooden sculpture of Samson grappling a lion's mouth was added. If the ancient hero was meant to symbolize Peter I in his victory over the Swedish, it has to be said that Kyiv's Samson was less of a tribute to the Tsar (as in Peterhof) than a parody. There is a legend that anyone who drinks water out of the fountain will become a resident of Kyiv. Over the pavil-

Podol market. From a watercolor painting by M.Sazhin.

ion stands a statue of the Apostle Andrew; at the end of the 19th century a sundial was placed over the columns. In the 1930s the fountain was demolished (they say that an official saw a heap of garbage in the pavilion and was misunderstood when he said "Clear it away!"). But in 1982 the architect-restorers Y.Lositskiy and V.Shevchenko rebuilt it in its former shape. Inside the pavilion there is a concrete copy of Samson and the lion.

GOSTINIY DVOR 11
Kontraktova Square

In 1809 construction began on a square building with shopping arcades in the middle of the square - Gostiniy Dvor (Hospitable Courtyard). It was designed by the Moscow architect Luigi Ruski. The first floor was barely completed when Podol was struck by fire. As a result, the shopping arcades were finished in haste, and remained only one story. Restorers subse-

The Church of the Blessed Virgin Pirogoshya

quently unearthed Ruski's blueprints, and in the 1980s, Gostiniy Dvor came to look the way it originally should have. Apart from shops and cafes, the building now houses the V.Zabolotniy Institute and the Library of Civil Construction of Ukraine.

Gostiniy Dvor

THE CHURCH OF THE BLESSED VIRGIN PIROGOSHYA 12
Kontraktova Square

Prince Mstislav Vladimirovich built the Church of the Blessed Virgin at the western end of the present square in 1132-1136. Before the construction began, the icon of the Blessed Virgin Pirogoshya was shipped from Byzantium (scholars believe that the name Pirogoshya comes from the Greek word "pirogotis" - "tower": this was the name given in Byzantium to icons displayed in the towers of monastery walls or in which towers were depicted). The hero of "The Lay of Igor's Campaign" - Prince Igor Sviatoslavovich - came to Pirogoshya to give thanks for his delivery from captivity among the nomads. The ancient church was rebuilt several times. In the first half of the 18th century it was the metropolitan church of Orthodox Kyiv (in those days, the church was known as Uspenskaya). During the period of the "Magdeburg Right," the magistrates' ceremonies took place here and the City Archive was kept here. This Podol shrine was demolished in 1935. The architects Y.Aseev, V.Otchenashko and others, rebuilt according to its original appearance in 1998.

THE FORMER THIRD GYMNASIUM 13
8, Pokrovskaya St.

This was originally a two-story classical mansion belonging to Nazariy Sukhota, a wealthy

The former Third Gymnasium

Kyivan. In the middle of the 19th century it was the seat of the City Council. Later it was given to the Third Men's Gymnasium. In 1876-1878, the mansion was extended and the part facing the square widened by the architects A.Shile and V.Nikolayev. Among the pupils of the gymnasium were the well-known doctor Feofil Yanovskiy, Lev Shvarzman (the son of a dry goods merchant, he became known as the idealist-philosopher Lev Shestov), and the poet Daniel Ruthouse. Now this is the district House of Children's Art.

THE FORMER GREEK MONASTERY 14
2b, Kontraktova Square

These adjoining modern-empire buildings (the architect V.Eysner, 1912-1914) originally belonged to St.Catherine's Monastery, which served the community of Greek colonists. The monastery's 18th century church, which was located at the end of the block, was demolished in 1929. The front buildings have survived, and are now used by the Kyiv and Regional Department of the National Bank of Ukraine. The destroyed bell tower over the right building was restored in 1996. It has now become a notable architectural feature.

The former Greek Monastery

GALSHKA'S DONATION

In 1615, the wealthy benefactress Galshka Gulevichevna offered the Kyiv Epiphany Fraternity a large plot of land for building an Orthodox cloister and school. The fraternity was created to protect Orthodoxy against the encroachments of Catholicism and the Uniate Church. Galshka's gift was used for the intended purpose. To protect the "brothers", Hetman Konashevich-Sagaydachny with his entire Cossack army became members of the fraternity.

FORMER FRATERNAL MONASTERY [15]
Grigory Skovoroda St.

The main temple of the Fraternal Monastery - Epiphany Cathedral - was created by Moscow architect Osip Startsev with funding from Hetman Mazepa in 1690-1693. The cathedral was considered a masterpiece of the Ukrainian Baroque. But it was destroyed in the 1930s along with the 18th century bell-tower. The two-level refectory church in the name of the Holy Spirit (17th-19th centuries) has survived. Near it there is a cook-house, cells, Host-house and the beautiful single-story house of the senior priest (1781). One can see all these buildings on

The old building of Kyiv Mogila Academy

entering the former cloister from the side of Grigory Skovoroda Street (now there is a hospital here). Among the old buildings there is a little park with a sun-dial in the form of a column. The sun-dial was built by the French mathematician and teacher Broulion at the end of the 18th century.

KYIV MOGILA ACADEMY [16]
Kontraktova Square

The year of foundation of the Academy and of the Fraternal Monastery is considered to be 1615, the year of the creation of the Fraternal School. In 1632 the school was reorganized as a collegium. Well-known educators of those times taught here - Iov Boretsky, Melety Smotritsky, Lazarus Baranovych, Innokenty Gizel and Sylvester Kosov. St.Metropolitan Piotr Mogila provided support for the collegium and turned it into a superb educational institution for those times. The name of Piotr Mogila was commemorated in the name of the collegium that became Kyiv Mogila Academy from 1701. The old building is preserved; the first floor was built under Mazepa in 1703-1704; the second floor was built in 1732-1740 by the architect Johann-Gottfried Schedel, who also completed the academic Annunciation Church with its Baroque dome (the picturesque gallery situated on the side of the courtyard was later blocked off). Here there was an excellent library, the Church Archaeological Museum, and the so-called "congregation" hall for academic meetings.

Memorial plaque of P.Mogila

GRADUATING STUDENTS OF THE MOGILA ACADEMY

In the old times, the whole course of education in the academy lasted 12 years. There were 8 classes: "Fara" or Analogy, Infima, Grammar, Syntax, Poetry, Rhetoric, Philosophy, and the most senior - Theology. The Academy provided a full theological and secular education. Meanwhile, the students ("spudeyi") were forced to show inexhaustible inventiveness in order to obtain funding and food: they wrote petitions for

Graduates of the Mogila Academy

ordinary Kyivans, organized paid performances, and sometimes they simply went begging (for which the Academy Board issued a special certificate). The list of famous graduate of the school, academy and collegium is extremely long. Among them were church figures who were canonized - St.Dmitry Rostovsky, St.Feodosy Chernigovsky, St.Ioasaph (Gorlenko), St.Paisy Velychkovsky; and also the well-known priests Pheophan Prokopovich, Grigory Konissky, Raphail Zaborovsky; the hetmans Ivan Vygovsky, Ivan Samoylovyich, Ivan Mazepa (who studied rhetoric), Filip Orlik, Piotr Polubotok; the statesmen Piotr Zavadovsky, Dmitry Trostchinsky, Prince Alexander Bezborodko; the writers Simeon Polotsky, Vasily Kapnist, Piotr Gulak-Artemovsky; the philosopher and poet Grigory Skovoroda; the historians Nikolay Bantysh-Kamensky and Maxim Berlinsky; the doctors Nestor Ambodik-Maksimovich

The central building of Kyiv Mogila Academy

Mikhail Lomonosov, who in 1734 took courses at Kyiv Mogila Academy and worked in its library.

BURSA 19
27, Naberezhno–Krestchatitskaya St.

and Daniil Samoylovich; the architects Ivan Grigorovich-Barsky and Ivan Zarudny; the composers Maxim Beresovsky and Artemy Vedel; the artist Grigory Levitsky; the traveller Vasily Grigorovich-Barsky. Until the mid-18th century Kyiv provided educated specialists for all the Moscow lands and other East Slavic lands.

NEW ACADEMIC BUILDING 17
Kontraktova Square

In 1819 Kyiv Mogila Academy was transformed into the Theological Academy and became a largely religious education establishment. On the corner of Iliyinskaya Street a new academic building was built (architects L.Sharleman', A.Melensky, 1822-1825, annex 1882-1883). Here studied the famous hermit-bishop Pheophan Govorov, Ukrainian writer Ivan Nechuy-Levitsky, the composers Alexander Kochits and Philip Kozinskiy, the future academicians Nikolay Petrov and Konstantin Vobly. The professors included Afanasy Bulgakov (the father of the famous writer Mikhail Bulgakov), the humanist-priest Alexander Glagolev and other famous theologians. During the Soviet era, the Theological Academy was closed,

and its buildings were used for training sailors. Between the old and the new academic buildings, a curved building was built for the needs of the naval school (earlier this area was occupied by the cloister shops, and overlooked by the bell tower). But since 1992 the university "Kyiv Mogila Academy" has been restored in its old buildings. The history of the Mogila Academy is a mandatory subject for all its students.

MONUMENT TO GRIGORY SKOVORODA 18

In the park on Kontraktova Square there is a bronze monument to the famous travelling philosopher and man of letters. Grigory Skovoroda looks as if he had come from far away wearing bast shoes with a bag on his shoulder and stopped in front of the academy. The monument was put up in 1976 (the author of the monument - sculptor Ivan Kavaleridze - was 89 years old at the time). A memorial plaque with the portrait of Skovoroda was put up on the wall of the old academic building nearby. Here we can also see the memorial signs in honour of Piotr Mogila, Galshka Gulevichevna and the great Russian scientist

Emblem of Kyiv Mogyla academy

Several buildings of the university "Kyiv Mogila academy" are located outside the former Fraternal Monastery. These include a two-story old building on the riverbank. In the olden days, this was a bursa - a dormitory for the academy's non-Kyivan students. The present building was built in 1778 by the architect I.Grigorovich-Barsky (in 1816 the architect A.Melensky extended and enlarged the bursa building including some features of classicism). There are many books about the bursa residents and their customs - it is enough to read the Gogol story "Viy." After the reform of the Kyiv academy, the seminary and afterwards the theological school were moved to the bursa building. On the front there is a memorial plaque to Semen Gulak-Artemovsky who studied in the seminary in 1824-1830 (the sculptor is G.Kalchenko). He was a poor student, but he had a beautiful baritone voice. When the composer Mikhail Glinka, who served as the bandmaster of the court choir, was selecting talented performers from Ukraine he took Semen away to Petersburg. The Kyiv seminarist became a famous singer and composer, the author of the immortal opera "Zaporozhets on the Danube".

The monument of G.Skovoroda

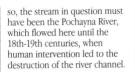

Museum of the hetmans

ILIYINSKAYA CHURCH [20]
2, Pochayninskaya St.

The stone Church of Saint Iliya the Prophet was built in 1692. The old Cossack family of the Hudims paid for its construction and renovation. The church has a single dome, which was recently gilded. Nearby there is a bell tower dating from the beginning of the 18th century with a hip-roof in the Moscow style. The gates leading into the courtyard of the church are notable: the brick arch dating from the middle of the 18th century picturesquely topped with a torn fronton and decorated with paired columns is a fine example of Ukrainian Baroque. On the metal door leaves are the letters "IP" - "Iliya the Prophet." The earliest known Christian church in Kyiv bore the same name. In the chronicle of 944 this church is described as "the Church of Saint Iliya Above the Stream." (The congregation of this church was made up of Varangians who had adopted Christianity.) According to one story, the present church is built on the site of the ancient church. If

Iliyinskaya Church

so, the stream in question must have been the Pochayna River, which flowed here until the 18th-19th centuries, when human intervention led to the destruction of the river channel.

NABEREZHNO-NIKOLSKAYA CHURCH [21]
12, Grigory Skovoroda St.

This well-shaped stone church with its single dome was built in 1772-1775 (architect I.Grigorovich-Barsky). This is a late work in the Ukrainian Baroque style and is close to Classicism. The dome was rebuilt later in Byzantine style. The church is named after Saint Nikolay. To identify it more precisely (since there are many churches of Saint Nikolay in Kyiv) it is named the Church of Nikolay Naberezhny (On the River Bank). Next to it there is a "warm" temple with a "genuine Russian" bell tower with hip-roof (architect M.Ikonnikov, 1861-1863). Nearby there is a granite memorial cross with the Ukrainian inscription "To those who sacrificed their life for Ukraine" (architect A.Ignashchenko, 1993).

MUSEUM OF THE HETMANS [22]
16–a, Spasskaya St.
☎ 416–16–13
Ⓜ Pochtovaya Square
Day off – Friday

In the heart of the area there is a 2-story stone building with a two-column ionic portico. It was evidently built at the beginning of the 18th century, and was later reconstructed more than once. Kyivans call this building "Mazepa's House," but the name is not confirmed by the documents. However, the story of Ivan Mazepa and the other Ukrainian hetmans is represented in the exposition at the Museum of the Hetmans,

which is located in this building. The museum collection contains about 2,000 exhibits. The building stands obliquely to the lines of the streets. This allowed it to survive the fire of 1811, as did the next building at 9b, Grigory Skovoroda St. In this part of Podol there are many living buildings from the 1980s, built in postmodern style. At 30, Spasskaya St. a huge contemporary business centre is wedged into the ensemble.

RESIDENCE OF APSHTEIN [23]
12, Spasskaya St.

This house was built in 1912 (architect V.Rykov) for the office of the iron-hardware trade of merchant Tovy Apshtein. To the present day, pictures of metal beams and chains have been preserved on the front of the building. During the Civil War the building housed the District Committee of the Komsomol. It is said that this is the building that was photographed with the famous notice: "The District Committee is closed. Everybody went to the front." In 1919 the Komsomol detachment left from here to suppress the peasant army of Ataman Zeleny (D.Terpilo). But the Komsomol members suffered a defeat near the village of Tripoliye. Many young lives were lost... Now The Capital Department for Protection of Monuments and the Historical Environment is located here.

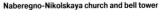

Naberegno-Nikolskaya church and bell tower

PODOL FIRE-TOWER 24
Khoriva lane

This well-shaped fire tower was built in the rational modern style (architect E.Bradtman, 1910). Next to it there is a memorial symbol in honour of the firemen who took part in the liquidation of the consequences of the Chernobyl accident. A museum is located here. The lane was previously called

Fire-tower

Voskresensky after the church of the same name opposite the fire tower (this church was demolished in 1930s). The Voskresensky housing estate on the left bank of the Dnieper is also named after this church.

"PETER'S HOUSE" 25
6/8, Konstantinovskaya St.

The building was built before the Podol fire around the beginning of the 18th century.

"Peter's House"

Its original appearance is difficult to recognize after the numerous reconstructions. Among the various facades the most picturesque is the one with the porch and the two-level gallery-arcade. There is a persistent legend that the emperor Peter I stayed here in August 1706 and January 1707, when he visited Kyiv to supervise the reconstruction of the Pechersk fortress. For that rea-

son, the building is named "Peter's House." At the turn of the 19th century, it housed a hospital for the insane. Later it became an orphanage. Now it is used for offices.

KHORIVA STREET 26

This street is called Khoriva due to a misunderstanding. The street begins near the Zamkovaya Mountain, which was once mistakenly named Khorevitsa. On the street there are some buildings from the period of classicism. Building #6/9 on the corner of Konstantinovskaya St. was built by architect P.Dubrovsky in 1830 for the district school for noblemen (the third floor was clumsily added on during the Soviet Era). In 1859 the first Sunday school for workers, artisans and peasants was opened here. Taras Shevchenko visited this school. On the opposite corner at 11-13/11, Khoriva St. there is an old building. Once it belonged to the architect Andrey Melensky, who was city architect for 30 years (1799-1829) and who created the finest examples of classicism in Kyiv.

CHURCH OF NIKOLAY PRITISK 27

At the end of Khoriva Street stands the Church of Nikolay Pritisk. Sometimes it is said that the name comes from the word for the old landing stages - "pritisk." However many people believe in an old legend that recounts how one night a thief tried to enter the church, but Saint Nikolay "pressed down on him" ("pritisnul") with the window arches so that he could not move. But even if it did happen, this event must have occurred in the times

Churhc of Nikolay Pritisk

of the old wooden church that existed up to the end of the 17th century. Later the burgher Petr, nicknamed Iron Coin, paid for construction of a stone church with a pear-shaped dome. The church bell tower acquired its present appearance in the 19th century. A memorial sign in honour of metropolitan Ivan Pavlovsky of the Ukrainian Autocephalous Orthodox Church was installed on the south front. He lived in the church building in 1935, and later perished in Stalin's camps.

DRUGSTORE MUSEUM 28
Pritissko–Nikolskaya St.
☎ 416–24–37
Ⓜ Kontraktova Square
Days off – Sunday, Monday

The first private drugstore in Kyiv opened in this building in 1728. The building survived, and since 1986 it has housed the drugstore museum, which has an interesting exposition devoted to the history of pharmacology in Kyiv.

FLOROVSKY MONASTERY 29
(see 150)

Drugstore Museum

THE UPPER VAL, THE LOWER VAL [30]

This is an example of the peculiar situation where two sides of one street have different names. The street follows the line of two earth ramparts (vals), which protected Podol until the end of the 17th century. Between them was a ditch filled with water, disrespectfully called "the gutter"

Podol streets

by Kyivans. Now a boulevard has replaced the "gutter".

KRESTOVOZDVIZHEN-SKAYA CHURCH [31]
1, Vozdvizhenskaya St.

This church is built in the late classical style. The history of its construction is very complicated - work started in 1811 shortly after the Podol fire, in 1823 a design by the architect A.Melensky was approved, and additional building was carried out right up until 1905. This was the parish church of the old craftsman's settlement of Gonchary-Kozhemiaki (the buildings of which are now under renovation). Drawings by the famous artist Grigory Svetlitsky have been

Krestovozdvizhenskaya church

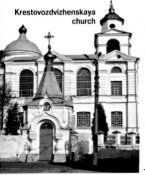

preserved in the northern side-chapel of the Mother of God of Kazan. The artist's house-museum is located at 30, Degtiarnaya St. in Kozhemiaki. Another memorial building in this area is the house at 10a, Vozdvizhenskaya St., where Mikhail Bulgakov was born. The new-born child was baptized in Krestovozdvizhenskaya Church.

THE CASTLE MOUNTAIN AND SHCHEKAVITSA

Beside the Upper Val is the Castle Mountain, where the wooden castle of the Polish and Lithuanian governors stood until the 17th century. The mountain is also known as Kiselevka after the last governor Adam Kisel, and as Florovskaya - after the Florovsky Monastery,

Shchekavitsa - the burial-site of Prince Oleg.
M.Sazhin

the remains of which are still preserved there. A staircase leading up from Andreyevsky Spusk can ascend the mountain. Alternatively, you can get there by taking a path leading up from the monastery. The Shchekavitsa Mountain (named after one of the founders of the city - Scheck) was the site of the city cemetery from the end of 18th century. The well-proportioned All-Saints Church crowned it. The cemetery was destroyed in the 1930s, and a broadcasting tower now stands where the church once was. Olegovskaya Street leads to the top of the mountain - reminding us that Prophetic Oleg was buried on Shchekavitsa.

Synagogue on Shchekavitskaya Street

A MULTITUDE OF FAITHS

Places of worship of different religions can be seen around Shchekavitsa. The low buildings on 28, Pochayninskaya St. belong to the Old Believer community. The Uspenskaya Church, which was built at the beginning of the 20th century, is still working here. The old Jewish Synagogue, built in the Moorish style in 1895 (the architect N.Gardenin), is situated at 29, Shchekavitskaya St. The romantic towers of the church of the Seventh Day Adventists - one of the branches of Protestantism - dominate 9/11, Lukyanovskaya St. The architect G.Duhovichniy built a big house of worship of evangelical Christian Baptists on Yaroslavskiy lane in the 1990s. The architect showed great respect for the old Podol architecture and the structure has been inserted unobtrusively among the older buildings. Finally, on the edge of Shchekavitsa near the old Muslim cemetery we can see the dome of a new mosque under construction (the architect A.Komarovsky).

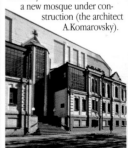

The House the Gospel

ARISTOCRATIC
LIPKI

ARISTOCRATIC LIPKI

The area on the hill to the south-east of today's Kreshchatik was known in ancient times as Klov - after the Klovskiy stream that flows by it (the name of the stream is perhaps due to its bubbling water). The chronicles mention a monastery on Klov, the remains of which were discovered by archaeologists on the territory of the school at 25, Shelkovichnaya St. Time passed, and this part of the town became known as Lipki after a pleasant linden alley (lipa - linden) that ran through it. In the 1830s, the Governor General V.Levashov ordered most of the lindens to be cut down, but the name was preserved. The Tsarina Elizabeth I chose this place to build a residence for travelling dignitaries. The presence of the tsarina's palace turned Lipki into an aristocratic district. This was where the highest gubernatorial officials and wealthy local people had their residences. Under the Soviets, the principal state institutions of Ukraine were situated in Lipki. The neighbourhood is virtually unmarred by ugly modern skyscrapers. Its shady streets are adjoined by parks and public gardens. Today it is perhaps the most prestigious area in Kyiv - comfortable, pleasant and well looked after.

The governor-general's palace at the corner of Institutskaya and Shelkovichnaya Streets was the residence of the governors of the south-western territory. It was surrounded by a large park. The last Hetman of Ukraine Pavlo Skoropadskiy lived here in 1918. In 1920 the Polish occupiers of Kyiv blew the building up. In 1934-1935 a complex of residential and governmental buildings was built in its place (architect S.Grigoryev). Among the residents were the Soviet functionaries D.Manuilskiy and D.Korotchenko, and the creative figures V.Vasilevskaya, A.Dovzhenko, F.Kozickiy, A.Korneychuk, A.Pashenko and others.

The Theatre for Young Viewers has been located at 15/17, Lipskaya St. in Lipki since 1955.

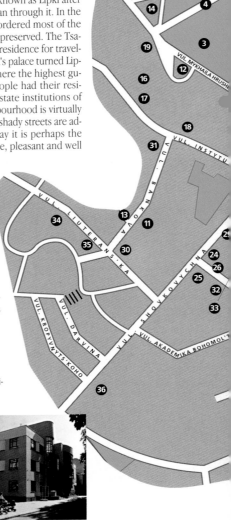

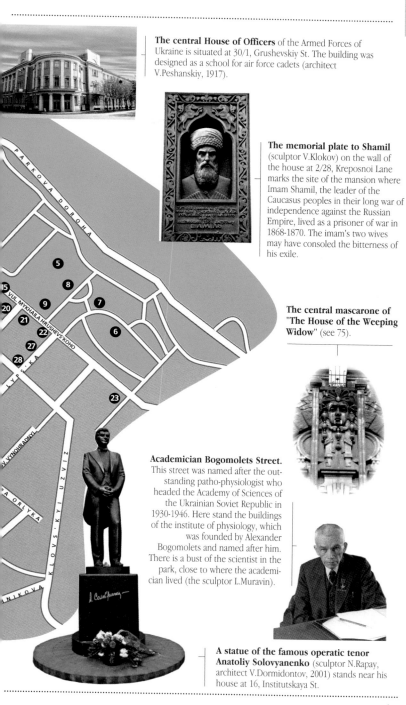

The central House of Officers of the Armed Forces of Ukraine is situated at 30/1, Grushevskiy St. The building was designed as a school for air force cadets (architect V.Peshanskiy, 1917).

The memorial plate to Shamil (sculptor V.Klokov) on the wall of the house at 2/28, Kreposnoi Lane marks the site of the mansion where Imam Shamil, the leader of the Caucasus peoples in their long war of independence against the Russian Empire, lived as a prisoner of war in 1868-1870. The imam's two wives may have consoled the bitterness of his exile.

The central mascarone of "The House of the Weeping Widow" (see 75).

Academician Bogomolets Street. This street was named after the outstanding patho-physiologist who headed the Academy of Sciences of the Ukrainian Soviet Republic in 1930-1946. Here stand the buildings of the institute of physiology, which was founded by Alexander Bogomolets and named after him. There is a bust of the scientist in the park, close to where the academician lived (the sculptor L.Muravin).

A statue of the famous operatic tenor Anatoliy Solovyanenko (sculptor N.Rapay, architect V.Dormidontov, 2001) stands near his house at 16, Institutskaya St.

65

KHRESCHATY PARK [1]

The chain of parks that border Lipki on the side of the Dnieper Hill begins with Khreshchaty Park. The name echoes those of the Khreschatitskiy Stream and Khreshchaty Ravine (see 102). A cultural and entertainment complex was established here by Kyiv merchants in 1881. The Merchants Garden enclosed a summer theatre, a summer club and a concert stage, which were popular in the city at the time. The shell of the stage survived until the 1970s, when it was demolished in order to make room for the pompous Arch of Friendship of the Peoples, which was dedicated to the unification of Russia and Ukraine (sculptor A.Skoblikov, architect I.Ivanov and others, 1982). The monument consists of a gigantic arch in the shape of a metal rainbow 30 meters in diameter, with the bronze figures of a Russian and a Ukrainian worker holding aloft the Soviet Order of Friendship of Peoples, and a granite image of the participants of the Pereyaslavska Rada of 1654. Only nine years after the opening of the monument, the Soviet Union broke up. There is a sightseeing platform near the monument, from where the Vladimir Hill, Podol, the Dnieper and the far bank of the river can be well seen. In the centre of

National Philharmonic

the park (which was known as Proletarskiy and Pionerskiy in Soviet times) formerly stood the "Dnieper" children's cinema (architects V.Zabolotny and others, artist B.Frolov, 1936 - 1937). It was later rebuilt as a stereo cinema. There is also an old water tower belonging to the municipal water system (architect A.Shile, 1876 - 1877).

NATIONAL PHILHARMONIC [2]
2, Vladimirsky Spusk

This building was erected in 1882 (architect V.Nikolayev) as a hall for the City Merchants Assembly. There was also a buffet, a room for card playing and so on. But the main part of the building was taken up by the auditorium, which was decorated in classical style. It is considered to offer the best

acoustics in the city. It is enough to mention that the interior columns are actually resonators in the form of wooden columns wrapped in horsehair and covered with special plaster to resemble marble. Among those who performed on the stage of the Merchants' Assembly were Tchaikovsky, Lysenko, Rakhmaninov, Skryabin, Shalyapin and Sobinov. Young Kyivans like composer Reinhold Gliere and pianist Vladimir Horovitz won recognition here. The building was also used for holding public meetings. In April 1917 the All Ukrainian National Congress was held here under the chairmanship of M.Grushevsky. In Soviet times, the Merchants Assembly Hall was by turns the City Hall, the Proletarian House of Art and the House of Communist Education. Then it was given to the young pioneers. But leading musicians continued to prefer the stage of this hall to all others. The Nazi occupiers held concerts here too (though that did not prevent them from setting up a brothel for army officers at the rear of the building). The building is now known as the N.Lysenko Column Hall of the Ukrainian National Philharmonic. During restoration work 1991-1996 (architect V.Khromchenkov) the unique features of

Friendship of the Peoples Monument

"Kissing Bridge"

the hall were retained and some lost details were restored on the front. Pope John Paul II met Kyivans here in 2001.

"DYNAMO" STADIUM [3]
3, Mikhail Grushevskiy St.

A popular entertainment venue, the "Chateau de Fleurs" (Castle of Flowers), which included a restaurant, vaudeville and alleys, functioned in this part of the park from 1860s. The "Chateau" was replaced by the "Dynamo" Stadium (architects V.Osmak, V.Bespalov and others), which was completed in 1936. The entrance to the stadium is in the form of a colonnade (architects N.Manucharova and V.Polischuk). After a number of reconstructions, the sports arena, which is picturesquely situated amidst the verdure of the park, has capacity for 18,000 spectators. FC "Dynamo" (Kyiv) plays its matches in the National Football Championship here. On the territory of the stadium there is a monument to the Kyiv footballers that died in Nazi concentration camps (sculptor I.Gorovoy).

PETROVSKAYA ALLEY [4]

In 1910 - 1911 a new road was built in the narrow gully between the Merchants Garden and the "Chateau de Fleurs." It was named Petrovskaya Alley in honour of Tsar Peter I (the 200th anniversary of the Battle of Poltava had recently been celebrated). In 1970s

a monument to the "leader of all Ukrainians" Grigoriy Petrovsky (sculptor A.Oleynik) was opened at the beginning of the alley. A metal footbridge was built over the alley according to a design by the engineer E.Paton. It is interesting that the bridge was constructed before the road was built under it. In 1983 it was replaced with an exact but more durable copy. Now enamoured couples often stop on the bridge, and for that reason it is called the "Kissing Bridge."

THE CITY GARDEN [5]

When the Mariyinskiy Palace (see 68) was built in the middle of the 18th century, a large garden was laid out beside it (it was earlier known as "Tsarskiy"). Kyivans found that the place had a special atmosphere filled with majestic peace and conducive to relaxation. One of the adornments of the present City Garden is an original concert stage (architect Y.Seryogin, 1982 - 1983) where public musical performances are held. Not far from the stage stand bronze statues of the classic of Ukrainian literature Lesya Ukrainka (sculptor V. Boroday, 1965) and of the great actress Maria Zankovetskaya (sculptor G.Kalchenko, 1974). There is also a bust of composer Mikhail Glinka amidst the greenery. The bust was originally placed in front of the City Musical School in 1910, and it was transferred here in the postwar years.

MARIYINSKIY PARK [6]

Until the 1870s this was a parade-ground for military training. But the Empress Maria Alexandrovna provided funds for laying out a park here, which was named "Mariyinskiy". At

the turn of the 20th century, a series of cast-iron fountains was installed (there are similar fountains in the City Garden). During the Civil War the park was used as a place of burial. Participants in the January Rebellion of 1918 were buried here in a mass grave. In 1967 a bronze statue of a proletarian with a flag (sculptors V.Vinaykin and V.Klimov, architect V.Gnezdilov) was placed over the grave. The revolutionaries I.Smirnov-Lastochkin and A.Ivanov are also buried here. In 1944 Army General

The Children's Side-Show in the Mariyinskiy Park

Nikolay Vatutin was buried in the park. He was the Commander of the 1st Ukrainian Front, which liberated Kyiv from the fascists. A granite statue of the general stands over his grave (sculptor E.Vuchetich, 1948). The Byzantine-style Alexandro-Nevskaya Parish Church (architect V.Nikolayev, 1889) stood in almost the same spot up to the 1930s.

THE FORMER APPANAGE OFFICE [7]
7, Mikhail Grushevskiy St.

The building in the middle of Mariyinskiy Park (architect V.Sychugov, 1875) was built for the local office of the Appanage Bureau, which took care of the property of the Tsar's family throughout the Empire. The Ukrainian writer Marko Vovchok (M.Vilinskaya) often stayed in the office room of this house.

Vatutin monument

MARIYINSKIY PALACE 8
5, Mikhail Grushevskiy St.

Before the arrival of the Tsarina Elizaveta Petrovna in 1744, there were no royal palaces in Kyiv. The tsarina stayed in the house of the Kyiv-Pechersk Archimandrites. Not finding that sufficiently comfortable, she ordered a palace for royal guests to be built at a point halfway on the road to the Lavra, where she went to prayer. In 1752 the architect I.Michurin completed a palace in the Baroque style of Bartholomew Rastrelli, the tsarina's favourite architect.

The building of the Verhovnaya Rada of Ukraine

The sculpture in front of the Verkhovnaya Rada

Originally the lower floor (for the courtiers) was made of stone, and the tsar's residence on the upper floor was made of wood. Catherine II was the first governing monarch to visit in 1787. The palace was sometimes offered as a residence to the highest officials of the land. Field-Marshal Piotr Rumyantsev-Zadunayskiy and General Nikolay Rayevskiy stayed here. But in 1819 the palace burned down. After the stone floor was rebuilt, the building was somehow transferred to the House of Artificial Mineral Water. Only after full-scale reconstruction (architects K.Mayevskiy and A.Shile, 1868 - 1870) did the palace go back to being a royal residence. A new upper floor in stone in the Baroque style of the Rastrelli epoch was added on. Subsequently all Russian monarchs and important foreign guests stayed here. The last to do so before the February Revolution of 1917 was the

The sculpture Charity and Justice

mother of Nikolay II, the Empress Mariya Fedorovna (by birth the Dutch Princess Dagmara). Since then the building has seen many ups and downs. At present the well-restored palace is used for ceremonial receptions of presidents and high-ranking government officials. It is called the Mariyinskiy Palace after the adjoining Mariyinskiy Park. The south facade of the building is the most impressive with its female statues symbolizing Charity and Justice. The fountains there are decorated with copies of French Rococo sculptures. The north facade is in a chamber style with a picturesque reflection in the basin of the City Garden. The most notable features of the interior are the vestibule, the marble stairs, and the main living room - the White Hall, which adjoins the Red and Green reception-rooms.

Mariyinskiy Palace

THE BUILDING OF THE VERKHOVNAYA RADA OF UKRAINE 9
5, Mikhail Grushevskiy St.

Built in 1936-1939 near the Mariyinskiy Palace according to a design by architect V.Zabolotny, this building was meant for the Upper Representative Institution, which was formerly housed in the Verkhovnaya Rada Palace

(Supreme Council). In 1945-1947 the building was enlarged with an annex on the side of the City Garden. Of all the administrative buildings in the Ukraine capital that were built in Soviet times, the Verkhovnaya Rada building seems the most harmonious and the most human. The main facade is decorated with classical simplicity and clarity. Sculptural groups representing the Ukrainian people (sculptor V.Znoba, 1985) stand along the

Lobby of the Mariyinskiy Palace

front of the facade. The building is crowned with a glass dome and a spire with a fluttering blue and yellow Ukrainian flag. The dome provides natural light to the 1300-seat session hall. The most notable feature of the interior is the picturesque ceiling "Blossom of Ukraine" (artists - the Scherbakovs). The Act of Independence of Ukraine was confirmed in the Verkhovnaya Rada on 24 August 1991. On 26 June 1996 the present Constitution of Ukraine was passed.

THE BUILDING OF THE CABINET OF MINISTERS OF UKRAINE 10
12, Mikhail Grushevskiy St.

A grandiose monument to the Stalin epoch. The building was designed to house the People's Commissariat of Internal Affairs of Ukraine (NKVD), which at the time was all-powerful. Some people say that the building was made semicircular for security reasons - so as to make it impossible to shoot from around the

corner. Eventually, though, the building was transferred to the government of the republic. It was built in the period 1936-1938. The author of the design, Architectural Academician I.Fomin, died at an early stage of construction, and it was completed by the architect P.Abrosimov. The giant building has a total volume of 235,000 cubic meters. It serves as an example of the active application of the legacy of classical architecture. The front facade is decorated with original columns. The lower floors are faced with labradorite, and the socle with polished granite. In general, the House of Government testified to the horrific might of the Soviet empire. At the same time, in spite of its size, the building is quite successfully "hidden" and has almost no negative influence on Kyiv's historic landscape.

THE BUILDING OF THE UKRAINIAN PRESIDENTIAL ADMINISTRATION 11
11, Bankovaya St.

This imposing building rises over Lipki district. It was originally two buildings constructed for the headquarters of the Kyiv Military Corps (architect A.Shile, 1877). Then

The building of the Ukrainian Presidential Administration

in 1936-1940 these were joined and extended (architect S.Grigiryev) to create the present monumental volume, which

The medallion and seal of the President of Ukraine

is decorated with a six-column Corinthian portico. From the end of the war until 1991, the Central Committee of the Communist Party of Ukraine was based here. N.Khrushchev, L.Kaganovich, N.Podgorny, P.Shelest, V.Shcherbitskiy worked there. Now the popularly elected President of Ukraine performs his duties from here (Leonid Kuchma holds this position since 1994).

The building of the Cabinet of Ministers of Ukraine

NATIONAL ARTS MUSEUM OF UKRAINE [12]

6, Mikhail Grushevskiy St.
☎ 228–64–29
Ⓜ Maydan Nezalezhnosti
Day off – Friday

The building was originally designed as The Museum of the Local Society for Antiquities and

Family.
F.Krichevskiy

the Arts - a group of patrons and connoisseurs of antiquities (after 1904 it became the Kyiv Museum of Arts, Industry and Science). Though the society was limited in its means, it did not want the building to look too skimpy. In 1898-1901 the architect V.Gorodetsky, who had reworked the original design by P.Boytsov, built the part of the structure that is visible from the street. However, his design was not fully realized until 1967-1972. The museum building now stands in the middle of a green

"island" like the image of an antique palace. The front may serve as a textbook for the study of classical architectural forms. Here we can see an exact reproduction

National Arts Museum

of the six-column portico of the Dorian order, with entablature, triglyphs and metopes, and a three-cornered pediment with the high relief "The Triumph of the Arts" placed in the tympanum. This composition was created by the sculptor E.Salya, as were the griffons and the giant cement figures of lions on both sides of the front steps. By the steps there is a memorial to Academician Nikolay Belyashevskiy (by the sculptor A.Kusch), who was director of the museum for many years. During Soviet times the History Museum was located here, and after 1936 - the National Art Collection. The museum displays show in detail

The portrait of V.Tomara
by G.Vasko

the different paths taken in Ukrainian art since the 13th century. They include a rich collection of iconography from the 14th-18th centuries, original Ukrainian portraits from the 18th century, paintings and graphics by Taras Shevchenko, paintings by 19th-20th century realists, the energetic creative explorations of the "Ukrainian avant-garde," and the most valuable artistic achieve-

A Guest from Zaporozhye.
F.Krasitskiy

ments of the Soviet period. For many years this large collection has been squeezed tightly into the compact museum. Part of the collection is due to be transferred to a new museum build-

Kazak Mamay. An unknown artist

....

ing that is currently under construction on Institutskaya Street.

THE GORODETSKIY HOUSE [13]

10, Bankovaya St.

In 1901 - 1903 the architect Vladislav Gorodetsky built a house for himself on the brow of the Kyiv Plateau. He is said to have made a bet with his colleague Alexander Kobelev, who did not believe that it would be possible to construct a building on such a steep slope. Gorodetsky won the bet. His friend and colleague, the mining engineer Anton Straus used drill driven piles of his own invention to create a stable foundation. Another friend of the architect, the Italian sculptor Elio Salya created the grandiose internal and external sculptural decoration in durable cement for which the building is often called "The House with Chimeras." At the corners and along the gutters young girls can be seen riding fantastic fishes. The cornices, the capitals of the columns, the arches and the walls are decorated with the contents of an entire zoo: elephants, rhinoceroses, antelopes, frogs, lizards, eagles, serpents and crocodiles... One statue depicting a fight between an eagle and a lion stands apart with the autograph of the author inscribed on the socle. The house is also decorated inside: in the vestibule, on the main stairs, and in the rooms of the first floor. Artistic tiled stoves and fragments of painting are preserved here. Specialists have praised the courage of the author, the resourceful completion of the design, and the easy play of sizes distinctive of the Modern style, which was just then coming into fashion. Meanwhile, the locals wove soulful legends around the history of the house: for example, that the architect built the house in memory of his drowned daughter. In reality, Gorodetsky was expressing his passion for hunting in the decoration of the house. By the way, he later went on safari in Africa and wrote a book about it, richly illustrated with photos and his own drawings.

V.Gorodetsky

In the Jungle of Africa.
V.Gorodetsky

HOW "THE HOUSE WITH CHIMERAS" HAS BEEN USED

On the side of Bankovaya St. the building has three floors with the basement, but there are three more floors in the depth of the hill. There were originally meant to be seven apartments. All the apartments except for the household rooms on the first floor and the studio beneath were rented out. All the apartments on each floor were designed as small private residences. There was even a cowshed in the courtyard for milk lovers. In 1913 Gorodetsky sold the house. The new owners rented the apartments until to the Revolution (in 1920 the architect left Kyiv forever, and 10 years later he died in Iran). Today "The House with Chimeras" houses a health centre.

"The House with Chimeras"

THE PARLIAMENT LIBRARY [14]
1, Mikhaila Grushevskogo St.

The building was built in 1910-1911 (architect Z.Kliave, A.Krivosheyev) for the city public library. The windows of the reading room face the Khreshchaty Park.

The Parliament Library

14, MIKHAILA GRUSHEVSKOGO STREET [15]

Noblemen participating in the Decembrists' plot against the tsarist tyranny held secret meetings in this old building in 1830s. It was once mistakenly believed that General Raevsky received Pushkin in this house. Now there is documentary proof that neither of them ever lived here.

THE FORMER INSTITUTE OF NOBLEWOMEN [16]
1, Institutskaya St.

The cross in memory of the victims of repression

The historical name of the street recalls the Institute of Noblewomen - an educational establishment for young ladies from noble and merchant families founded in 1838. The building of the Institute was built in the classical style during 1838-1843 (architects V.Beretti, A.Beretti). The students lived in the Institute. The course of instruction lasted seven years, not counting the preparatory class. Graduates of the Institute received a certificate as a home teacher. The famous opera singer N.Zabella-Vrubel was a student here. The composer N.Lysenko was a music teacher here. After the revolution the notion of "noblewomen" was abolished. Military units and different establishments occupied the building. The most terrible page in the building's history was the period 1934-1941 when the NKVD (People's Commissariat of Internal Affairs of the USSR), the principal body of repression, was based here. Thousands of victims of repression passed through the cellars of the NKVD. Now this period is commemorated by a memorial cross. In the 1950s the building was reconstructed after being destroyed in the war (architects G.Severov, A.Zavarov and others). A cinema hall with seating for an audience of more than 2,000 was arranged here. The former Institute of Noblewomen was restored as the October Palace of Culture (now it is the International Centre for Culture and the Arts). On October 23, 1965 Kyiv was awarded the "Golden Star" of a hero city in the October Palace. Among the guests of events held in the hall of the palace were the first cosmonaut Yuri Gagarin, academician Andrey Sakharov, Britain's Princess Anne and others. In 1904 a large annex with a four-columned portico (architect E.Tolstoy) was built on the south side of the former institute. The

The International Center for Culture and the Arts - the former Institute of Noblewomen

The griffon on the front of the National Bank

annex now houses the modern "Kinopalats" cinema.

THE OLD EXCHANGE BUILDING 17
7, Institutskaya St.

The creation of an exchange in Kyiv was evidence of progress in the business life of the city. The exchange building was built in 1873 (architect A.Shile). The front is decorated with elements in the style of the "Peter Baroque." From time to time, concerts were held in the hall of the exchange. For example, the great pianist and composer Anton Rubinstein performed here in 1880. The rapid growth of trade transactions meant that within ten years the exchange building was already insufficient, and work began on construction of a new exchange, which has not survived. For some time a Land Bank operated in the old exchange. Now this building houses the Club of the Cabinet of Ministers.

NATIONAL BANK OF UKRAINE 18
9, Institutskaya St.

The main building of the bank originally had two storeys (architects A.Kobylev, A.Verbitsky, 1902-1905). This structure in the style of the early renaissance became the decoration of the Lipki district. The building is faced with artificial stone. The sculptor E.Salya decorated the corners with sculptures of griffons. Vertically on two sides from the central front there are the symbols of Kyiv, Podol and Volyn provinces and the symbols of commerce, transport, industry and agriculture. Obliquely to the front space there is a spacious, sumptuously decorated opera-

The building of the National Bank

tional hall. Recently the image of the symbol of Kyiv, Archangel Mikhail, was restored on the glass of the ceiling. During the Soviet era, when Kyiv was the capital of the Ukrainian Soviet Social Republic, the old state-bank building turned out to be too small. In 1934 the architects V.Rykov and A.Kobelev constructed two additional stories. After this the building became even grander. Those who do not know about the reconstruction would never guess that the building was once half as high. The departmental museum, with a rich collection of materials about the currency of Ukraine, was created within the bank's building.

The Ancient Greek hetaera Phryne

THE RELIEF PICTURE "THE TRIUMPH OF PHRYNE" 19
4, Muzeyny Lane

The sculptor Fedor Balavensky created this design on the front of a revenue house in the modern style (architect V.Rykov, 1909). The theme for the composition came from ancient literature. The famous Greek hetera Phryne (who, by the way, was the model for the great sculptor Praxiteles) was so beautiful that the Athenians worshipped her as a goddess. The supporters of the law were so afraid of the anger of the gods that they put Phryne on trial, accusing her of blasphemy. Phryne's lover, the orator Hyperid, vainly tried to convince the judges of Phryne's innocence. At last he resorted to extreme measures. Tearing off Phryne's shawl and pointing to the naked beauty, Hyperid exclaimed: "Look at this woman! Is she not worthy of a god's honours!" The astonished judges unanimously acknowledged her worthy. Absolved, Phryne left the courtroom in triumph. This moment is depicted on the relief. The moral: True beauty is invincible!

The Athenians admiring the beauty of Phryne.
A fragment of the design

MANSIONS OF LIPKI

The "House of the Weeping Widow"

In the days when dignitaries were constantly staying at the Tsar's Palace, and the head of the southwestern territory resided in the governor-general's palace at the present 8, Shelkovichnaya St. on the corner of Institutskaya St. (destroyed in 1920), the wealthy and the aristocratic felt flattered to live near the mighty. No wonder that there are numerous old mansions in Lipki district. Most of these mansions now serve as venues for ceremonial receptions, as the offices of influential establishments or as diplomatic missions. So it may be difficult to arrange visits.

18, MIKHAIL GRUSHEVSKY STREET [20]

This is a masterly imitation of the style of a Venetian Renaissance (architect V.Nikolaev 1889). The sugar magnate and philanthropist Moisey Galperin owned this house.

20, MIKHAIL GRUSHEVSKY STREET [21]

The mansion was built in 1897 to the order of brick manufacturer Markus Zaytsev. The architect V.Nikolayev decorated the front in the Neo-Greek style.

22, MIKHAIL GRUSHEVSKY STREET [22]

The luxurious front is decorated in the style of modernized baroque (architect F.Troupiansky, 1910s). The owner of the mansion was Yakov Poliakov - a doctor and the son-in-law of the "Sugar King" Lev Brodsky, he was the manager of the Lazar Brodsky mill in Podol. In Soviet times, the Bolshevik leader P.Postyshev lived here.

15, Shelkovichnaya St.

32, MIKHAIL GRUSHEVSKY STREET [23]

The front of this house is decorated in Renaissance style with molded representations of the symbols of military endeavour - armor, helmets and weapons. This was the residence of the commander of the Kyiv military district. The mansion was built specially for General Mikhail Dragomirov - a hero of Russian-Turkish war, and a famous military theorist and pedagogue. A wounded knee meant the general had difficulty climbing stairs, so what was perhaps the first lift in the city was installed between the first floor and the second. The next resident of the mansion was General V.Sukhomlinov. After the revolution, Soviet military leaders who commanded the Kyiv military district resided here: the heroes of civil war I.Yakir, I.Fedko and I.Dubovoy, and the future marshals of the Soviet Union S.Timoshenko and G.Zhukov. Now the embassy of the Chinese People's Republic is located here.

15, SHELKOVICHNAYA STREET [24]

This mansion was built in 1912 for Nikolay Kovalevsky - a wealthy member of the Kyiv City Council who in his spare time was an Esperanto enthusiast. The architect P.Aleshin evidently reflected his impressions of Old Armenian architecture in the exterior of the mansion with its massive corner

tower. The columns in the galleries are decorated with original molding (according to rumor, the round face with a moustache is a caricature of the architect). On the first floor there was a wonderful room with an interior like a railroad car. It is said that in this way the owner of the house immortalized his first meeting with his beloved wife, which took place aboard a train.

"CHOCOLATE HOUSE" [25]
17, Shelkovichnaya St.

The timber merchant and philanthropist Semen Mogilevtsev owned this mansion built at the turn of the 20th century. The

18, Mikhail Grushevskiy St. at the beginning of the last century

brown painting of the building and its big rustics looking like chocolate lobules explain the common "nickname" for the house. The sculptures of dog's muzzles indicate that the owner was fond of dogs. After the revolution, the mansion was at different times occupied by Internal Affairs Minister I.Kistiakovsky, Soviet state figure and diplomat H.Rakhovsky, and the members of the All-Ukrainian Academy of the Sciences. Later the Palace of Weddings was located here. Now the mansion is being turned into a children's picture-gallery.

HOUSE WITH THE CARYATIDS [26]
3, Orlika St.

The architect I.Bieliayev built this small but expressive building in the Neo-Empire style in 1911 for the engineer Vsevolod Demchenko, a city figure, and a deputy of the fourth State Council. On the front there are relief caryatids. The origins of the word "caryatid" are to be found in ancient history. When the Ancient Greeks were at war with the Persians, all the Greek cities supported the common cause. Only the city of Carya refused to resist Persian. After the Greek victory, the citizens of Carya were cruelly punished. All the men of Carya were killed, and all the women - Caryatids - were enslaved. To intensify their humiliation, the women were obliged to do the most shameful work dressed in the most luxurious of attires. Since then female figures used in architecture as supports are called "caryatids." But in the Demchenko mansion they do not support anything and play only a decorative role.

2, LIPSKAYA STREET [27]

This small single-story mansion with garden was built for the family of Ivensen (architects V.Sychugov and V.Katerinich, 1883). The walls are decorated with intricate molded details and filigree brickwork. For a long time the owner of the mansion was Mikhail Filipov, lawyer and banker. Under the Soviet regime the People's Commissar for Education V.Zatonsky lived here.

4, LIPSKAYA STREET [28]

At first this also was a one-storey building, and the property of the Ivensen family, but in 1896 according to the project by the architect A.Krauss the house was considerably enlarged to fit the needs of its new owner - the wealthy sugar manufacturer

Fragment of the front of the "House with the Caryatids"

Markus Zaks. The front of the building is decorated in Renaissance style.

16, LIPSKAYA STREET [29]

Nataliya Uvarova, daughter of sugar manufacturer Fedor Tereshchenko, ordered the construction. The front is decorated with elements in Neo-Imperial style (architect P.Gallandsky, 1912). The bas-relief panel in the frieze presents the various sides of human life: work, creativity, and sacrifice to the gods. After the revolution, the building was occupied by the punitive bodies:

4, Lipskaya St.

the Cheka, NKVD and KGB. But now the mansion has been transferred to humanitarian structures (in particular, the Ukrainian Fund for Culture is located here).

"HOUSE OF THE WEEPING WIDOW " [30]
23, Luteranskaya St.

This is a masterpiece in the modern style (architect E.Bradtman, 1907). The mansion was built on the order of Poltava merchant Sergey Archavsky. The central decoration of the front is a big portrait of a beautiful woman. When it is raining the drops run down her cheeks. From it the folklore name of the mansion was born.

2, BANKOVAYA STREET [31]

This modest apartment house was rebuilt when sugar manufacturer Simkha Liberman bought it from General Fedor Trepov (architect V.Nikolayev, 1898). The building was transformed into a little palace decorated in Renaissance style. The "surprises" of the interior include the special ceiling of one of the rooms on the upper floor: during the Jewish holiday Succot, part of the roof can be disassembled to form an opening with branches to resemble a hut (during this holiday Orthodox Jews live in temporary huts for several days). Since 1953 in the mansion is located the Writers Union of Ukraine.

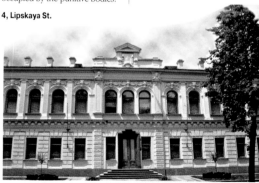

KYIV
CITY MUSEUM [32]
8, Orlika St.
☎ 293-60-71
Ⓜ Arsenalnaya
Day off – Friday

This two-storey building in Baroque style (architects P.Neyolov and S.Kovnir, 1753 - 1755) was called the Klovskiy Palace and was designed for the VIP guests of the Lavra. In 1811 - 1857 the first Kyiv Gymnasium was housed in the Klovskiy Palace. Among its students was the artist N.Ge. Later on it was a Women's Theological Seminary that prepared teachers for parish schools. Restored after being destroyed in the Civil War, the building passed through a number of owners, until in 1981 it was transferred to the Kyiv City Museum. Its carefully assembled collection gives a detailed picture of the past and present of the Ukrainian capital. The museum has been recognized as a center of knowledge about Kyiv.

FORMER BUNGE
SCHOOL [33]
18/5, Lipskaya St.

This elegant building (the architects G.Shleifer and E.Bradtman, 1904) was first built as a primary school founded by the followers and admirers of the outstanding Kyivan economist and state figure N.H.Bunge.

Kirche

"SULIMOVKA" [34]
16, Luteranskaya St.

This house was built in 1833 - 1835 at the order of landowner Akim Sulema, who was involved in its design. The building stood empty for some time, and Kyivans were afraid of the evil spirits living in it. But from 1859 an institution for old people and orphans run by the Kyiv

"Sulimovka"

Charitable Society functioned here. It included orphanages, school shops, pensions and so on. The philanthropic complex was named "Sulimovka." Over the left wing of the building was erected the head of the Alexander Nevskiy Home Church. In Soviet times, the church was destroyed, and "Sulimovka" was turned into an ordinary dwelling house.

KIRCHE [35]
22, Luteranskaya St.

The name of the street comes from the Lutheran community that lived here from 1812. The Kirche decorated in Romanesque style has survived (architects I.Strom and P.Shleifer, 1855 - 1857). After restoration (architect Y.Doroshenko, 2000) public worship was renewed here after disruption in the Soviet epoch. In the nearby buildings at ## 18 and 20 were

Klovskiy Palace - Kyiv City Museum

the Lutheran educational institutions: the Real School for boys and the Gymnasium for girls.

THE CENTRAL
CLINICAL HOSPITAL [36]
39, Shelkovichnaya St.

This medical institution founded by the city authorities has been functioning since 1875. At first the hospital was named Alexandrovskaya in honour of Tsar Alexander III. For many years medical students practised here under guidance of experienced professors. A monument-bust (the sculptor M.Vronsky) was put up in honour of one of the professors, Vasiliy Obraztsov. A memorial plate is dedicated to the neuropathologist Boris Minkovskiy. Now the hospital buildings can accommodate over 1,200 patients. The hospital church of Saint Mikhail (architect V.Nikolayev, 1895 - 1901) was destroyed in 1931, but now it has been restored on the surviving founda-

The monument to V.Obraztsov

tion. During the restoration a way was cleared to the underground burial-vault, and the headstone of the founder of the church, the well-known philanthropist Mikhail Degtyarev, was found.

SACRED PLACES AND
STRONGHOLDS OF PECHERSK

SACRED PLACES AND STRONGHOLDS OF PECHERSK

The name of the large elevated area to the southeast of Lipki comes from the Kyiv-Pecherskaya Lavra. This neighborhood was formerly an isolated area of Kyiv that arose around the largest monastery in Rus. At the end of 17th century, "Pechersk town" was fortified with earth ramparts at the order of Hetman Ivan Samoylovich. The subsequent history of the Pechersk district is closely connected with the fortifications. There were two main stages of construction works - under Peter I and Nikolay I. The Old and New Fortresses were built as a result. The belligerent Emperor Nikolay was very proud of the Pechersk fortifications. Once he said condescendingly to Kyiv Metropolitan Filaret: "And now I hope that your sacred places are effectively protected by our strongholds." But the wise old man objected: "I think, Your Majesty, that our sacred places will protect your strongholds." Only at the turn of the 20th century were the military limitations on the development of Pechersk removed. During recent decades entire districts of modern buildings have appeared here.

The Museum of Cultural Heritage (a branch of the Kyiv History Museum) was founded on the basis of private collections and reflects the cultural activity of the Ukrainian Diaspora connected to Kyiv. The museum is located in a restored building resembling a classical Pechersk house of the 19th century.

The monument of Lesia Ukrainka (sculptor G.Kalchenko, architect A.Ignashchenko, 1973) stands on L.Ukrainka Square on the Avenue of the same name.

Slava Square

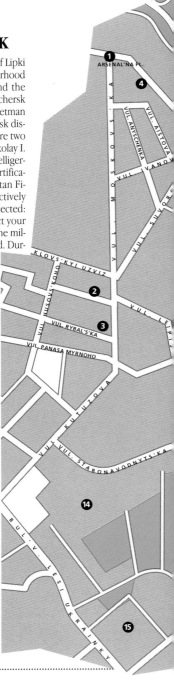

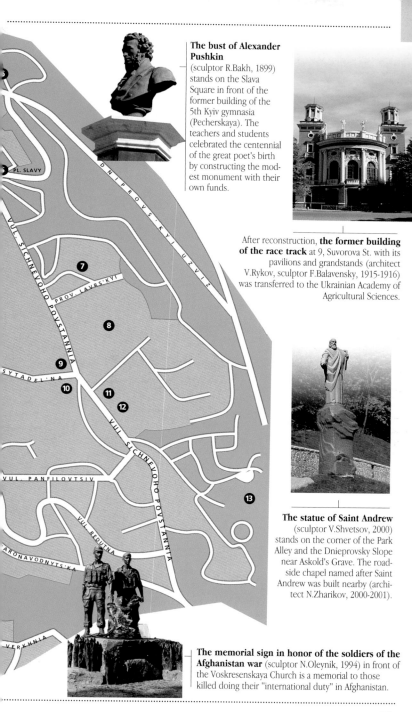

The bust of Alexander Pushkin (sculptor R.Bakh, 1899) stands on the Slava Square in front of the former building of the 5th Kyiv gymnasia (Pecherskaya). The teachers and students celebrated the centennial of the great poet's birth by constructing the modest monument with their own funds.

After reconstruction, **the former building of the race track** at 9, Suvorova St. with its pavilions and grandstands (architect V.Rykov, sculptor F.Balavensky, 1915-1916) was transferred to the Ukrainian Academy of Agricultural Sciences.

The statue of Saint Andrew (sculptor V.Shvetsov, 2000) stands on the corner of the Park Alley and the Dnieprovsky Slope near Askold's Grave. The roadside chapel named after Saint Andrew was built nearby (architect N.Zharikov, 2000-2001).

The memorial sign in honor of the soldiers of the Afghanistan war (sculptor N.Oleynik, 1994) in front of the Voskresenskaya Church is a memorial to those killed doing their "international duty" in Afghanistan.

ARSENALNAYA SQUARE  1

The building of the military commandant's office is situated here. The former barrack in Pseudo-Gothic style (architect P.Tamansky, 1846-1850) served also as the gate of the New Pechersk fortress (see 96). Now the arches of the gate are blocked. The new buildings of the Arsenal military enterprise were built nearby. Since they had access to firearms, the Arsenal workers were often the initiators of revolutionary insurrection. At the beginning of 1918,

The memorial to the Arsenal workers

they organized the January revolt against the Ukrainian Central Rada under Bolshevik slogans. The forces of the Central Rada suppressed the revolt. The traces of bullet holes are visible on the plant's walls. In the middle of Arsenalnaya Square in front of the entry to Arsenalnaya metro station there is a monument to the workers of Arsenal plant (architect G.Granatkin and others, 1960) - in 1923 a gun was installed on a pedestal that was previously part of the monument to Iskra and Kochubey (sculptor P.Samonov, 1914, the statues have not survived).

Vvedenskaya community

WOMEN'S GYMNASIUM BUILDING 2
2, Reznitskaya St.

Among the students of the former O.Pletneva women's collegiate (architect A.Kobelev, 1903) was Alla Tarasova - the daughter of a Kyiv dentist, later the star of Moscow Arts Academic Theatre and film star, a people's artist of the USSR.

VVEDENSKAYA COMMUNITY 3
42/2, Moskovskaya St.

This was originally a convent founded in 1878 by a captain's widow, Matrena Egorova, who bought for it the Empire-style corner building (built in 1804 for Kyiv commander G.Rybalsky). In

The Ypsilanti house

1901 the community was reorganized as a convent. The Soviet authorities closed it twice. A monastery has functioned here since 1996. Its sanctuaries consist of a miracle-working icon of the Blessed Virgin, "Attend to Humility," and relics of the founder of the community, who took the veil with the name Demetra before her death.

HOUSE OF YPSILANTI 4
6, Yanvarskogo Vosstaniya St.

Konstantinos Ypsilanti, the Greek-born former Turkish governor of Moldova and Wallachia, lived here in 1807-1816. He was persecuted for his participation

The monument to the Arsenal workers

in the struggle for the liberation of Greece from the Ottoman yoke and took refuge in Kyiv. The sons of Ypsilanti, Alexander and Dmitry, struggled for the liberation of their nation. Contemporaries were struck by the exotic eastern decoration of the Ypsilanti house. It is said that the house is discussed in A.Dumas' novel "The Count of Monte Christo". The house was later rebuilt. In 1880 the art scholar and archaeologist A.Prakhov lived here. The famous painter Iliya Repin visited him here.

SLAVA SQUARE 5

In 1890s a park was laid out in Pechersk district at the initiative of General A.Anosov, the commander of the Kyiv fortress. The park was called Anosovsky. In 1957 the park was converted into a memorial to the Eternal Glory of the Heroes of the Second World War (architects A.Miletsky, V.Baklanov, L.Novikov). A 27-meter obelisk was erected above the tomb of the Unknown Soldier. Marshal V.Chuykov ignited the Eternal Flame. 34 heroes of the defense and liberation of Kyiv, fallen for Motherland, were interred along the alley leading from the Slava Square to the monument. The laying of wreathes on the tomb of the Unknown Soldier became a sacred tradition. On Slava Square we can see such original buildings as the Palace of Children's Creativity (architects A.Miletsky, E.Bylsky, 1962-1965; the State Award of the USSR in 1967) and the Salute hotel (architects A.Miletsky and other, 1982). The bell tower (1750) in front of the Voyenno-Nikolskaya

Lighting of the Eternal Fire.
1957

church, a Ukrainian baroque structure from the end of the 17th century (architect O.Startsev), stood on the site of the hotel. In 1930 the bell tower and cathedral were demolished.

ASKOLD'S GRAVE 6

According to the legend told in the chronicles, Varangian leader Oleg captured Kyiv and killed the local rulers Askold and Dir in 882. Askold's name remained in the memory of Kyivans. There are reports that he was baptized in Tsargrad in the 860s taking the name Nicholas and that he tried to convert Rus to Christianity. The burial place of the prince is known as Askold's Grave. Many notable Kyivans from the end of the 19th and the beginning of the 20th centuries were buried in the city cemetery nearby. The architect A.Melensky built the Saint Nikolay church (1810) here in the form of a classic rotunda. But in 1934-1936 the cemetery was destroyed, and the

The memorial of Eternal Glory

church was turned into a park pavilion. Only in 1998 was the church restored. A wooden cross indicates that the young Ukrainian patriots killed in the battle with the Bolsheviks near the Kruty station were buried in the cemetery in 1918. A memorial (architect Y.Vig, 1997) to the stay of the Hungarians on their way from the Volga to the territory of present-day Hungary, as described in the chronicle, was placed nearby.

The Savior Church at Berestov

THE SAVIOUR CHURCH AT BERESTOV 7

Berestov (from the word for "elm forest") was the name of a village where Prince Vladimir Sviatoslavovich had a palace. He died here. A little wooden cloister was founded nearby. At the end of the 11th century, the stone Church of the Saviour (God's Transfiguration) was built on the territory of the cloister. It is known that Prince Yuri Dolgoruky, founder of Moscow, was buried here (on the occasion of the 800th anniversary of Moscow in 1947, a symbolic headstone was placed in the church). After the

The Salute hotel

Mongol invasion the cloister was ruined. Only the narthex survived. In 1640-1647 Metropolitan Piotr Mogila added new apses. Frescos from the 17th century have survived. One of them depicts Piotr Mogila on bended knees presenting Christ with a model of the church. Later on the church acquired the elements of Ukrainian baroque style. The architect A.Melensky added a bell tower in classic style (1813-1814). For some time it was a parish church. In 1825 General Sergey Volkonsky married young Mariya Raevskaya here (later the princess Volkonskaya voluntarily followed her Decembrist hus-

The church at Askold's grave

band to Siberia). Now the Church of the Savior at Berestov is a museum. In the interior, visitors can see Old Russian frescos, and part of the original stonework. Church services take place here on Sundays.

HOLY ASSUMPTION KYIV-PECHERSK LAVRA 8

The miracle-working icon of the Assumption of the Blessed Virgin

The full name of the monastery indicates its principal sanctuaries. The miracle-working icon of the Assumption of the Blessed Virgin was kept in the Uspenskiy (Assumption) Cathedral on the territory of the Upper Lavra. The word "Pechersk" is derived from the network of caves ("pechery"), where the imperishable tombs of hermit saints were preserved. The Greek word "lavra" means "street, village." The word is used for big and populous monasteries. The oldest and most venerated lavra in Rus is in Kyiv.

YOUR TONGUE WILL LEAD YOU TO KYIV

This saying goes back to olden days, when thousands of pilgrims from throughout the Russian Empire went to pray before the relics in Kyiv-Pechersk Lavra. They sometimes had to walk for thousands of kilometres. Many of them were illiterate, and only a few knew anything about geography. But wherever they were in the country, they could always find someone to direct them to Kyiv.

HISTORY

Kyiv-Pechersk Lavra is the oldest Orthodox monastery of Rus and Ukraine. Its founder was the monk Antoniy of Lubeck, who took his monastic vows on Mount Athos. He came to Kyiv to spread monasticism in Rus and dwelled in a cave above Dnieper, where the metropolitan of Kyiv - the elder Illarion - had previously sought solitude. One of Antoniy's first disciples, Feodosiy, became the co-founder of the monastery. At first the cenobites lived in caves and prayed in underground temples. Later on surface structures were built. Prince Sviatoslav

Antoniy

CHRONICLES

1051 - *Founding of a monastery with a subterranean church in the Far Caves by the Reverend Antoniy.*
1062 - *Creation of the Near Caves.*
1073-1089 - *Construction of the Uspenskiy Cathedral.*
1223-1233 - *Writing of the Kyiv-Pechersk Paterik.*
1688 - *Monastery was given the name of Lavra.*
1696-1702 - *Stone construction on the territory of the monastery funded by Hetman I.Mazepa.*

Yaroslavovich gave the monastery the plateau on which was erected the so-called Upper Lavra. The strict statute of the ancient Studiyskaya Cloister provided the basis for the life of the monks. Over the centuries, Kyiv-Pechersk Lavra attracted numerous hermits and a multitude of pilgrims. Beautiful stone churches decorated with drawings, as well as cells, towers and other buildings arose here. The Lavra played a major role in the cultural history of Russia and Ukraine. It is connected with the names of the scribe Nestor, the painter Alipiy, the educator Piotr Mogila, the scientist-encyclopedist Pamva Berinda, the historian Innokentiy Gizel and many others. At the beginning of the 17th century the Lavra archimandrite Yelisey Pletenetskiy founded the first printing-house in Kyiv here. More than once the Lavra buildings were destroyed (in 1718, when a horrible fire devastated the monastery, and under the Nazi occupation of 1941-1943), but every time the Lavra rose from the ashes. Under the Soviet regime, the monastery complex was used as a "museum town" under the Kyiv-Pechersk Historical and Cultural Reserve. Now there is an acting congregation on the territory of the Lavra. Kyiv-Pechersk Lavra has been on the UNESCO Register of World Heritage since 1990.

The Uspenskiy Cathedral. 1702

EXTRACT FROM THE ESSAY "THE THREE CAPITALS" BY THE PHILOSOPHER GEORGIY FEDOTOV

From the hills of old Kyiv, Pechersk, Shchekavitsa - from everywhere, the boundless azure expanse that takes your breath away stands out from the green. It seems that a man is not worthy of such beauty; he cannot stand it for long. So that is why they hid themselves in caves - out of self-preservation...

Feodosiy

1731-1744 - *Building of the Great Bell Tower.*
1893-1895 - *Construction of the new refectory and the adjacent church.*
1926 - *Creation of the Kyiv-Pechersk Historical and Cultural Reserve.*
1929 - *Closure of the monastery.*
1941 - *Destruction of the Uspenskiy Cathedral.*
1988 - *Restoration of monastic life on the territory of the Lavra.*
1998-2000 - *Reconstruction of the Uspenskiy Cathedral.*

Mitre.
18th century

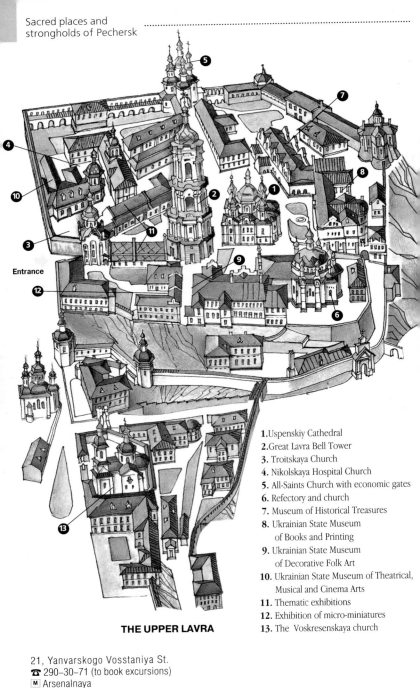

THE UPPER LAVRA

1. Uspenskiy Cathedral
2. Great Lavra Bell Tower
3. Troitskaya Church
4. Nikolskaya Hospital Church
5. All-Saints Church with economic gates
6. Refectory and church
7. Museum of Historical Treasures
8. Ukrainian State Museum of Books and Printing
9. Ukrainian State Museum of Decorative Folk Art
10. Ukrainian State Museum of Theatrical, Musical and Cinema Arts
11. Thematic exhibitions
12. Exhibition of micro-miniatures
13. The Voskresenskaya church

Entrance

21, Yanvarskogo Vosstaniya St.
☎ 290–30–71 (to book excursions)
Ⓜ Arsenalnaya

Plan of the National Kyiv-Pechersk Historical and Cultural Reserve

14. Gallery leading to the Far Caves
15. Gallery leading to the Near Caves
16. Church of the Elevation of the Cross
17. Church of the Life Source
18. Church of the Birth of the Blessed Virgin
19. Bell tower of the Far Caves
20. Annozachatiyevskaya Church

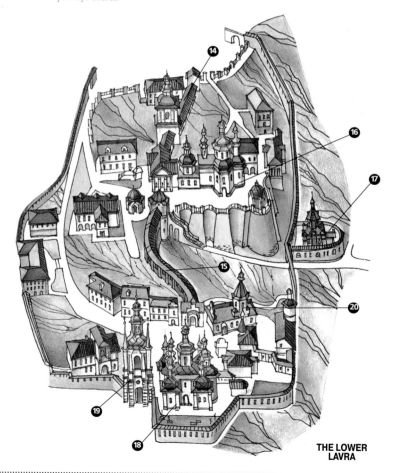

THE LOWER
LAVRA

THE USPENSKIY CATHEDRAL ❶

According to legend, the main

Faces of the Holy Martyrs. 18th century. Troitskaya Church

church of the Kyiv-Pechersk Lavra was built by architects from Constantinople, who came to Kyiv following a divine command. The length of the golden belt presented to the Reverend Antoniy by Shimon the Varangian was used as a measure. Construction began in 1073. By 1089 the cathedral was decorated with paintings and mosaics. The cathedral was subsequently rebuilt. At first it had a single dome. In the 18th century it was turned into a seven-domed building, abundantly decorated in the Ukrainian baroque style. This is the burial place of the first Kyiv Metropolitan Saint Mikhail, the Reverend Feodosiy, the Kyiv commander and patron of the arts Konstantin Ostrozhskiy, the Saint Metropolitan Piotr Mogila, the Ukrainian scientists Pamva Berinda and Innokentiy Gizel, the romantic heroine Natalia Dolgorukova and Field-Marshal Duke Piotr Rumiantsev-Zadunaiskiy. In Soviet times the Cathedral was turned into a museum. On 3 November, 1941

Troitskaya Church

the Cathedral was blown up (it has never been established who was responsible - the Nazi occupiers or the Soviet underground). The Uspenskiy Cathedral was rebuilt in its original form in 1998-2000 (architects O.Grauzhis and others). In the north part of the interior there is a replica of the baptismal church of St.John the Baptist, which adjoined the original cathedral. Thanks to the restoration, the Lavra ensemble has recovered its original integral appearance.

GREAT BELL TOWER ❷

The Great Bell Tower of the Lavra is one of the most notable buildings in the Kyiv landscape. It is the highest free-standing bell tower in the former Russian Empire. Its height with cross is 96.5 m. The four-tier structure was built in 1731-45 (architect I.-G.Shedel). The diameter of the lower tier at the base is 28.8 m. The second tier is decorated with 32 Dorian columns; the third tier with 16 Ionic columns; and the fourth tier with 8 Corinthian columns. There were hanging bells on the third tier (three small 18th century bells have been preserved). There is a viewing platform

here, which gives a bird's eye view of the landscape. On the fourth tier there is a chiming clock (the mechanism weighing 4.5 tons was manufactured in 1903). The clock bells chime every quarter of an hour.

Great Bell Tower

TROITSKAYA CHURCH ❸

The church is situated above the Holy Gates - the main entrance to the territory of the Upper Lavra. In its present state after renovation and decoration in the 17th - 20th centuries, it is an elegant Ukrainian Baroque building with a golden dome, front figures and rich decoration. But the base of the building is an ancient stone church built in 1106-08 (you can see old Russian architectural motifs on the southern front of the building). According to legend, this church was founded by the Chernigov Prince Sviatoslav, who became a Pechersk

The Uspenskiy Cathedral

monk under the name of Nicholas the Saintly. Vivid and dynamic compositions from the 18th century have been preserved inside the temple (by the painter A.Galik and others): "Faces of the Holy Martyrs," "Jesus Casting the Moneychangers from the Temple," "The Council of Nicaea."

The refectory and church

NIKOLSKAYA HOSPITAL CHURCH ❹

In the north-western part of the Upper Lavra there was formerly a separate monastery for elderly and ailing monks. It was founded at the beginning of the 12th century. On this territory is preserved the Nikolskaya Church from the turn of the 17th century - an elegant Ukrainian baroque building with an adjacent hospital barrack (now the premises are occupied by the lectorium). The State Historical Library of Ukraine is housed in the former Lavra Apothecary near the cells.

THE ALL-SAINTS CHURCH AND THE ECONOMIC GATE ❺

The Economic Gate led to the Economy Building of the Lavra. This was where the Economist - the manager of the Lavra economy - had his cell. In 1696-98 the stone All-Saints Church with its five gold-plated pear-shaped domes was built above the gate. Its harmonious composition recalls the five-domed wooden churches of the Ukrainian

Nikolskaya Hospital Church

baroque. The church was erected with funds provided by Hetman I.Mazepa (the hetman's coat of arms on the front of the church was recently restored). The interior was painted in 1906 by the pupils of the Lavra icon-painting school under the direction of the painter I. Izhakevych.

THE REFECTORY AND THE CHURCH ❻

The vast refectory where the Lavra monks took their meals and the adjoining church of St.Antoniy and Feodosiy were built in 1893-1895 (architect V.Nikolayev), when there were more than a thousand monks. The sturdy dome of the church recalls the buildings of ancient Byzantium. The well-known architect A.Shchusev directed the interior decoration. The marble icons are in the neo-Russian style. The expressive paintings in the refectory and the church (by the painters I.Izhakevych, G.Popov and others, the beginning of the 20th century) are

marked by a modernist influence. Behind the refectory there is a viewing area, which provides a beautiful panoramic view of the Far and Near Caves, the Dnieper and the far bank.

THE TOMB OF P.STOLYPIN

Under a black stone cross lies the Russian Prime Minister Piotr Arkadyevich Stolypin - the initiator of the well-known agrarian reform. In 1911 he was shot by a terrorist-provocateur in the Kyiv Opera. In Soviet times the tombstone of this staunch supporter of the monarchy was dismantled, but in 1989 it was restored.

THE TOMB OF I.ISKRA AND V.KOCHUBEI

Colonel Ioann Iskra of Poltava and the supreme judge of the Zaporizhyan Host Vasiliy Kochubei warned Tsar Peter I that Hetman Mazepa was planning to defect to the side of the Swedish King Charles XII. Peter did not believe them, and he handed the informers over to the hetman, who ordered them to their deaths by decapitation (1708). When Mazepa later betrayed the Tsar, Iskra and Kochubei were buried in the Lavra as martyrs. On the tombstone there is an original verse epitaph, which A.Pushkin cited in the notes to the poem "Poltava."

V.Kochubei

UKRAINIAN MUSEUM OF HISTORICAL JEWELLERY ❼

☎ 290–13–87
Day off – Monday

The museum is located in the so-called "Kovnirovsky building" - a stone edifice that once housed the Lavra bakery and bookstore. It was built in the 18th century by the architect S.Kovnir in the baroque style with a picturesque figured fronton. The museum of historical jewellery was opened here in 1969. It houses a collection of

Breakfast. 1950. K.Bilokur

unique pieces produced by the ancient Scythians (including the famous golden pectoral from the Tolstoy grave), different pieces by the jewellers of Kyivan Rus, masterpieces by Ukrainian makers of gold jewellery, rare examples of silver Judaic ritualistic accessories, a collection of coins and other exhibits.

UKRAINIAN STATE MUSEUM OF BOOKS AND PRINTING ❽

☎ 290–22–10
Day off – Tuesday

This museum is located in the space formerly occupied by the Lavra typography, which was built in the 18th century. The museum was opened in 1975. The collection includes manuscript volumes from the times of

**"Horseman." Tile.
19th century**

Kyivan Rus, the first Ukrainian printed editions - the Lvov "Apostle" (1574) of the first printer Ivan Fedorov, the "Ostrog Bible," and the Kyiv Pechersk "Book of Hours," as well as fine examples of old Ukrainian book illustrations and many other rare exhibits. Old printing equipment is also on display here. The museum has first editions of Ivan Kotliarevsky, Taras Shevchenko, Ivan Franko, Lesia Ukrainka and other classics of the national literature printed during their lifetime.

STATE MUSEUM OF UKRAINIAN DECORATIVE FOLK ART ❾

☎ 290–13–43
Day off – Tuesday

The museum has operated as an independent entity since 1964. The original art of the Ukrainian people is widely represented here: icons, decorated eggs, embroidery, examples of clothes, pottery, glass, faience and others. There are special displays devoted to the work of the famous artists Katerina Bilokur and Mariya Primachenko. One of the museum's buildings is known as the house of the metropolitan. This structure dating from the 18th-19th centuries was the residence of

Folk woman's costume

the Kyiv metropolitans, who were also the archimandrites of Kyiv Pechersk Lavra. Tsar Peter I and Tsarina Elizabeth Petrovna stayed here. Near the metropolitan's house stands the Metropolitan Church of the Annunciation (architect E.Yermakov, 1905).

STATE MUSEUM OF THEATRE, MUSIC AND CINEMA ARTS OF UKRAINE ❿

☎ 290–51–31
Day off – Tuesday

The museum was created in 1923. The exposition has been functioning in its present format since 1977. Here we can see the so-called "vertep" - the Ukrainian puppet theater of the 18th century, playbills and pictures of the plays of different Ukrainian theatre troupes,

Decorative sculpture "The Goat." 1970. D.Golovko

personal effects of famous artists and musicians, autograph notes by the greatest composers, and old musical instruments.

Kolkhoz Field. 1948-1949. K.Bilokur

SUBJECT EXHIBITIONS ⓫

Secular exhibitions devoted to the history of the Kyiv Pechersk Lavra, the restoration of the Lavra complex and the Ukrainian art of the Baroque period were created on basis of the stock of the Kyiv Pechersk Preserve. This stock includes numerous rare treasures - old icons and engravings, jewelry pieces, jewel embroidery. Two parallel stone buildings from the first half of the 18th century contain the exhibitions. These are the so-called "cells of the cathedral elders," where the Lavra's senior clergy once resided.

The Gospel case.
17th century.

EXHIBITION OF MINIATURES ⓬

On the territory of the Upper Lavra there is an exhibition of works by the contemporary master N.Siadristy. It is made up of miniature pieces created with the aid of a microscope. The hero of the famous story "The Lefthander" by N.Leskov shod a flea, but the works of N.Siadristy are even more delicate than those of the Lefthander. Some of these works have no equal anywhere in the world.

Riza (metal plating) on the icon of John the Warrior.
18th century

WALLS AND TOWERS

The strong stone walls surrounding the Upper Lavra were built around the turn of the 18th century. In times of danger they turned the monastery into a real fortress. The construction of the walls was financed by Hetman I.Mazepa. The fortress complex consists of four towers: The Southwest Tower (also named the tower of Ivan Kushchnik - from the name of the church that was planned to be opened in the tower); the South Tower (or the Horlogium,

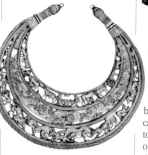

Pectoral (breast decoration).
4th century A.D.

because up to 1818 it had a clock); the North Tower (or the Painting Tower, because it once held a painting studio); the East Onufriyevskaya Tower with the church of Saint Onufry, (also known as the Chamber Tower, because

"Apostle". 1574.
Lvov. Printed by Ivan Fedorov

Alb. 18th century.
Silk, gold and silver embroidery

Hetman Ivan Mazepa had chambers here. Near the tower of Ivan Kushchnik on the side of Yanvarskogo Vosstaniya Street another tower decorated with a brickwork pattern can be seen. This tower is not part of the fortifications, however: it is a water tower built for the needs of the Lavra (architect V.Sychugov, 1879).

Chalice.
18th century.
Author F.Levitsky

THE CAVES

Underground path in the caves

S pecial overland galleries lead from the Upper Lavra to the Near and Far Caves. The Lavra caves are a complex system of narrow underground corridors 1 - 1.5 meters wide and 2 - 2.5 meters high, along which there are numerous shrines and relics. In ancient times people settled in underground dwellings dug in the solid layers of loam, sand and boggy loess on the high bank of the Dnieper. Here they were protected from bad weather and wild animals. In 1051 the Reverend Antoniy settled in an old cave in one of the hills. This was where the Far Caves appeared. Antoniy and his disciples extended the underground corridors and built a church there. In 1062 Antoniy moved to a cave near the Upper Lavra, which was the beginning of the Near Caves. The most remarkable Pechersk ascetics chose to live as hermits. They dug narrow caves linked to the main corridor only by small holes for food and air and stayed there permanently. Two or three times a week, monks left the host and holy water at the holes. If the host and holy water were left untouched this indicated that the ascetic had died. They buried the dead monks in the caves. The remains were embalmed and have been preserved to the present day.

Nestor the Chronicler.
1702. L.Tarasevich

THE UNDERGROUND LABYRINTHS

The solemn and mysterious appearance of the underground labyrinths made a striking impression. Foreign travellers in the 16th - 17th centuries wrote that the catacombs of the Lavra stretched for hundreds of kilometres - even as far as Moscow and Novgorod. The fame of the wonders of the Lavra spread throughout the world.

THE PECHERSK BURIALS

The Orthodox Church canonized the ascetics of the Lavra caves as saints. Soviet atheistic propaganda tried to prove that the reason why the remains do not decay is the natural character of the ground and air in the caves. But right up to the present, new evidence is appearing of the extraordinary character of

the Pechersk burials. Apart from the remains of the saints whose names are known, the caves also contain the heads of unknown ascetics, which shed a holy chrism. There have been many examples of their healing influence. Today visitors can view the caves escorted by monks. Everyone who enters should take a candle. One should remember that the Lavra caves are a very holy place, and one should enter in appropriate clothes and keeping peace and silence.

THE NEAR CAVES

The underground corridors of the Near Caves have a total

The Pechersk burials

The entrance to the Near Caves of the Lavra. V.Timm. 1859

length of 383 meters, and they are situated at a depth of 5 - 20 meters. They are also called the Antoniyevskiye Caves as the remains of Saint Antoniy are buried here. The Near Caves contain the underground Church of Saint Antoniy, the Church of the Entry of the Mother of God into the Temple and the Saint Varlaham Church. There are 79 surviving burial sites. Among them are Nestor the Chronicler, the first known Russian artists Alipiy and Grigoriy, the doctor Agapit, the prince-ascetic Nikolay Svyatosha, the holy martyr Kuksha. The remains of the epic hero Ilya Muromets are also buried here. During the examination of the remains, it was established that Ilya died from a stab wound. According to legend, a force of angels transported him from the place where he met his death to the Lavra caves.

A fragment of the icons from the underground Varlaham Church. 19th century

MEMORIALS OF THE NEAR CAVES 🔟

The main temple of the Near Caves ensemble is the Church of the Elevation of the Cross (Krestovozdvizhenskaya) in Ukrainian Baroque style (1700 - 1704). The magnificent carved icons of 1769 have survived here. From the 19th century the church served as a burial-vault for the Kyiv metropolitans. The old refectory of the church is connected to the brothers' cells (classical housing decorated with a four-column portico, dating from the 1830s). At the brow of the hill stands

the bell tower (architect S. Kovnir, 1760). The headstones of a number of well-known Kyivans can be seen in front of the Kresto-vozdvizhenskaya Church and the entrance to the caves. The tomb of the general-governor A.Bezak (the architect M.Ikonnikov, 1860) is particularly noteworthy. The headstone was restored.

THE DRAW-WELLS 🔟

Beneath the Near Caves, under a strong 18th century breastwork

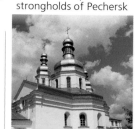

Krestovozdvizhenskaya Church

(engineer D.Debosket) two old draw-wells under tracery have survived. According to legend, one of them was dug by Saint Antoniy and the other by Reverend Feodosiy. Beside the draw-wells a chapel was built over an artesian well (architect E.Yermakov, 1913). Now it is the "The Life-Giving Source," a church in honour of the Icon of the Mother of God.

The Near Caves. The tomb of Varlaham

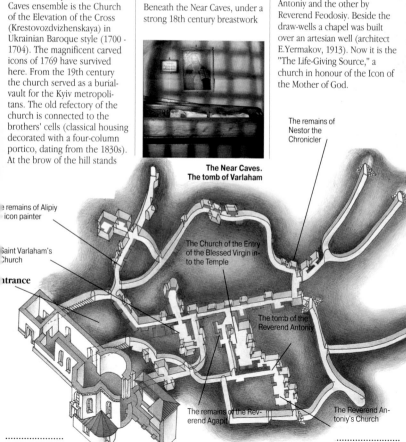

The remains of Nestor the Chronicler

The remains of Alipiy icon painter

Saint Varlaham's Church

entrance

The Church of the Entry of the Blessed Virgin into the Temple

The tomb of the Reverend Antoniy

The remains of the Reverend Agapit

The Reverend Antoniy's Church

Plan of the Near Caves of the Kyiv Pechersk Lavra

91

Icon painter Alipiy

THE FAR CAVES

The cave corridors have a total length of 293 meters, and the depth is 5.20 meters. The remains of Reverend Feodosiy were buried here in 1091. That is why they are also called Feodosiyevy. The Far Caves contain the underground churches of the Blessed Virgin, the Reverend Feodosiy, and Christ's Nativity. 46 tombs have survived from ancient times, among them those containing the relics of Longin the Pechersk porter, Moses the miracle-worker and Archbishop Feofil of Novgorod. The Far Caves are adjacent to the so-called Varangian cave - the oldest part of the underground labyrinth of the Lavra. According to legend, the incredible treasures of the Varangian brigands are stored here. The recovered remains of the Kyiv metropolitans Filaret (Amfyteatrov) and the saint martyr Vladimir (Bogoyavlenskiy), who was murdered near the Lavra by revolutionary soldiers in 1918, were recently moved to the underground crypt of the Far Caves.

The church of The Life giving Source

ARCHITECTURAL MONUMENTS OF THE FAR CAVES 🔞 🔞 🔞

Above the Far Caves stands the picturesque baroque church of the Birth of the Blessed Virgin (1696). The central three-domed building is linked to four corner edifices with decorative domes. The bell tower of the Far Caves is 42 meters high. This is one of the most expressive baroque buildings in Kyiv (erected in the 1750s by the architect S.Kovnir). A fanciful dome crowns the building and the corners are supported by counterforts bearing faceted broaches. The walls are decorated with colorful stucco molding. Above the entrance to the Caves stands the Annozachatiyevskaya Church (1679, subsequently rebuilt). The residence of the metropolitan of Kyiv and Ukraine is situated on the territory of the Far Caves.

CEMETERY OF THE FAR CAVES

On a bastion behind the church of the Birth of the Blessed Virgin is a small cemetery, where among others many outstanding military commanders are buried. Under a modest cast iron plate lies the Field-Marshal Prince Fabian Osten-Saken. When the troops of the anti-Napoleon coalition occupied Paris in 1814, he was appointed governor general of the French capital. In recognition of his nobility and justice, he was presented with a gold sword bearing the inscription "To General Saken from the City of Paris". Also buried here are: the generals Paisiy Kaysarov

and Afanasiy Krasovskiy, heroes of the war of 1812; the brothers Nikolai and Stepan Leonov, cavalry generals who were heroes of the liberation of Bulgaria from the Ottoman yoke; and Admiral Ephymiy Putyiatin (with whom

The part of the Annozachatiyevskaya Church under the dome. 19th century

the writer I.Goncharov traveled on board the frigate "Pallada").

"KYIV-PECHERSK PATERIK"

IIn 1223-1233, the Reverend Simeon (the Bishop of Suzdal, who is buried in the Near Caves) and his spiritual son the Reverend Polikarp (a Pechersk monk) wrote down the legends that formed the basis of the "Kyiv-Pechersk Paterik." The word "paterik" is derived from the Greek word for "father." This collection of stories about the saints of Pechersk and their miracles is an important historic monument and a significant source of information about the Lavra hermits.

LEGENDS OF "KYIV-PECHERSK PATERIK"

Reverend Mark the Undertaker dug out the tombs of many of the deceased cenobites with his

own hands. Once he was ill and
didn't manage to prepare a wide
enough tomb. When the coffin
was put in place it turned out
that it was not possible to pour
anointing oil on the body. The
brothers started to reproach
Mark for not finishing the job.
And then he addressed the
deceased: "Brother! There is no
space. So please do the work
yourself and pour anointing oil
on your body." The deceased
stretched out his arm, leaned
forward a little, took the oil and
poured it onto his face and chest
in a cross, and then returned to
his eternal slumber.
Reverend Alipiy - the Pechersk
cenobite - was known as a mas-
terful icon painter. One wealthy
Kyivan asked two monks to
arrange with Alipiy to draw seven
large icons. He provided the
boards for the icons and a fair
sum of money as payment. But
the greedy monks said nothing
to Alipiy. They asked the cus-
tomer for the payment twice
more, and then they accused
Alipiy of taking three times the
price and doing nothing. The
indignant rich man came to the
monk to demand his order. The
innocent Alipiy was called to
account. But when the

**Fragments of icons from the under-
ground Feodosiyivskaya Church.**
18th century

untouched boards were brought
in, beautiful icons miraculously
appeared on them.
The chemist Siluyan - a righteous man of the Far Caves - was
the sexton of the monastery garden. Once thieves sneaked in.
The holy man was praying in his
cell, but he foresaw their arrival.
Through his prayers, he made
the thieves stand motionless for
three days. This miracle brought
them to repentance. Siluyan
brought them to reason and let
them go.
In the Near Caves lay the relics
of Prokhor the Miracle-Worker.
In his religious endeavors he
deprived himself of usual bread
and ground flour from bitter
goose-foot. But he was rewarded
for his patience, when the food
he prepared miraculously
acquired the taste of real bread.
One time famine came to Rus,
but there was a lot of goose-foot
everywhere. So Prokhor indus-
triously baked bread and generously gave it to the hungry and

the poor.
Another time
internal wars
were preventing
merchants from
bringing salt to
Kyiv. The mira-
cle-worker again
came to the res-
cue: by his
prayers he transformed the ashes
gathered in the cells into salt.
At Easter 1463 Dionisiy Shepa, a
holy cenobite of the monastery
came to burn incense over the
remains of the holy hermits of
the Near Caves. When he did so,
he said: "Holy fathers and brothers! This is a glorious day: Christ
is risen!" And a thunderous
answer came from all the saints:
" He is risen indeed!"

**Entrance to the gallery leading to
the Far Caves.**
1859. V.Timm

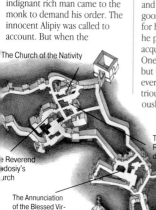

The Church of the Nativity

e Reverend
dosiy's
urch

The Annunciation
of the Blessed Vir-
gin. The burial
place of the mar-
tyred Metropolitan
Vladimir

The cell of the
Reverend Feo-
dosiy

**Plan of the
Far Caves of
Kyiv-Pechersk Lavra**

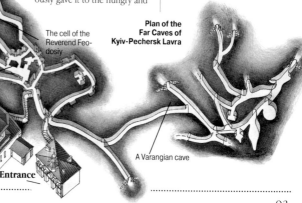

A Varangian cave

Entrance

93

THE CITADEL

In 1706 Tsar Peter I feared an attack by Swedish troops on Ukraine. He actively began to fortify Kyiv, and he personally drafted a project for a fortress in Pechersk. The earth ramparts of this fortress surrounded the walls of the Lavra and Pechersk in a half-ring, open in the direction of the Dnieper. The fortification was of the bastion type: it consisted of nine bastions and one half-bastion connected by "crutinas" (intermediary stretches of the ramparts). The ramparts were 6 meters high, on slopes - 20 meters. In front of the ramparts were dry moats 5-6 meters deep. The fortress was built by Russian "street" troops (elite troops) and Ukrainian Cossacks, who were mercilessly harried by the tsar's officials. When the new fortifications built in the mid 19th century under Nikolay I encompassed a larger area of Pechersk, the building of Peter's times - the Old Pechersk Fortress - became the Citadel of the New Pechersk Fortress. Most of the old ramparts have survived to the present day, though later construction means it is hard to get an idea of the citadel as a whole today. Passages were cut through some sections of the rampart.

The Voskresenskaya Church

For example, Yanvarskogo Vosstaniya Street passes through it between the former Spasskiy and Petrovskiy bastions. Here you can easily go up to the top of the bank and take a walk along the flat top.

THE OLD ARSENAL [9]
30, Yanvarskogo Vosstaniya St.

This large square building, which served as a manufacturing workshop and a fortification. It was one of the first Kyiv buildings to be built in the style of Classicism. It was designed in 1783 (Lieutenant-General I.Meller), but the construction was not carried out until 1797 - 1803. At the time the church of the Voznesenskiy Women's

The old arsenal

Monastery was demolished, and the Arsenal was built in its place. Its workshops produced and repaired guns and gun-carriages, and manufactured cannon balls, grenades and case-shot. Arms depots were arranged here. Yakov Andriyevich, an active participant in the Decembrists' movement worked in the Arsenal planning department. The question of creating here a cultural complex - the Arsenal of Art - is currently being considered.

THE CHURCH OF THE REVEREND FEODOSIY PECHERSKIY [10]
14, Citadelnaya St.

This church was built in 1698 - 1700 in Ukrainian Baroque style with the funds of Colonel Konstantin Mokiyevskiy of Kiev. According to legend, the church was built on the spot where the funeral procession of the Reverend Feodosiy stopped for a rest while carrying the remains from the Far Caves to the Uspenskiy Cathedral (the church's altar was placed where

Moscow Rampart Gates

the casket with the remains was laid down). A small monastery has been arranged on the basis of the Feodosiyskaya Church.

THE VOSKRESENSKAYA CHURCH [11]
27, Yanvarskogo Vosstaniya St.

This church was also founded by Colonel Konstantin Mokiyevskiy, a relative of Hetman Mazepa who distinguished himself during Peter I victorious Azov campaign. Built in 1698, it served as the parish church for the inhabitants of the Pechersk borough and the Lavra peasants living nearby. The church burned down several times. Despite being rebuilt, it has retained the features of the Ukrainian Baroque. In 1991 it was trans-

The Feodosiyskaya Church

ferred to the Society of Veterans of the Afghanistan War, so the church is now often called Afghanskaya.

THE IVAN HONCHAR MUSEUM [12]
29, Yanvarskogo Vosstaniya St.
☎ 573–92–68
Ⓜ Arsenalnaya
Days off – Saturday and Sunday

The museum is situated on the site of the former residence and office of the Kyiv governors and governors-general built in 1757 - 1759 by the architect S.Karin. The house burned down in 1783, and only a quarter of a century later was it rebuilt as the "Comissariatskiy magazin" (the store of the commissary office). The Ukrainian Center for Folk Culture, "The Ivan Honchar Museum," has been established here. The museum display is based on the private collection of the artist, sculptor and ethnographer Ivan Makarovich Honchar (1911 - 1993), who managed to preserve the expressions of national peculiarity in the period of "stagnation" under Brezhnev.

THE GREAT PATRIOTIC WAR HISTORY MUSEUM [13]

44, Yanvarskogo Vosstaniya St.
☎ 295–94–57
Ⓜ Arsenalnaya
Day off – Monday

Yanvarskogo Vosstaniya Street leads to the south fortifications of the Old Pechersk Fortress. The gunpowder cellar from the end of the 18th century (there is a cafe there now) inside the Alexeevskiy Bastion and the nearby brick Moskovskiye Fortress Gate, which is now free from the thick of the bank, have survived. The grandiose complex of the Great Patriotic War History Museum are visible behind them. It covers a territory of 20 hectares. The idea for the gigantic memorial was suggested by the Russian monu-

**The exhibition of
defense technology**

mental sculptor E.Vuchetich shortly before his death. It was carried out by the Ukrainian authors V.Boroday, F.Sogoyan, V.Yelizarov, G.Kisly and others. The main building of the complex is the museum house, which

The Rodina-Mat statue. The Great Patriotic War Museum

is surmounted by the high conical pedestal on which the Rodina-Mat (Motherland) statue stands. The 530-ton statue is constructed as a carcass of metal beams surfaced with sheets of non-corrosive chrome-nickel steel. Lifts operate inside the carcass, in the torso of the Rodina-

**The Museum of
the Great Patriotic War**

Mat. There are special stairs for sightseeing and maintenance in the hands. On the head of the statue there are the caps of technical hatches. Rodina-Mat holds a shield with the image of the state symbol of the USSR in its left hand, and a 12-ton sword in its right. The height of the whole construction, from the bottom of the building to the tip of the sword, is 108 meters. The huge statue has impudently intruded into Kyiv's historic panorama, but there is nothing to be done now. On the inside of the cone pedestal the names of the Heroes of the Soviet Union and Socialist Labor, who performed their feats during the war years, are written. When the Soviet leader Leonid Brezhnev opened the complex on 9 May 1981, he could see his own name

at the top of the list - his entourage of flatterers regularly awarded him with Gold Stars. Now the name of Brezhnev has been taken away. The present museum display contains many interesting exhibits. The Memorial Hall with its huge number of funeral letters for dead warriors leaves a strong impression. On the territory of the memorial, there are thematic sculpture compositions showing the defense of the border, the inhabitants of the occupied territories, the struggle of the partisans, the heroes of the front and the home front, the forcing of the Dnieper. Every year on Victory Day, the Fire of Glory is lit in its gigantic cup. The exhibition of defense technology occupies a separate area. The two tanks standing in front of the museum are made into toys for the children. One wants to believe that they would not be used for any other purpose. The Pechersk Landscape Park borders the territory of the memorial. Exhibitions of flowers are held here regularly. The open-air Singing Ground for popular concerts is arranged here.

Sculptural composition

95

THE NEW PECHERSK FORTRESS

The belligerent policy of the Russian Empire under Tsar Nikolay I allotted to Kyiv the role of an outpost of autocracy in the southwestern territory. But given the then level of weaponry, the old earth ramparts were a poor defence for Pechersk. In 1831 work began on the construction of a vast new system of fortifications according to plans drawn up by the engineer K.Opperman. These did not form an uninterrupted line of defence. Instead they formed a set of buildings arranged singly and in groups, the lines of fire from which covered the whole surrounding area. To create the New Pechersk Fortress and the esplanade (the vacant space on the outer side of the fortifications), the dwellers of Pechersk were forcibly resettled to other regions. However, as soon became apparent, the result was not worth the expenses: the development of artillery soon

Modern decor of fortress buildings

made the fortress obsolete, and in 1897 it was turned into a fortress-warehouse. The basic buildings from the mid-19th century were the lines of the Hospital and Vasilkov fortifications, as well as a number of buildings along the slopes of the Pechersk heights. These included the barrack with gates. In order to cover the Waterfront Highway, two mighty support walls were built below it (in 1949, one of them was used for the Green Theater - a concert and cinema space in the open air). In the vicinity of Moskovskaya Street, there are several former barrack-fortifications. The long building of the so-called "barrack of military singers" (1835-1839) at 45, Moskovskaya St. was later turned into an infantry cadet school (now it is the Military Institute of Communication). Among its students were the future military ministers of the Ukrainian People's Republic V.Salskiy and A.Galkin, as well as the future commander of the White Volunteer Army A.Denikin.

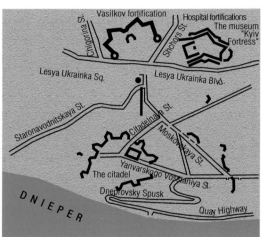

The plan of the Pechersk Fortress

Prospect of Kyiv-Pechersk Fortress and a part of the Fortress Wall from Moscow side. 1783

THE HOSPITAL FORTIFICATIONS

A polygonal defense system was used for the western complex of the New Pechersk fortress, built in 1836-1851. Parts of the lines of fortification were formed by the so-called polygons, where the fire from the ramparts was sustained by caponiers - special fortifications at the front of the ditch. The buildings of the garrison hospital, which was established back in 1755, became part of the Hospital Fortifications. The oldest part is shaped in a gigantic half-square and was built in 1836-1842. Now this is the Central Clinical Hospital of the Ministry of Defense of Ukraine. The central entrance to the hos-

**The caponier.
Hospital Fortifications**

pital is also part of the former fortifications: the way to the gates leads over a bridge over the ditch. The adjacent stretch of the rampart was recently restored. To the north of the bridge behind a vast drill square, there is a curved building - the Half Tower (1839-1842), which for a long time was occupied by a school for military doctors. Among the school's graduates were the Ukrainian cultural and religious figure I.Ogiyenko, the Soviet army commander N.Shchors, and the writers Demian Bedniy and Ostap Vishnya.

KYIV FORTRESS MUSEUM

24a, Hospitalnaya St.
☎ 224–19–70
Ⓜ Arsenalnaya
Day off – Monday

One of the caponiers of the Hospital Fortifications got the name Kosoi ("Crooked") because of its asymmetrical plan. After 1863, the Tsarist authorities began to use it as a military-political prison for revolutionaries. The execution of prisoners also took place in the fortress. Prominent participants in the Polish rebellion of 1863 - M.Druzbatski, A.Zielinski, P.Kryzanowski, R.Olszanski, V.Padlewski, T.Rakowski, and K.Rudzki - were executed by firing squad near the Kosoi caponier. A memorial plate was put up in their honour, though the list of those killed is neither full nor exact. In 1907 garrison soldiers who took part in revolutionary riots were executed at the same spot. There is a monument to them at the place of execution (the architect I.Sigalov, sculptors Y.Sinkevych, M.Gritsuk, 1971).

Memorial to the revolutionaries of 1905-1907

In Soviet times the Kosoi caponier became a historic

Memorial to the executed Polish revolutionaries

museum. Now this is the Kyiv Fortress history and architecture museum. The display presents the city's unique fortifications.

The restored fortress rampart

VASILKOVSKIYE FORTIFICATIONS

The south-western part of the Pechersk elevation was covered by the Vasilkovskiye fortifications built in 1831-1844 according to a design by K.Opperman. This complex included star-shaped earth ramparts about 10 meters high, the flanks of which ended in two identical ring-shaped towers, each of them capable of housing a battalion. One of those, now known as the Round Tower, is situated at 44, Shchors St. and faces Lesia Ukrainka Boulevard. Now it is a shopping centre. The other tower located at 34, Shchors St. is called Prosorovskaya, as its chapel contains the tomb of Field-Marshal Prince Alexander Prosorovskiy, who took part in the annexing of Bessarabia and the Crimea to Russia. The Prosorovskaya tower is still used by the military, as is the central building of the Vasilkovskiye fortifications - "Tower #1". Not far from the Vasilkovskiye ramparts stands the buildings of the State University of Culture and Arts (36, Shchors St.), which is now

The Round Tower

popular due to the frequent appearances, in concerts and on TV of the "singing rector" M.Poplavskiy.

"THE TSAR'S VILLAGE" 14

On the slopes of the picturesque "Navodnitskaya Gully" (named after the ancient Navodnitskaya crossing, the road to which led along the gully) a line of identical skyscrapers arose in the 1980s-1990s forming a separate micro-district. The buildings here were designed for the Soviet (and then for the commercial) elite. Kyivans gave the area the nickname "The Tsar's Village".

I.BOGUN MILITARY LYCEUM 15
25, Lesia Ukrainka Blvd.

The neo-imperial style building of the Lyceum was built for the Alexeevskiy Military School (architect N.Shekhonin, engineer I.Lilye, 1915-1916). Under the Soviet regime this was a military high school, named after the Communist commander S.Kamenev. The famous generals N.Vatutin and I.Panfilov studied here. In the years after the war it housed the Suvorov Vocational School - a military school for

boys. The well-known scriptwriter and poet G.Shpalikov was a graduate of this establishment. Today the school is named after Ivan Bogun, a Cossack colonel and comrade of Bogdan Khmelnitsky. However, a cop-

The Military Lyceum

per monument of the invincible Russian commander Alexander Suvorov still stands in front of the Lyceum (the work of the amateur sculptor Major I.Zarechniy, 1974).

Students of the Suvorov School

The Tsar's Village

ALONG
KRESHCHATIK

ALONG KRESHCHATIK

Two hundred years is not a long period for ancient Kyiv, but the 1,300 meter long Kreshcha Street remains the most popular place in the city all year round - its Broadway, its Champs ysees, its Nevskiy Prospekt. Kreshchatik has been praised by bards and poets, reproduced artists and cinematographers, and depicted on postcards and stamps. The beauty of the sha chestnuts in bloom competes with that of the human-built ensembles of post-war buildings. though the street has plenty of shops and offices, most people come here not on business, just to relax, to sit in one of the countless cafes, to breathe the distinctive and truly metropoli air (which has recently became much cleaner, since the street is closed to traffic on weekend On major holidays a lot of people visit the festivities on Kreshchatik. But this popularity does have its reverse side: Kyiv's aggressively ambitious and pushy modern architects are ready to go to any lengths to leave their mark here, and for the moment it is difficult to judge what consequences this will have for the appearance of this much-loved street.

The front of the "Youth Theater" at 17, Proreznaya St. bears a memorial plate to Les Kurbas - the great reformer of Ukrainian theater, who headed the company in 1918-1919.

The bas-relief on the pediment of the former apartment house at 6, Kreshchatik St. (architects I.Zetsker, D.Torov, 1911) is decorated with a copy of the relief "Industry" by the Belgian sculptor K.Menier.

The building at 32, Kreshchatik St. (architect F.Lidval, 1911-1913), which today houses the Architecture Department, was built for the local branch of the Russian Bank of Foreign Trade. The statues above the cornice symbolize Trade and Navigation. Some of the reliefs on the front were scorched during the fire of 1914.

The monument to Nikolai Yakovchenko (sculptor V.Chepelyk and others, 2000). The much-loved comic actor is depicted resting with his dachshund near the Franko Theater.

"The Ukrainian House" - is the name given to the cultural centre located at 2, Kreshchatik St. (architects V.Gopkalo and others, 1982). Now, not everyone remembers that this used to be the Lenin Museum (by the way, the leader of the proletarians never visited Kyiv).

The Danish artist Herluf Bidstrup makes a drawing on the Kreshchatik. Photograph made in 1962.

L. PUSHKINS'KA

VUL. PRORIZNA

VUL. KHRESCHATYK

⑤

④

VUL. KHRESCHATYK

⑦

MAIDAN NEZALEZHNOSTI

⑪

VUL. KOST'OL'NA

⑧

NKOVETS'KOI

VUL. HORODETS'KOHO

OSCHA IVANA RANKA

VUL. INSTYTUTS'KA

⑨

YEVROPEIS'KA PLOSCHA

The Bessarabskiy covered market (architects G.Gai, M.Bobrusov, 1908-1912) was erected in modern style and decorated with reliefs on the subject of agricultural labor (sculptors A.Teremets, T.Rudenko). The place where the market stands was formerly an open trading area where peasants from Bessarabia (Moldova) brought their wares.

HOW KRESHCHATIK BEGAN

In the place of the present Kreshchatik, under the rampart of the Old Kyiv Fortress, there used to be a road leading from the hollow called "Kreshchatiy Yar" in the direction of Vasilkov. According to one version, the name of the ravine comes from a stream beginning at the Kreshchatik Spring and flowing to the place where the Kyivans were christened. Another version

Autumn in the city. S.Kaplan. 1973

is that the toponym came from the ravines that met and crossed here. A street with urban estates in grounds was established here at the end of the 18th century. At first it was called "Teatralnaya" - after a wooden theatre that stood in the place of the present "Ukrainskiy Dom" in the first half of the 19th century. Then the theatre was replaced by the "Yevropeyskaya" hotel, which is now recalled in the name of Yevropeyskaya Square. As the city developed further, Kreshchatik turned into a central arterial road. At the beginning of the 20th century, it was a rich and elegant street with the City Duma, the exchange, a post office, bank offices, different trade companies, luxurious apartment houses, theatres and cinemas. Only a few isolated buildings have survived from the Old Kreshchatik to the present day (see 104).

THE SUICIDE-STREET

During the first days of the Nazi occupation in September 1941, the houses along Kreshchatik began to blow up one after another. It emerged that the Soviet Secret Services left radio-controlled bombs in many of the central buildings when they left the city.
  The victims of this suicidal action included not only the Nazi occupiers, who had taken comfortable lodgings on Kreshchatik, but also civilian residents. The street was on fire, and in order to prevent it from spreading, the Germans demolished the houses surrounding the fire. In this way, the city centre was quickly turned into ruins.

THE POST-WAR RENAISSANCE

Soon after the liberation of Kyiv, an All-Union contest to find a design for a new Kreshchatik was held. While the Kyivans enthusiastically contributed to the restoration of their favorite street by clearing the ruins, the architects prepared their creative proposals. After long discussion, the design proposed by a group led by the Moscow architect A.Vlasov was approved. The design was marked by the pomp of the Stalin epoch. However, it should be noted that as a result,

Captured German soldiers on the ruined Kreshchatik. August 1944

View of Teatralnaya Square at the end of 1840s. M.Sazhin

the architects created a unified complex truly befitting a capital - festive, ceremonial and distinctive. The first forerunners of the new construction were the dwelling houses at ## 13 and 17, Kreshchatik St. (architects A.Vlasov, A.Dobrovolskiy and B.Pryimak, 1949 - 1951). Like most of the subsequent buildings, they were faced with light ceramic tiles and the socles were decorated with granite. In the course of the reconstruction, Kreshchatik was widened considerably. The earlier width of the street (50 meters) was retained in only one place by the surviving pre-war house at # 5. A passage had to be cleared through its first floor.

HOUSES ## 23 - 27

This spectacular ensemble of apartment blocks (architects A.Dobrobolskiy, A.Malinovskiy and P.Petrushenko, engineer I.Skachkov, 1951 - 1956) closes the perspective of Bogdan Khmel'nitsky Street. The central 14-storey building at # 25 is crowned with a spire. Due to the variation in elevation, it is raised 16 meters above street level, and a handsome granite staircase leads up to it. Similar tower blocks stand on either side at # 23 and 27. Their developed socles are occupied by shops. The balanced proportions, the distinctive silhouette and expressive details make this ensemble the most successful element of the post-war Kreshchatik.

KYIV CITY COUNCIL 2
36, Kreshchatik St.

View of the main
street from
Besarabskaya
Square

The building of the City Council of Peoples Deputies (architects A.Vlasov, A.Zavarov and A.Malinovskiy, 1952 - 1957) - which currently houses the Kyiv Council and Kyiv City State Administration - recalls the austere classical traditions. An extension at the rear contains a large meeting hall. The Kyiv Council consists of 75 deputies under the City Head, who is elected by the entire population of the city (since 1999 - Alexander Omelchenko). High metal flagstaffs stand in front of the City Administration. This was where the national flag was raised in front of an official institution for the first time in modern Ukrainian history.

UKRTELERADIO 4
26, Kreshchatik St.

At the end of 18th century, the manor of the landowner O.Golovinskiy stood in roughly this location. It was the first stone house on Kreshchatik. The City Post Office stood here

The ensemble of apartment blocks at # 23 - 27 Kreshchatik Street

after 1849. In 1914 the old building was demolished to make way for a new post office (it has not survived). By that time the building of the City Telephone Station had already risen behind it. This building was reconstructed after the war and organized as a center for television and radio broadcasting. Its renovated facade, decorated by the architect V.Yelizarov in the style of the Ukrainian baroque, is not visible from Kreshchatik. It is blocked by the administrative building at # 24, which follows the bend of the street in the form of a supple curve (architects N.Shilo and others, 1952 - 1957).

THE CENTRAL SUPERMARKET 3
38/2, Kreshchatik St.

The construction is based on a pre-war retail building put up in 1936 - 1939 according to a design by architects from the Moscow studio of A.Shchusev. The facade was given rationalized shapes, and the corner is emphasized by an original step-form termination. The Central Supermarket was reconstructed after the war (architects L.Gomoliaka and V.Zhoga, 1958 - 1960). Its external appearance has been brought into line with the new construction of the street.

The Central
Department
Store

AT THE CORNER OF KRESHCHATIK AND PROREZNAYA STREET 5

The name "Proreznaya" recalls that, in the middle of the 19th century, the street was, as it were, "cut" ("prorezali") through the former fortress rampart. If you pass from Proreznaya St. through the arch onto B.Grinchenko St., you can see a remaining fragment of the old rampart rising opposite the Architects House. The building of the Architects House (7, B.Grinchenko St.) is part of the former complex of the Music College, which was rebuilt after the war. The complex was based around the old Conservatory, where the pianist Vladimir Horowitz studied and the composer Reinhold Gliere was director (that building is now located on the territory of the State Television and Radio and is not available for observation).

Muzykalniy Lane, which formerly led to the Conservatory, has now been turned into the gateway of the post-war house at 6, Proreznaya St. In the square in front of the house stands a bronze statue of Mikhail Panikovskiy, the well-known character from Ilf and Petrov's novel "The Golden Calf," as portrayed by the screen actor Z.Gerdt (sculptors V.Shchur and V.Sivko, architect V.Skulskiy, 1998). In the novel, the pickpocket Panikovskiy worked on the corner of Kreshchatik and Proreznaya Street, pretending to be a blind man and robbing the people who helped him to cross the road.

"The great blind man" - Mikhail Panikovskiy

The Alexander Church

THE OLD BLOCK [6]

At 40/1-52, Kreshchatik St. there is a string of historical buildings. In the house at # 40/1 (architect V.Nikolayev, 1873 - 1874) on the corner of B.Khmel'nitskogo St. the landlord I.Kane opened a private hotel. The artist M.Vrubel and the actor Panas Saksaganskiy stayed here. The future Hetman of Ukraine Pavel Skoropadskiy lived here at the beginning of 1918, as the influential circles gradually came to realize the necessity of the forthcoming change in power. The house at # 42 (architect A.Krivosheyev, 1894) was built on the order of Olga Dyakova - the granddaughter and heir of the wealthy businessman and former Kyiv mayor G.Eysman. Her father, an officer, fell in love with Eysman's daughter, but the mayor was afraid the young man was only interested in wealth, and he was reluctant to give his consent for the marriage. However, the couple married against his will. The mother died giving birth to their daughter, and the inconsolable officer threw himself from the Chain Bridge into the Dnieper. Only then did Eysman realize his mistake. He did everything for his orphaned grandchild, who later married Ippolit Dyakov - a future mayor of Kyiv. O.Dyakova immigrated after the revolution

and became a well-known editor. A cinema was established in the house at # 52 (architects A.Gross and V.Nikolayev, 1875 - 1878) at the beginning of the 20th century. After 1922, the Lysenko Music and Drama Institute was located here. The institute (after 1934, the Theater Institute) played a considerable role in the development of Ukrainian culture. Among the institute's teachers were the composers M.Verikovskiy and V.Kosenko, the vocal teacher E.Muravyova, the dramatic actors Les Kurbas and L.Gackebush, and the playwright V.Miller. Among the pupils were the opera singers Z.Gayday and O.Petrusenko, the conductor N.Rakhlin, the dramatic actress O.Kusenko, and the comedy duo Y.Timoshenko and E.Berezin (Tarapunka and Shtepsel). Designs for the internal renovation of the Old Block of Kreshchatik are currently being considered, but its front is recognized as a historical and architectural monument.

Sculpture on the facade at 50 Kreshchatik Street

THE PASSAGE [7]

15, Kreshchatik St.

"Passage" means "crossing" in French. This is the name given to a double row of shops between two parallel streets. The two large buildings forming the Kyiv Passage were built in 1913 - 1915 (architect P.Andreyev) at the order of a wealthy investor - the "Rossiya" Insurance Company. Many

well-known people lived in apartments on the Passage, including the writer Victor Nekrasov. In his book "Notes of an Idler," he recalls how for a long time he paid no attention to the bas-reliefs decorating the walls of the buildings, and then he suddenly noticed that one of them represented children trying to give wine to a lion. After the war, a new building with a monumental arch (architects A.Vlasov, A.Dobrovolskiy and B.Priymak, 1949 - 1951) was attached to the Passage from the side of Kreshchatik.

THE BANK BUILDINGS [8]

The two adjoining buildings at 8 and 10, Kreshchatik St. are decorated in Neo-Empire style. The building at # 8 belonged to the branch office of the St. Petersburg Account Loan Bank. The building at # 10 belonged to the branch office of the Volga-Kama Bank. They were built in 1914 - 1916 by the architect P.Andreyev: the first on the design of Academician L.Benua, the other on his own design. The bas-relief compositions on the facade of the Volga-Kama Bank have been preserved. The central figures are the ancient gods Hephaestos (Vulcan), Poseidon (Neptune) and Hermes (Mercury). They symbolize industry, navigation and trade respectively, and these were the sectors financed by the bank.

The house of contractor Ginsburg

KOSTIOLNAYA STREET

A pleasant old street runs next to Kreshchatik. It was named after the St.Alexander Catholic Church, which was built in 1817 - 1842 (after

A fragment of the facade of the house at 13 Gorodet-skogo Street

the design was revised several times, construction works were completed under the supervision of F.Mekhovich). In the

Soviet period, the Church was transformed into a planetarium. Only in 1995 was it reconsecrated after restoration.

The impressive buildings in modern style at ## 7 and 9, Kostiolnaya St. were built in 1913. The facade of the building at #7 is decorated with an image of embracing giants (the sculptor F.Sokolov). Now you hear that this was a hint at the sexual orientation of the owner. The rocket constructor Sergey Koroliov lived in the house at #9, when he was a student of the Kyiv Polytechnic Institute.

THE MERING ESTATE

Up to the end of the 19th century, this large space adjoining Kreshchatik was occupied by the private estate of the well-known doctor and Kyiv University Professor Fedor Mering. He bought over 1.5 hectares of land here. It was said that Mering's wealth was due to his altruism. He treated poor Jewish people free of charge, and they used

their commerce ties to provide him with information about profitable deals. The estate had a patriarchal appearance: low buildings, a pond with a bathing hut and a garden. After the professor's death, his heirs sold the estate to the newly created Kyiv Landlords' Society. In 1895, the Society divided it into lots for building apartment houses, laying out a plan for a square and four streets: the present Architectora Gorodetskogo, Olginskaya, Zankovietskoy and Stanislavskogo. As if by the wave of a magic wand, the former city estate was filled with substantial buildings. The most imposing of them, 9, Architectora Gorodetskogo St. (architects G.Shleifer and E.Bradtman, 1900 - 1901), was built on the order of the "King of Kyiv Contractors" Lev Ginsburg. The astonishing luxury of the facade decoration served as an advertisement for the landlord's construction office.

View of the Mering estate. 1880s

"DO NOT BELIEVE YOUR EYES" 9

Given the development of the Mering estate began only in 1895, how is it that the facade of the beautiful Renaissance-style house at 13, Architectora Gorodetskogo St. bears the date "1884"? You should remember the words of Kozma Prutkov: If the word "Buffalo" is written on an elephant cage, do not believe your eyes. The matter is that the building was built on the

order of the furniture manufacturer Iosif Kimayer, and the company was founded in 1884.

I.FRANKO THEATRE 10
3, I.Franko Square

The theater building was constructed in Neo-Greek style (architects G.Shleifer and E.Bradtman, 1896 - 1898). At first a Russian drama troupe led by N.Solovtsov performed here. Such remarkable actors as S.Kuznetsov, L.Leonidov, E.Nedelin, E.Polovietskaya, M.Tarkhanov, E.Shatrova and V.Yureneva appeared in the Solovtsov Theater. Since 1926 the building has been occupied by the troupe of the present Ivan Franko National Academic Drama Theatre. The names of such masters of the Ukrainian stage as G.Borisoglebskaya, A.Buchma, O.Kusenko, I.Maryanenko, N.Uzhviy, Y.Shumskiy, G.Yura and many others are linked to the theater. The first place among the present cast is rightly given to B.Stupka. Beside the theater on the square of the same name, there is a memorial to Ivan Franko (sculptors O.Suprun and A.Bielostotskiy, architect N.Ivanchenko, 1956). The building of the former 8th Kyiv Gymnasium (architect N.Dobachevskiy, 1897), where the future ballet soloist Sergey Lifar studied, stands on Ivan Franko Square.

The memorial to Ivan Franko

I.Franko Theater

The Monument to Independence.
The sculptor A.Kushch and others

THE MAIN SQUARE [11]

Maydan Nezalezhnosti
(Independence Square) is the
recognized center of Kyiv. During
official holidays, the governmental podium stands here. The former names of the square are:
Kreschatitskaya, Dumskaya,
Sovietskaya, Kalinina and October
Revolution. In tsarist times, the
square was situated on only one
side of Kreshchatik. The City
Duma and Noble Assembly were
situated here. The present
appearance of the square arose in
the post-war years. It includes the
building of the Central Post Office
(architect B.Pryimak and others,
1952 - 1957), the Trade Union
House with its tower and electronic clock (architects
A.Malinovskiy and A.Komarovskiy,
1975 - 1980), the Ukraina
Hotel (before 2001, the
Moskva Hotel. The original
design by the architect
A.Dobrovolskiy and others
was simplified considerably
during construction works
in 1953 - 1961), the Opera
Studio of the Conservatory
(architect L.Katok, 1955 -
1959). In 1976 - 1981 a
group of architects
(A.Komarovskiy and others)
conducted the general
reconstruction and completion of the square, for
which they received the USSR
State Award. But now the
same A.Komarovskiy has
launched a radical mod-
ification of the square,
demolishing all that
was built previously.

LIADSKIYE GATE, PECHERSKIYE GATE

The Liadskiye Gate, the
southeast entrance to the
"City of Yaroslav," once
stood at the crossroads of
the present Mikhaylovskaya,
Malaya Zhitomirskaya and
Sophiyskaya streets and
Shevchenko Lane. Later the
Pecherskiye Gate of the Old
Kyiv Fortress was built in its
place. The remains of the
Pecherskiye Gate were found by
archeologists. It is now restored
as a replica arch.

CITY DUMA

One of the previous names of

The fountain in Maydan Nezalezhnosti

Maydan Nezalezhnosti -
Dumskaya Square - came from
the building of the City Duma,
the seat of Kyiv's municipal self-
government, which stood in the
center (the architect A.Shile,
1874 - 1878). A statue of the
Archangel Mikhail, the protector
of the city, was set on
the spire surmounting
the building. After the
revolution, when
Soviet bodies took up
residence in the for-
mer Duma, the
archangel was
replaced with a five-
pointed star. During
the post-war recon-
struction of
Kreshchatik, the build-
ing was not restored.

A SUCCESSION OF MONUMENTS

A surprising feature of Kyiv's central square is that no monument
there lasts for long. For example,
in 1913 a monument to P.Stolypin
(sculptor E.Ksimenes) was put up
in front of the City Duma.
But only four years later, it
was cast down from its
pedestal. The Soviet authorities replaced it with a sculpture of Karl Marx (sculptor
I.Chaykov) with his hand
behind the breast of his coat.
At that time, Kreshchatik was
temporarily renamed
Vorovskogo Street, and the
Kyivans joked about the statue of the author of "Capital":
"Marx guards capital on Thief
["Vor"] Street." The unimpressive
sculpture was removed from the
square in 1931. A monument to
Stalin was due to be installed here
after the war, but this project was
never realized. A monument to the
October Revolution with a granite
Lenin (the sculptor V.Boroday and
others) was set in front of the
Moskva Hotel in 1977, but it was
demolished soon after the unsuccessful Communist coup in August
1991. Time will show whether this
strange tradition will be broken by
the current Monument to
Independence - a 12-meter bronze
sculpture of a girl holding a branch
of a snowball tree set on a 50-
meter column - unveiled here during the celebration of the 10th
anniversary of Ukraine's
independence.

The monument to Stolypin in front of the City Duma

AROUND THE OPERA

AROUND THE OPERA

Just behind the Golden Gate and outside the former Old Kyiv fortifications, streets that were marked afterwards with tremendous expressions of the city's versatile cultural life were laid out in the middle of 19th century. Here the City Theatre was built for performance of operas. Not far away, in the other theatre hall, theatrical troupes performed. A whole system of educational institutions was opened here. The complex of quarters for the Ukrainian Science Academy was built here. Many newspapers and magazines had their offices here. Many well-known writers lived here. The fusion of intellect and the sharp word was realized in the Ukrainian Central Council, which propagated the ideas of national revival throughout Ukraine from this part of town. A lot of old buildings have survived in the pleasant green streets around the Opera. They not only recall the heights of science, literature and art, they are also recognized as great monuments of architecture.

Dmitriy Gnatiuk in the role of Sultan (from the opera "Zaporozhets za Dunayem").

In 1918 - 1919 a whole galaxy of talents studied in the studio of the well known avant-garde artist **Alexandra Exter** at 1/27, Leontovicha St.: V.Meller, A.Petritskiy, I.Rabinovich, A.Tyshler. The poet O.Mandelshtam, whose wife N.Mandelshtam was also taught by Exter, called in here too.

The former hospital at 33, Gonchara St. is an intricate building in Modern style (architect I.Ledokhovskiy, 1908). P.Stolypin died here in September 1911 after being wounded by a terrorist in the Opera House. In the photo: **the coffin with the body of Stolypin is carried out of the hospital.**

The image of Pallas Athena against the background of the building of the Ministry of Emergency Situations (formerly the Women's High School).

Olesia Gonchara Street holds a record for the number of name changes. Originally it was Malo-Vladimirskaya Street. It subsequently bore the names of the Russian reformer P.Stolypin, the SR-terrorist G.Gershuni, the Marxist Lado Hetskaveli and the pilot V.Chkalov. Now it is named in honor of the writer O.Gonchar.

The bronze bust of Boris Paton (sculptor A.Skoblikov, 1982). This commemorates the great scientist in the field of electric welding and twice "Hero of Socialist Labor" during his lifetime.

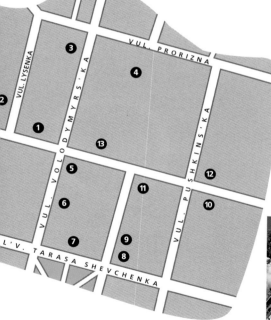

The building at 43, Vladimirskaya St. (architect V.Nikolayev, 1888). The newspaper "Kyivskoye Slovo" had its office here. In the residence of the newspaper worker N.Vertinskiy in the same building, the future poet and singer Alexander Vertinskiy was born.

T.SHEVCHENKO NATIONAL ACADEMIC THEATRE OF OPERA AND BALLET OF UKRAINE [1]

50, Vladimirskaya St.

The comparatively small City Theater was built here in 1856. After it burned down in 1896, the city authorities announced an international competition for the design of a new theater building. The winner was Viktor Shreter, an academician from Petersburg. In 1901 his idea for a large and elegant building in Renaissance style was realized. The theater was generally used for opera and ballet performances. As well as talented local performers, foreign stars such as the opera soloists Giuseppe Anselmi,

Ukrainian National Opera

S.Turchak

Mattia Battistani, Maria Gai, Felia Litvin, Antonina Nezhdanova, Leonid Sobinov and Fedor Shalyapin, and the ballerinas Ekaterina Geltser and Matilda Kshesinskaya appeared on its stage. The most unpleasant episode in the history of the theater occurred in 1911, when the terrorist and provocateur D.Bogrov assassinated Prime Minister P.Stolypin. After the revolution, the theatre was reorganized as the Ukrainian National Opera. The singing talents of Ukrainians are well known throughout the world. This has been demonstrated on the Kyiv stage by such

excellent performers as Zoya Gayday, Boris Gmyrya, Mikhail Grishko, Mikhail Donets, Maria Litvinenko-Volgemut, Ivan Patorzhinskiy, Oksana Petrusenko, Larissa Rudenko, Anatoliy Solovyanenko and others. Leading Ukrainian ballet artists, producers, conductors, musicians, stage artists have made a worthy contribution to the success of the theatre. A general reconstruction of the building (architects B.Zhezherin, O.Grauzhis and others) was carried out in the 1980s. The front of the building is decorated with images of the semi-nude muses Melpomena (the muse of tragedy) and Terpsichore (the muse of dance) by the sculptor E.Salya. In recent years, a huge bust of Taras Shevchenko (sculptor A.Kovalyov) was installed beneath them in the central loggia, violating the style. The theater has been named after the Kobzar since 1939. In the large square to the right of the theater, there is the monument to the composer Nikolay Lysenko (sculptor A.Kovalyov, architect V.Gnezdilov, 1965), the author of the classic Ukrainian operas: Natalka-Poltavka, Taras Bulba and Eneida.

ADMINISTRATION OF THE SOUTHWEST RAILWAY [2]

6, Lysenko St.

The street behind the theater used to be called "Teatralnaya," but now it bears the name of N.Lysenko. Here stands the huge building of the Administration of the South-West Railway (architects V.Kulikovskiy and A.Von Hogen, 1887 - 1889). Its facades are decorated with brick facing and Gothic elements. Outstanding figures of the railway, including Alexander Borodin, Klavdiy Nemeshayev and Piotr Krivonos, worked here. During the Revolution of 1905, the Marxists Gleb Krzhizhanovskiy and Alexander Shlikhter actively incited discontent throughout Kyiv from here.

THE BUILDING OF THE "UKRAINIAN CLUB" [3]

42, Vladimirskaya St.

Lysenko Monument

In 1908 the "Ukrainian Club" was opened in the semi-basement of this house. It was a union of national public figures headed by Nikolay Lysenko. Meetings were attended by writers Ivan Nechuy-Levitskiy, Lesya Ukrainka, her mother Olena Pchilka and Maxim Rylskiy (then a gymnasium pupil), and the actors Maria Zankovetskaya and Nikolay Sadovskiy. Mikhail Kotsubinskiy, Panas Mirny and Ivan Franko visited the club when they were in Kyiv. In 1912 the authorities closed the Ukrainian Club accusing it of subversive activity. But soon

The Administration of the Southwest Railway

another Ukrainian society "Rodina" was arranged in the house. When the city administration gave permission, it assumed the stress mark was on the first syllable to mean motherland. But the members of the club called it "Rodyna" ("family" in Ukrainian). The Ukrainian Scientific Society headed by Mikhail Grushevskiy

The building of the "Ukrainian Club"

also functioned in this house. This was where the Ukraine Central Rada was founded in March 1917. Now the building houses the escalator leading to one of the most beautiful metro stations in the city "The Golden Gate" (architects B. and V.Zhezherin, artists G. Koren and V.Fedko). The underground

The House of Scientists

Caryatid

part is decorated in the style of Old Russian architecture with a gallery of mosaic portraits of characters from the chronicles.

THE HOUSE OF SCIENTISTS 4
45, Vladimirskaya St.

The impressive building in the Renaissance style and the annex in the yard were built in 1891 - 1892 (architect A.Khoynatskiy) for the engineer Vasiliy Kochala and his wife Maria (her initials "MK" may still be seen in the decorations of the facades). Before the Revolution, the popular liberal club "Kyiv Social Meeting" functioned in the annex. Now the House of Scientists is situated here.

THE COMPLEX OF THE UKRAINE NATIONAL SCIENCE ACADEMY 5
55, Vladimirskaya St.
15, B.Khmel'nitskogo St.

In 1914 the architect P. Alioshin started constructing a Women's Gymnasium here. But the unfinished building was transferred to the Academy, and it served as a basis for a whole complex of buildings. Now the National Natural Science Museum is located at 15, B.Khmel'nitskogo St. It includes archeology, geology, paleontology, zoology and botany expositions (Telephone: 225-01-85, days off - Wednesday and Thursday). The Conference Hall of the Ukraine National Science Academy is situated at 55, Vladimirskaya St. Since 1919, the Presidium of the Academy of Science has worked on the opposite side of the street, at 54, Vladimirskaya St., in the building formerly occupied by the Countess Levashova's Pension for Girls (architect A.Beretti, 1850s).

The Conference Hall of the Ukrainian Academy of Science

THE HOUSE OF TEACHERS 6
57, Vladimirskaya St.

The house was built in 1911 for the Pedagogic Museum (architect P.Alyoshin). The neo-classical building is simple, as all great structures are. It proportions are perfect and the modest decorations are harmonious. Along the front there is the bas-relief frieze (sculptors L.Ditrich and V.Kozlov)

The memorial sign in the vestibule of the House of Teachers

representing more than 200 figures from the history of education. The masks of Alexander the Great and Socrates can be seen above the side entrances. A 500-seat auditorium is situated under a glass dome. In 1917 - 1918 the future of Ukraine was considered in this auditorium, when the Ukrainian Central Rada met here (see 16, 17). The first steps of the independent state are linked with the names of Mikhail Grushevskiy, Vladimir Vinnichenko, Dmitriy Doroshenko, Sergey Yefremov, Vladimir Naumenko, Simon Petlura and others. Now a memorial sign (1995) in the vestibule of the building commemorates them. In the Soviet times the building was used as a state institution. In 1982 it was restored to its original function, when it was made the House of Teachers.

THE FORMER 1ST GYMNASIA [7]
14, Shevchenko Ave.

This notable monument of late classicism (architect A.Beretti, 1847-1850) was designed as a gymnasium, but for the first seven years it served as a military school (Tsar Nikolay I considered the latter more important). Among the students of the Kyiv gymnasium were the future president of the Ukrainian Academy of Sciences Alexander Bogomolets, aircraft designer Igor Sikorski, Soviet People's Commissar for Education Anatoly Lunacharsky and many others. Gymnasium graduates Mikhail Bulgakov and Konstantin Paustovsky described their alma mater in their works. It is here that Colonel Turbin says farewell to the cadets in Bulgakov's play "Days of the Turbins." The trustee of the educational district occupied a state apartment adjoining the gymnasia building. Nikolay Pirogov, the famous surgeon and teacher, lived here when he occupied this post. After 1917 the bodies governing Ukrainian education were based in the building.

Now one of the buildings of the Kyiv National Taras Shevchenko University is located here.

The former first gymnasium

THE STATE TARAS SHEVCHENKO MUSEUM [8]
12, Shevchenko Ave.
☎ 224–25–56
Ⓜ Teatralnaya
Day off – Monday

Kyiv Mayor Pavel Demidov San-Donato owned this elegant mansion in the second half of the 19th century. Then sugar manufacturer and philanthropist Nikola Tereshchenko acquired the mansion (during his lifetime, the perpendicular street overlooked by one of the fronts of his residence was named Tereshchenkovskaya). Since 1949 the museum of the Kobzar has been located here. The collection includes Shevchenko autographs and personal effects, his paintings and graphics, photograph and numerous documents. Among the exhibits is the portrait of poet Vasily Zhukovsky by Karl Brullov that was raffled off in a lottery to redeem Taras from serfdom.

The portrait of V.Zhukovsky.
K.Brullov

THE LITERARY MEMORIAL MUSEUM-APARTMENT OF P.TYCHINA [9]
5, Tereshchenkovskaya St.
224–43–90
Ⓜ Teatralnaya
No days off

The museum is located in a government apartment house built in 1934 (architect S.Grigoriev). The biography of Pavlo Tychina demonstrates how the totalitarian regime remade a talented and intelligent lyric poet in its mold.

THE NATIONAL ACADEMIC LESIA UKRAINKA THEATRE OF RUSSIAN DRAMA [10]
5, B.Khmel'nitsky St.

The present appearance of the theater is the result of a reconstruction carried out in 1937-

The pioneers visiting P.Tychina

1938 (architect E.Kodner). The original two-story building was owned by French businessman A.Bergonier and contained a hotel, shops and a circus (architect V.Nikolayev, 1875). The circus was later converted into a theater. Famous Russian and Ukrainian dramatic actors appeared on its stage. The first cinematic performance in Kyiv

The sitting room in the mansion of N.Tereshchenko.
A photo from the end of 19th cent.

took place in the Bergonier Theater in 1896. The present theater has been based here since 1926. Among the actors of the Lesia Ukrainka theatre were such favorites as Mikhail Belousov, Oleg Borisov, Lubov Dobrzhanskaya, Yuri and Kyril Lavrov, Pavel Luspekayev, Eugenia Opalova,

Ada Rogovtseva, Mikhail Romanov, Victor Khalatov and many others. Near the theatre there is the entrance to the "Teatralnaya" metro station. The decoration of the station has survived from the time when the station was called "Leninskaya": the design is composed of numerous citations from the leader of the proletariat and now it resembles a theater of the absurd.

THE NATIONAL LITERATURE MUSEUM OF UKRAINE 11

11, B.Khmel'nitsky St.
☎ 225–13–70
Ⓜ Teatralnaya
Day off – Sunday

The museum is located in the building of the former Collegium of Pavel Galagan. The Collegium was an educational establishment created by the landlord and patron Grigory Galagan in memory of his son who died young (architect A.Shile, 1871). The students here were the coevals of the late Pavel - sixteen-year-old boys who had completed the senior classes of the gymnasia and were preparing to enter the university. The Collegium had a friendly attitude towards Ukrainian culture. Among the students were the future president of the Academy of Sciences V.Lipsky and other prominent scholars. The famous Russian poet Innokenty Annensky was the director of the Collegium for some time. In Petropavlovskaya house church in 1885 the writer Ivan Franko got married to Olga Khoruzhynska from Kyiv, relative of the teacher Tregubov (it is said that the classic author almost was late for the wedding

The former Fundukleyev gymnasium

- he took a great interest in the library of Tregubov). During the period of the Central Rada, the General Secretariat of Military Affairs headed by S.Petlura was located here. The museum was created in 1981. One of the halls in which the original interior is preserved is devoted to the history of the Collegium.

THE FORMER FUNDUKLEYEV GYMNASIA FOR WOMEN 12

6, B.Khmel'nitsky St.

The wealthy philanthropist and former Kyiv governor Ivan Fundukley played a decisive role in the establishment of the first gymnasium for women in Kyiv in 1859. He offered his own residence with all its buildings to the gymnasium, and provided it with a permanent income. The grateful citizens of Kyiv named not only the gymnasia but also the street in his honor. Among the students of the Fundukleyev gymnasium were the poetess Anna Akhmatova, the singer of the Moscow Bolshoi Theatre Ksenia Dzerzhinskaya and the Ukrainian historian Nataliya Polonskaya-Vasilenko. A graduate of the gymnasium Katia Desnitskaya became the wife of a Siamese prince. The building obtained its

Ivan Fundukley

The former hotel "Ermitazh"

present appearance in the post-war years, when the former Fundukleyevskaya Street was named after Lenin (in 1992 the street was renamed in honor of Bogdan Khmelnitsky).

THE FORMER HOTEL "ERMITAZH" 13

26, B.Khmel'nitsky St.

The building is in the style of "Kyiv Renaissance" (architect A.Krauss, 1902-1905). The poets Alexander Blok and Andrey Bely stayed in the hotel during their performance in Kyiv (1907). In the Soviet period it was the hotel "Intourist." Here stayed the artists Alexander Vertynsky and Gerard Philippe, the painter Pavel Korin, the scientist Norbert Wiener and others. The annex in the yard once held the editorial office of the magazine "Lights," on the pages of which the first stories by Konstantin Paustovsky (1912) and Isaak Babel (1913) appeared.

THE HOUSE "ROLIT" 14

68, B.Khmel'nitsky St.

This house was built in two stages (architects V.Krichevsky, P.Kostyrko, 1930-1934, corner annex - architect N.Sdobnev, 1936-1939) as an apartment house for the "Rolit" writers' society (the name is an abbreviation of the Ukrainian for "workers of literature"). The residents required due immortalization: 23 memorial plaques have been installed on the front of the building.

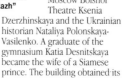

**The interiors of
the Medical Museum**

MUSEUM
OF MEDICINE 15
37, B.Khmel'nitskogo St.
☎ 224–15–73
Ⓜ Teatralnaya
Days off – Sunday, Monday

This is the former dissecting room of Kyiv University. The building was designed in late classical style (architect A.Beretti, 1851-1853). Today this is one of the most original museums in the city. Its displays present a detailed history of the famous European medical schools. The display cases with statues of famous doctors treating their patients are especially attractive.

THE FORMER WOMEN'S
HIGH COURSES 16
55a, O.Gonchara St.

This building is a garish example of the Neo-imperial style built by the architect A.Kobelev in 1912-1914. It was built for the Women's High Courses - an educational establishment that prepared women for pedagogical activity. Before it was built, the Courses were located nearby at 51, B.Khmel'nitskogo St. At that time Anna Akhmatova was a student of the juridical department of the school. She quit her studies after her marriage to the

poet Nikolai Gumilev in 1910. The central pediment of the building is decorated with the image of Athena Pallada - the ancient goddess of wisdom. Now this is the home of the Ministry of Emergency Situations.

GEOLOGY INSTITUTE 17
55b, O.Gonchara St.

The building is separated from the previous one by a square with an old fountain. It was built at the same time and in the same style according to a design by the above-mentioned A.Kobelev. This was originally a department of the Russian technical society - a recognized center for scientific and engineering thought. In Soviet times the

The Institute of Geology

house was given to different educational and scientific institutions. Among those who worked here when it was home to the Institute of Electrical Machinery of the Academy of Sciences of

**The former Women's High
Courses**

the Ukrainian Soviet Republic was Academician Sergey Lebedev, under whose guidance the first electrical computing machine in the USSR and Europe was built in 1950.

CHAPAYEV STREET 18

Historically this street was named Sviatoslavskaya. This is the "youngest" street in this part of the city. It was laid out along the bottom of a gully in 1898 and was lined with houses in "Kyiv renaissance" style. The writer K.Paustovskiy spent his youth in #9 (the architect N.Gardenin, 1901). In his "Story about Life" he describes the visits of an old organ-grinder to the gully. The poet Boris Pasternak lived in the same house for some time. At the end of the street, there is a square with a monument to the writer Oles' Gonchar (sculptor V.Chepelik, 2001).

**The monument to
Oles' Gonchar**

QUARTER OF PROFESSORS
AND PATRONS

QUARTERS OF PROFESSORS AND PATRONS

The Latin Quarter of Paris is the area near the Sorbonne, where medieval students learned Latin. Ever since the Kyiv University was built on the vacant ground above the Lybyd river gully, the area around it has been more or less the same. They used to say that there was not a single house in the area from the Lybyd to the University where there was not either a student or a professor living. This part of the city became a focal point for Kyiv's intellectual elite. The masters of Ukrainian culture lived here. Among the historical buildings, the mansions of the famous entrepreneurs of the Tereshchenko family stand out. They contained the priceless art collections that subsequently became the basis for the museum collections. Near the monumental building of the University there are two spacious green oases - the Shevchenko Park and the Botanical Garden. Nearby a straight row of poplars marked the direction of a beautiful boulevard. After it was paved under the Governor-General D.Bibikov, it became known as the Bibikov Boulevard. Now it is named after Taras Shevchenko.

The monument of V.I.Lenin (sculptor C.Merkurov, 1946) is located at the beginning of Shevchenko Avenue. Nikita Khrushchev unveiled this monument in person. Thanks to its modest size and its clear artistic value, this monument to the leader of the proletariat has survived to the present time.

The building in modern style at 21, Vetrova St. (architect I.Ledokhovsky, 1910-1911).

In the mansion on 34 Shevchenko Avenue lived the manufacturer and philanthropist Ivan Tereshchenko. His son, **Mikhail Tereshchenko**, a future minister of the Provisional Government, grew up here.

The mansion at 7, Tolstogo St. (architect P.Boytsov, 1890s) was owned by the sugar manufacturer Alexander Tereshchenko. Now **the Library of Medicine** is located here.

The obelisk on Victory Square was raised in honor of the Hero-City Kyiv (architect V.Lashko, L.Semenuk. 1982). The monument is 43 meters in height.

The memorial plaque to Vladimir Horowitz (12, M.Kotsubinskogo St.). The family of the future pianist lived in this building in year of his birth. The school in the courtyard of the house is the former gymnasium #7, where Vladimir studied.

"House of Moroz" at 61/11, Vladimirskaya St. (architect I.Zektser, 1910-1912). The Kyivans persistent in calling it the "Morozov House," though the manufacturer Berl Moroz, who built this massive apartment house in modern style, was no relation to the Morozov family.

KYIV NATIONAL
TARAS SHEVCHENKO
UNIVERSITY 1
60, Vladimirskaya St.

THE RED BUILDING

Kyiv University was founded in 1834 and named after St.Vladimir. The main building was built in 1837-1843 according to a design by the Petersburg architect V.Beretti. There are various explanations for the red color of the front - there is even a legend that it was ordered by Nikolay I after student riots to show that the university was ashamed of its students. A more likely explanation, however, is that the colors of the building - red walls with black fragments on the columns and eaves - correspond to the red and black stripes on the ribbon of the order of St.Vladimir.

V.Beretti

HISTORY: NAMES AND FACTS

The pages of the history of the university are packed with outstanding names and dates. Taras Shevchenko worked here as a member of the archeographic commission. Mikhail Grushevskiy studied here. Its walls seethed with student free-thinking under tsarist rule and in the years of the Brezhnev stagnation. Outstanding schools in different branches of science were formed at the university. The names of several professors

View of the university from the Botanical Garden. 1846. M.Sazhin

The Red Building of the University

became legendary. Professor Nikolai Bunge, the outstanding economist, became Minister of Finance, and then the Head of the Committee of Ministers of the Russian Empire. For almost half a century, Professor Vladimir Antonovych, the founder of the history school, was a leader of Ukrainian political and social life in pre-revolutionary Kyiv. Doctor Vasiliy Pokrovskiy became a professor when he was only 28 and died at 39 after becoming infected with typhoid while fighting an epidemic. Professor Boris Bukreev provided an outstanding example of lifelong creativity - he taught mathematics at the university for more than 75 years. Anatomy professor Vladimir Bets made a number of fundamental discoveries in the study of the human brain. Chemistry professor Sergey Reformatskiy developed a new organic reaction that is now named after him and is used widely in the world. It is impossible to enumerate all the outstanding graduates of Kyiv University, so we will name only a few of them: Luka Voyno-Yasenskiy, an archbishop and doctor who became the president of the Academy of Sciences of Ukrainian Soviet Republic; the presidents of the Academy of Sciences of Ukraine O.Levitskiy, V.Lipskiy, D.Zabolotniy and A.Bogomolets; the philosophers N.Berdiayev and L.Shestov; the

historians D.Doroshenko and E.Tarle; the mathematician, geophysicist and polar explorer O.Schmidt; the doctors F.Yanovskiy and N.Strazhesko; the painter N.Ge; the Ukrainian literary figures M.Staritskiy, V.Vinnichenko, M.Rylskiy and A.Korneichuk; and the Russian writers M.Bulgakov and K.Paustovskiy. In the first year of its existence, the university had only two faculties - philosophy and juridical with a total of 62 students. Now there are about 20 thousand students in 17 facul-

University diploma of M.Bulgakov

ties. Numerous new buildings of the Kyiv National University, which has been named after Taras Shevchenko since 1939, were built in the southern part of the city.

THE LIBRARY BUILDINGS 2

The buildings symmetrically situated on two sides of the Red Building together form a harmonious ensemble, although they were built much later (architect V.Osmak). The building on the left, 62, Vladimirskaya St. (1914-1929), is occupied by a branch of the V.Vernadskiy National Library of Ukraine. It holds the collections of rare works, a collection of scrolls. Royal bookcases from the 18th century (donated to the university by the Kremenets Lyceum together with a collection of books belonging to the Polish King Stanislaw-Augustus) are preserved in the department of old printed periodicals. The building to the left (1940) houses the university's scientific library, which is named after the first rector M.Maksimovich.

"THE RECTOR'S HOUSE" 3
64, Vladimirskaya St.

For a long time, this late classical building (1840s) belonged to Ivan Rakhmaminov - a professor of the physico-mathematical faculty and rector of the university in the first half of the 19th century. Now this is the office of the rector of the Kyiv National Taras Shevchenko University. According to a memorial plaque, the graphic artist Georgiy Narbut, one of the creators of Ukrainian national artistic style, lived here in 1917.

METEOROLOGICAL OBSERVATORY 4
14, L.Tolstogo St.

This small classical building dating from the middle of the 19th century (architect A.Beretti) was designed for the university specialists taking meteorological measurements and making calculations. On the right are the university chemistry buildings. On the left - a fine propylaeum leading to the Botanical Garden.

THE A.FOMIN BOTANICAL GARDEN 5

The garden was organized by Kyiv University in 1839 on the slopes of a vacant ravine. Since 1935 it has been named after the academician A.Fomin, who directed the garden for many years. The garden contains a collection of more than 8,000 plant species, including 143 species recorded in Ukraine's Red Book of rare species. Visitors are attracted to the immense 30-meter high glass environmental chamber (1977), which contains the oldest species of palm trees in Ukraine. The garden occupies an area of 22.5 hectares. Not only a scientific laboratory, it is also a pleasant place for walking and recreation. The "University" metro station adjoins the garden. The underground platform is decorated with busts of outstanding writers and scientists of Russia and Ukraine.

UNIVERSITY CLINICS 6
17, T.Shevchenko Blvd.

The environmental chamber

The clinics were founded in the days when the medical faculty was part of the university. This set of buildings (architect M.Ikonnikov, 1885-1886) was subsequently renovated and enlarged. Today it is used as a hospital. Some well-known Kyiv doctors worked here. One of the patients of the hospital's therapeutical department was the Ukrainian writer Mikhail Kotsubinskiy.

Shevchenko Park

SHEVCHENKO PARK 7

One hundred and fifty years ago in the place where the park is now there was an immense, dusty parade-ground. It was subsequently decided to put up a monument to Tsar Nikolay I. The

The playground

landscape-gardener K.Khristiani created a new park here, which was originally called after the university. Ever since it was opened to the public in 1889, it has been a favorite with students and pupils. The park was fenced and closed at night. The monument to the tsar (sculptor M.Chizhov) was put up in 1896. It was removed by the Soviet regime. In 1939, on the same spot was placed a monument to Taras Shevchenko, who was severely persecuted by Nikolay I (sculptor M.Manizer, architect E.Levinson). The closing lines of the poem "Testament" are carved on the red granite pedestal under the bronze statue. Today Shevchenko Park is an attractive place for recreation. Especially popular are the playground and the area for chess players. In the eastern side of the park the old fountain called the Black Sea, whose basin is in the shape of the Black Sea, has been preserved.

Quarter of professors and patrons

A model. S.Konenkov

KYIV RUSSIAN ART MUSEUM ⑧
9, Tereschenkovskaya St.
☎ 224–61–07
Ⓜ L'va Tolstogo
Days off–Wednesday, Thursday

Originally a small mansion stood here on the left side of the plot (architect V.Nikolayev, 1877). Then at the order of the new owner, sugar magnate Fedor Tereschenko, a luxurious two-storey palazzo (architects A.Gun and V.Nikolayev, 1882 - 1884) was attached to it. The front of the building is richly decorated. The frieze contains high relief compositions, where scenes of sacrifice alternate with scenes of festivity. The interior is even more luxurious: the vestibule, the main stairs and the owner's apartments on the second floor; the Gold and the Silver sitting-rooms; the spacious White Hall; the study and the dining-room, which are artistically decorated with wood; the Turkish-style smoking room. Like his brother Nikola, Fedor Tereshchenko was an outstanding philanthropist. He supported a charitable complex in the Podol district (49, Nizhniy Val St.). He gathered a rich collection of paintings in the mansion. Tereshchenko bought

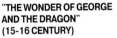

In the Wild North.
I.Shishkin

high-class paintings by Russian artists, many of whom he knew personally. An art gallery was opened in the nationalized mansion in 1922 on the basis of the Tereshchenko collection and other private collections. The Kyiv Russian Art Museum is a real treasure. The most valuable items include Old Russian Iconography and the works of Dmitriy Levitskiy, Vladimir Borovikovskiy, Vasiliy Tropinin, Nikolay Ge, Ivan Kramskoy, Nikolay Yaroshenko, Vasiliy Vereshchagin, Ivan Shishkin, Vasiliy Polenov, Mikhail Vrubel, Mikhail Nesterov, Zinaida Serebryakova and other masters. The gallery also has several works by Ilya Repin, a famous Russian artist born in Ukraine. Tereshchenkovskaya Street was formerly named after Repin. A statue of Repin (sculptor O.Komov) was installed in front of the museum in 1984.

"THE WONDER OF GEORGE AND THE DRAGON" (15-16 CENTURY)

An icon of the Rostov-Suzdal School dedicated to the dragon-slaying exploit of Saint George. It symbolizes victory over the dark powers of evil. It is notable for its bright festive colours.

"PORTRAIT OF THE GREAT PRINCESS ALEXANDRA PAVLOVNA" BY D.LEVITSKIY (1791)

The official character of the portrait of the granddaughter of

Catherine II did not prevent the artist from creating a delicate and tender image of the girl. On her chest she wears the star of the order of Saint Catherine, which was awarded to the Great Princesses at birth.

"IN THE WILD NORTH" BY I.SHISHKIN (1891)

The picture was inspired by the poem by Lermontov. By exact representation and the use of various shades of blue, the landscape painter was able to reproduce the rugged grandeur of northern nature.

Portrait of the Great Princess Alexandra Pavlovna. D.Levitskiy

"A GIRL AGAINST THE BACK-GROUND OF A PERSIAN CARPET" BY M.VRUBEL (1886)

The exotic world of the east is

Girl against the Background of a Persian Carpet. M.Vrubel

transferred to the canvas. Actually, Vrubel saw these carpets, ornaments and silk in the loan office of the Kyiv moneylender Dakhnovich, to whom he was led by poverty. Manya Dakhnovich, the daughter of the owner of the office, posed for the artist.

The Wonder of George and the Dragon

B.Khanenko

BOGDAN AND VARVARA KHANENKO ART MUSEUM 9

15, Tereshchenkovskaya St.
☎ 225–52–69
Ⓜ L'va Tolstogo
Days off–Monday, Tuesday

Kyiv is obliged to the selfless collectors and patrons Bogdan Khanenko and his wife Varvara (born Tereshchenko) for this museum. A wealthy lawyer and businessman, Khanenko collected pictures by Western European artists and Eastern art works. The couple housed the collection in their mansion (architect R.Meltser, 1887 - 1888), whose halls are designed in the European styles: Gothic, Rococo and Baroque. The Khanenko family coat of arms is placed on the front of the building. Khanenko died in 1917 and bequeathed his collection to Kyiv as a future public museum. Varvara Khanenko took care of the art treasure during the tempestuous times of the Civil War and man-

Madonna with Child.
G.Bellini

The god of the river Scheldt, Cybele and the goddess of Antwerp.
P.P.Rubens

aged to carry out the last will of her husband. The museum was opened in 1919. Eventually it filled up with other works, but the Khanenko collection remains the basis. The Kyiv museum may look modest in comparison with the grandiose collections of the

Louvre, the Metropolitan Museum and the Hermitage, but art lovers will be struck with the masterpieces of painters of universal importance. Among the artists on display are: the Italians: Giovanni Bellini, Pietro Perugino, Francesco Guardi, Giovanni Batista Tiepolo; the Spaniards: Diego Velasquez, Louis de Morales, Juan Surbaran; the Flemings: Peter Paul Rubens, Anthony Van Dyke, Jacob Jordans; the Dutch: Jacob Van Reisdal, Jan Sten, Gerard Terborgh; the French: Francois Boucher, Jean-Batiste Greze, Jacques-Louis David; the British: Joshua Reynolds. The art of the East is represented by some interesting designs. The museum collection includes Old Egyptian statues, Coptic cloth, Chinese classical art, Japanese engravings, Indian bronze figures and Persian miniatures. It also includes artistic relics of ancient times and unique Early Christian Byzantine Icons from 6th - 7th centuries created from wax paints.

"MADONNA WITH CHILD" BY G.BELLINI

The intense colors of the picture sound like musical chords. It is filled with a mood of great peace and secret sorrow. The artist, Giovanni Bellini, was one of the founders of the Venetian Art School, and a teacher of Giorgione and Titian.

"THE GOD OF THE RIVER SCHELDT, CYBELE AND THE GODDESS OF ANTWERP" BY P.P.RUBENS

This small sketch by the Great Fleming remained as an idea for a never-to-be-realized picture - an allegory of the hope that the earth goddess Cybele would yield fruit to the city of Antwerp through the river Scheldt (the North Netherlands had blocked the mouth of the Scheldt and paralysed the trade and economics of Antwerp).

"A PORTRAIT OF INFANTA MARGARET" BY D.VELASQUEZ

The youngest daughter of King Philip IV of Spain is presented in the portrait as if shackled in a heavy court dress. The artist does not conceal the irregularity of facial features characteristic of the Habsburg dynasty, but he conveys with amazing mastery the sad charm of the child pining in the Court.

Portrait of the Infant Margaret.
D.Velasquez

"A PORTRAIT OF LAZAR HOCHE" BY J.L.DAVID

Restless and vacillating color expresses the romantic spirit of the French Revolution. One of its heroes was the young commander Lazar Hoche, who is shown in the portrait. On the handle of his sword is inscribed the motto "To win or to die."

Portrait of Lazar Hoche.
J.L.David

PAN'KOVSHCHINA

The lands of the Kyiv metropolitans once stretched along the Lybid River. In the 16th century, the Pan'kovich family managed these lands. The family gave its name to this stretch of land on the outskirts of town. The buildings of the present Pan'kovshchina were planned during the construction of the university. According to legend, the students named Tarasovskaya, Pan'kovskaya and Nikolsko-Botanicheskaya streets in honor of the Ukrainian patriots Taras Shevchenko, Panteleymon Kulish and Nikolay Kostomarov.

THE FORMER ESTATE OF M.GRUSHEVSKY 10
9, Pan'kovskaya St.

In 1908-1909 the family of history professor Mikhail Grushevsky bought the lot on the corner of Pan'kovskaya and Nikolsko-Botanicheskaya Streets. The owners lived in a three-story annex in the courtyard on the hill. On the corner of the two streets a large apartment house was built in Ukrainian modern style (architect V.Krichevsky, 1909). In January 1918 when

The building at 58, Saksaganskogo St.

M.Grushevskiy was heading the Central Rada, the corner house was destroyed during the bombardment of Kyiv by the Red Army (in the 1950s a new residential building was built in its place). The annex survived and Grushevsky lived there as a Soviet academician after his return from emigration. There are now plans to build a memorial museum here. Unfortunately the renovation of the building has been going on for several years already.

THE BRIDES OF FAMOUS WRITERS

The original owner of the expressive-looking building in updated gothic style at 33-35, Saksaganskogo St. (architect I.Zektser, 1910-1911) was the manufacturer B.Gronfayn. As a student, Isaak Babel fell in love with the manufacturer's daughter. The wealthy Gronfayn considered that Babel was not a good match for his daughter. The young people ran away to Odessa and married there. The father-in-law was furious. After the revolution, however, when Babel became a famous writer, the elderly and impoverished Gronfayn made up with him. Not far away from this house, at 22, Saksaganskogo St. lived the doctor M.Kozintsev. His son Grigory Kozintsev became a famous film director. The daughter was a talented artist and a beautiful woman. The writer Iliya Erenbourg fell in love with her. This was the time of the Civil War; the situation was difficult and unstable. But the marriage contracted in Kyiv in 1919 survived all the trials of these difficult times.

Panas Saksagansky

THE HOUSE OF SINGER O.KAMIONSKY 11
58, Saksaganskogo St.

A solid apartment house with elements of neo-empire style (architect I.Zektser, 1914) was built at the request of the opera singer Oscar Kamionsky - a baritone; he was an unsurpassed performer of the parts of Figaro,

The former Mariinskaya Society

Demon, and Onegin. His wife Klara Brun (a dramatic lyric soprano) also was a soloist of Kyiv Opera, and later she became a professor at the Conservatory.

THE BUILDING OF MARIINSKAYA SOCIETY 12
75, Saksaganskogo St.

The Mariinskaya Society was founded in 1878 and prepared nurses to care for wounded soldiers. The former name of this street - Mariinsko-Blagoveshchenskaya Street - originated from the Mariinskaya Society and the name of the Annunciation (Blagoveshchenskaya) church (architect V.Nikolayev, 1887, demolished in 1935). The society's building was constructed in accordance with a design by the architect V.Rykov (1913). The author's nostalgia for the Italian Renaissance and the divine

SRSTPG

fronts of Andrea Palladio is obvious. The pure Palladio front is decorated with a relief on the theme of care for the wounded (sculptor F.Balavensky). Four female figures rise above the central part of the building. The statues symbolize Charity, Life, Love and Medicine. Now the Institute of Occupational Hygiene is located here.

THE HOUSE OF M.STARITSKY [13]
93, Saksaganskogo St.

Several prominent figures of Ukrainian culture lived in close proximity on the former Mariinsko-Blagoveshchenskaya Street. Now these historic monuments have been united in a museum complex. In house #93 (it has been reconstructed as it was before) lived the family of the writer, actor and director Mikhail Staritsky - the author of the famous play "Between Two Stools".

The memorial symbol of N.Lysenko

N.LYSENKO MUSEUM [14]
95b, Saksaganskogo St.
☎ 220–02–91
Ⓜ Dvorets Sporta
Day off – Monday

Staritsky's brother-in-law - the classic of Ukrainian music Nikolay Lysenko - lived in the annex. It was during this period that he wrote the operas "Eneida," "Nocturne," as well as many vocal pieces. Lysenko was permanently at the center of the

social life of the city. His friends and associates often visited his house. In 1980 a memorial exposition opened. It contains the composer's personal effects, documents and manuscripts, note editions, as well as his collection of Ukrainian folk instruments. Lysenko's piano and his conductor's baton have survived.

Admirers of the composer's legacy gather in the musical hall attached to the museum.

LESIA UKRAINKA MUSEUM [15]
97, Saksaganskogo St.
☎ 220–57–52
Ⓜ Dvorets Sporta
Day off – Tuesday

The Ukrainian writer, folklore specialist and social figure Olena Pchilka (Olga Dragomanova-Kosach) lived on the first floor of this beautiful building dating from the end of 19th century. Very often her daughter, the great poetess Lesia Ukrainka (Larissa Kosach-Kvitka) stayed at her mother's house. Here she wrote many poems, worked on literary translations, articles and reports, and prepared her collected poems. In 1962 a literary memorial museum was opened here presenting the life and creative development of Lesia Ukrainka, her struggle against serious illness, literary triumphs and persecution by the authorities. The museum also contains ethnographic materials collected by Olena Pchilka.

A stamp in honor of the centenary of Lesia Ukrainka

Lysenko museum

THE HOUSE OF P.SAKSAGANSKY [16]
96, Zhilianskaya St.

One of the pillars of the Ukrainian theater, Panas Saksagansky (Tobilevich) passed the lasts decades of his life here. A brilliant character actor and director, he organized theatrical societies and performed with them on tour all over Ukraine and abroad. He was a born pedagogue and spotter of new talents. His brother Nikolay Sadovsky (Tobilevich) - a famous artist and theatrical figure - also lived in an apartment on the first floor for some time.

SRSTPG [17]
108/16, Saksaganskogo St.

The mysterious abbreviation SRSTPG stood for the South Russian Society for Trade of Pharmaceutical Goods. This large enterprise owned the magnificent building on the corner of Saksaganskogo and Kominterna Streets (architect A.Khoynatsky 1898-1899). The building's front with its sumptuous portico is decorated with designs on a medical theme. Above the front sculptures of owls (symbolizing wisdom) have survived. The central statue of Mercury, the patron of the trade, was lost however.

FORMER GYMNASIUM #2 18

18, T.Shevchenko Blvd.

This is a building in the Late-Classical style (architect P.Shleifer, 1854 -1856). Among the pupils were the poet Semyon Nadson, the composer Reinhold Gliere, the future academicians Agafangel Krymskiy and Otto Schmidt, and the economist and poet Pavel Chubinskiy - the author of words to the National Anthem "Ukraine is still alive."

UKRAINIAN DRAGOMANOV PEDAGOGIC UNIVERSITY 19

22–24, T.Shevchenko Blvd.

This educational institution began to develop in 1906, when the restored Kyiv Commerce Institute was established here. Its founder was the well-known historian Professor Mitrofan Dovnar-Zapolskiy, who studied the influence of economics on historical processes and hoped to educate competent economists for the improvement of society. But many of those who studied here became famous outside their specialities. They include the writers Isaak Babel, Pavlo Tychyna and Vasiliy Ellan Blakytny, the screenwriter and director Alexander Dovzhenko, and the actor and theatre producer Solomon Mikhoels (Vovsi). During the turbulent times of the revolution, the units of the Ukrainian Army known as Sech Sagittarius were formed on the territory of the institute. In Soviet times eco-

Pedagogic University

nomic, engineering and pedagogic institutions operated here.

ST.VLADIMIR'S CATHEDRAL 20

20, T.Shevchenko Blvd.

St.Vladimir Cathedral

THE HISTORY OF THE CONSTRUCTION

When the monument to Saint Prince Vladimir, the Christener of Rus, was raised, religious Kyivans were troubled: Vladimir destroyed the idols, and now he will stand as an idol himself. The Moscow architect I.Shtrom came up with a design for the Kyiv Saint Vladimir's Cathedral in monumental Byzantium style crowned with 13 domes. However the donations collect-

The Last Judgment.
V.Vasnetsov

ed for constructing of the cathedral were not sufficient to cover the costs. The eparchy architect P.Sparro "reduced" the design to only 7 domes. But this would make the cathedral too small. They appealed to the well-known Kyiv architect A.Beretti for help. He confidently suggested enlarg-

ing the 7-dome project by half as much again. They trusted his judgement, and in 1862 the construction work began. The main bulk of the structure was completed, and the builders were ready to add the domes, when suddenly it turned out the transversal arcs could not hold the weight of the upper circle, and they began to crack. The architect blamed the contractors and the workers. The cracks were growing, and Beretti was dismissed in 1866. The architects spent a long time searching for a solution to the problem. Only in 1875

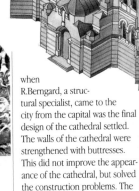

when R.Berngard, a structural specialist, came to the city from the capital was the final design of the cathedral settled. The walls of the cathedral were strengthened with buttresses. This did not improve the appearance of the cathedral, but solved the construction problems. The treasury assigned the necessary funds. Berngard recommended his student V.Nikolayev as chief constructor. The young and energetic architect justified the hopes of his teacher. The construction work was completed in 1882, but it was not until 1896, after decoration, that the Vladimir's Cathedral was solemnly consecrated in the presence of Tsar Nikolay II.

DECORATION OF THE INTERIOR

V.Nikolayev proposed a design for the simple and rapid decoration of the

St. Vladimir Cathedral

Cathedral, which was approved by the local church and the archeological society consulting the work. But one of the members of the society had a special opinion. This was Adrian Prakhov, a St.Petersburg professor and a noted specialist in

church history who had supervised the decoration of the old frescos of the Kirilovskaya Church in Kyiv (see 136). Prakhov turned to his Moscow contacts with the great opportunity for turning the provincial cathedral into an artistic masterpiece. The professor proposed covering the interior walls with paintings and to invite leading artists to participate. Prakhov's feverish activity was crowned with success. He was appointed the manager of interior design. In order to solve the problem successfully, the professor cunningly underestimated the cost of the work. Later on, he had to obtain new installments using different methods. As a result, work on the decoration slowed down. Finally, due to Prakhov's enterprising nature, the impossible became reality. The brilliant talent of V.Vasnetsov and M.Nesterov, the genius of M.Vrubel, the flying brush of V.Kotarbinskiy and other Europe-known artists turned the Kyiv Vladimir Cathedral into a place of pilgrimage for aesthetes and a symbol of the new religious art.

THE MAIN ART COMPOSITIONS

The central composition of the cathedral wall-painting, "The Mother of God with Child" was painted by the outstanding Russian artist Victor Vasnetsov. Vasnetsov's other important works are "The Eucharist", "The Consecrators" and "The Prophets" on the walls of the altar, "The Christ-

God the Son. V.Vasnetsov

The Threshold of Paradise. V.Vasnetsov

Pantocrator" inside the main dome, "God the Father", "God the Son" and "The Holy Spirit" on the vault of the main nave, and "The Christening of Vladimir" and "The Christening of the Kyivans" on opposite sides of the entrance. In all he painted about 3,000 square meters of walls. The Russian ascetics and martyrs Boris and Gleb, Nestor the Chronicler, Mikhail of Chernigov, Alexander Nevskiy and others appear on the columns of the cathedral. V.Vasnetsov and M.Nesterov made the icons. Nesterov also painted the compositions on the gallery "The Birth of Christ" and "The Resurrection of the Lord." The paintings on the lower circle belong to brushes of the artists Wilhelm Kotarbinskiy and Pavel

The Pantocrator. V.Vasnetsov

Svedomskiy. Part of the decoration was based on the sketches of Mikhail Vrubel. Among the participants of the decoration of the chapel were the Ukrainian artists V.Zamiraylo, S.Kostenko and N.Pimonenko. Many of the compositions first created here were repeated in the interiors of other Orthodox Churches throughout the country. The wall-paintings of the cathedral left a bright impression and a festive mood that could not be forgotten.

THE MONUMENT TO N.SHCHORS [21]

This monument was erected in 1954 (sculptor M.Lysenko, architects A.Vlasov and A.Zavarov) to honor the memory of N.Shchors. This Red Army divisional commander, who was killed in the Civil War, was turned into a romantic myth by Soviet propaganda. It is known for a fact that the future president of Ukraine Leonid Kravchuk served as a model for the statue of the horseman. A monument to count Alexey Bobrinskiy - the pioneer of sugar-beet industry in Kyiv region (sculptor I.Shreder, architect I.Monigetty, 1872) - stood in more or less the same location until 1920.

THE FORMER "PRISONER COMPANIES" [22]
27, T.Shevchenko Blvd.

This is a sturdy building with thick walls (engineer A.Tillo, 1845-1849). It was originally a sort of prison for vagrants and petty criminals who were employed for construction works in the city. Now it houses a vocational school.

THE PHARMACIST'S HOUSE [23]
36, T.Shevchenko Blvd.

This fine house with small towers resembling a castle (the architects V.Nikolayev, P.Sparro, 1873-1874) belonged to the rich pharmacist Nikolai Fromett. He

Central railway station

was a notorious miser who saved every coin, and his son - the heir to a fortune of half a million - received pocket money of no more than 30 kopeks a day. One day the pharmacist was paralyzed. Two other intrepid pharmacists became his guardians. After giving some money to Fromett Junior, they managed to quickly embezzle all the fortune of the unfortunate miser.

POBEDY SQUARE [24]

The square was once known for its market. In 1860 this place on the edge of the city was given to Jewish traders. It was called "the Jewish Bazaar" or Jewbaz for short. In 1867-1871, the Church of Saint John Chrysostom was built on the square. Plated in cast iron, it was built according to a design by the engineer R.Nikkles. This unusual building was called "the Iron Church" (it hasn't been preserved; this was the place where the poet Maximilian Voloshin was christened). Now the former Jewbaz, which was renamed Pobedy Square in 1952, has quite a different look. The most prominent buildings are the circus under its vast dome (architect V.Zhukov, 1960), the Ukraine department store (architect

I.Gomoliaka, 1960-1966), the Lybid hotel with the sculpture of the sister of the legendary founders of Kyiv on the end wall (architect N.Chmutina, sculptors M.Gritsuk, Y.Sinkevich, 1965-1970).

THE RAILWAY STATION [25]

The first train arrived to Kyiv in 1870. At the time the railway station was a modest gothic building (the architect I.Vishnevskiy). In 1927-1932 the current station building (the architect A.Verbitskiy) was built. It combines a slight hint of the Ukrainian Baroque with the general construction design. The suburban railway station with a clock tower (the architects A.Dobrovolskiy,

The monument to N.Shchors

I.Maslenkov, 1960) also stands on Vokzalnaya Square. In 2001 the station complex was renovated. The work was completed with astonishing speed, worthy of mention in the Guinness Book of World Records. Apart from renovation of existing buildings and platforms, a new southern building of the station was built with all modern facilities. In front of it the Church of St.George the Victor was built on a new square.

The circus

THE ROAD TO
VASILKOV

THE ROAD TO VASILKOV

Back in the times of Kyivan Rus, the road to Vasilkov (Vasilevskiy) was considered one of the most important transportation arteries in Kyiv. Vasilkov, today a district centre in Kyiv region, was then a significant town - Vasilev, named after the Christian name of its founder - the Prince Vladimir (Vasili) Svyatoslavich. The road to Vasilkov afterwards provided communication between Kyiv and the south-eastern part of the country. Until the first part of the 19th century, only a short stretch of the Vasilkov Road (up to the Bessarabka block post) was within the city limits. But then Kyiv started expanding and the old road turned into the busy Bolshaya Vasilkovskaya Street, more than 3.5 km in length. In the middle of the 19th century, the New Building area adjacent to the Lybyd River and the railroad formed along it. In 1919 the Bolshaya Vasilkovskaya Street was renamed Krasnoarmeyskaya. There are no historic monuments here, but it is difficult to imagine our city without such structures as the Ukraine Palace, the National "Olympics" Sports Complex and the Nikolayevskiy Roman-Catholic church.

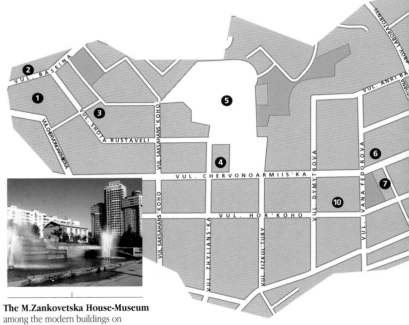

The M.Zankovetska House-Museum among the modern buildings on Krasnoarmeyskaya Street.

The houses on the corner of Pushkinskaya Street and Tolstogo Square. The apartment house at #45 crowned with a turret and slanting attic (on the right, architect M.Artynov, 1901) a distinctive example of "pseudo-Russian" style. The office building at #42/4 (on the left, V.Zhezherin, 1980s) is an example of modern architecture. A sculpture dedicated to the memory of the famous Kyivan Alexander Arkhipenko was put up in the courtyard.

On the right - **the building at 14, Krasnoarmeyskaya St.** (architect P.Svatkovsky, 1911). A distinctive example of an apartment house in the northern modern style.

The Kyiv literary and artistic society met in the house at 1, Rognedinskaya St. in 1896-1901. Among the members of this popular union were the writer A.Kuprin, the architect V.Nikolayev, the philosophers N.Berdiayev and S.Bulgakov, the painter N.Murashko, the composer V.Pukhalsky, the historians V.Ikonnikov and E.Tarle, the artist and director N.Solovtsev, the classics of Ukrainian culture N.Lysenko, M.Staritsky, Lesia Ukrainka and many others.

The sculpture that crowns the front of the Saint Nicholas Roman Catholic church. (see 131).

According to the legend, **the mascaron above the entry to the courtyard of the house at 14, Krasnoarmeyskaya St.** is a portrait of the former owner I.Slinko.

Planetarium on Krasnoarmeyskaya Street.

"BESSARABIAN SQUARE" 1

1–5, Krasnoarmeyskaya St.,
2–6, Basseynaya St.

This block has been under reconstruction for a long time. The most remarkable historic building here is the commercial property that formerly extended along Bessarabskaya Square from Krasnoarmeyskaya Street to Basseynaya Street It was built in three stages in 1894 - 1901 by the architect A.Krauss. It formerly contained the hotels "Orion" and "Berlin" as well as numerous apartments and shops. The first stage of the property was built for A.Danilevsky, a banker who created Kyiv's first "pyramid" trust company. He was sent to Siberia for defrauding his investors. In 2001 new attics were built in. During the reconstruction, the adjoining house on Krasnoarmeyskaya Street, where the writer Sholom-Aleichem lived for several years, was demolished. The small detached house where the composer R.Gliere spent his childhood once stood on "Besarabian square."

THE KYIV ADDRESS OF GOLDA MEIR 2

5a, Basseynaya St.

The name of Basseynaya Street comes from the "basin gutter" -

an open reservoir for waste-water that stretched along the street until the XX century. Itsko Mabovich, a joiner, occupied a little flat in the courtyard of house #5. His daughter Golda, who was born in Kyiv, eventually became the Prime Minister of Israel Golda Meir. The Maboviches left Kyiv in 1903. Now there is a memorial plaque in honor of Golda Meir on the front of the house (sculptor V.Medvedev).

The memorial plaque to Golda Meier and a 10 shekel banknote

THE CENTRAL SYNAGOGUE 3

13, Shota Rustaveli St.

This part of town contains several memorials to Jewish community. The most notable is the Central (Choral) Synagogue founded by the multi-millionaire "sugar king" Lazar Brodsky (architect G.Shleifer, 1898). It was not possible to get permission to build the Synagogue at once, because the tsarist authorities at the time restricted the rights of Kyiv's Jewish community. Brodsky had to use a ruse. He applied to the Senate with a design for a normal house, which was only partially planned as a meetinghouse. In 1926 the Soviet authorities closed the synagogue. After the war, it was reconstructed as a theater. The puppet theater was situated here until 1997. Now the synagogue has been restored.

The monument to Sholom-Aleichen

The Operetta House

The Central Synagogue

The restored prayer hall was opened in 2000 (the architect Y.Paskevich). Incidentally, the "Kinopanorama" cinema occupies the building of the former Merchants' Synagogue (built in 1899 by Leo Brodsky, the younger brother of Lazar), but it was rebuilt unrecognizably in 1958.

OPERETTA HOUSE 4

53, Krasnoarmeyskaya St.

The building was constructed in 1901 - 1902 (the architect G.Antonovskiy) as the Troitskiy People's House of the local Literacy Society. The name came from the neighboring Troitskaya Church, which was built in the middle of the XIX century and has not survived. In the People's House, the Literacy Society introduced people to cultural values and attempted to direct them away from drunkenness. The front of the building is decorated with busts of Gogol and Shevchenko. Mariya Zankovetska, Nikolay Sadovskiy, Panas Saksaganskiy and other notables of the Ukrainian theatre played on the stage. In 1905 the first Kiyv trade union was founded here. Now the troupe of the Operetta House (founded in 1934) performs in this hall. Old residents remember the gorgeous Vera Novinskaya in the role of Silva and Vasiliy Kozaretsiy as Mister X.

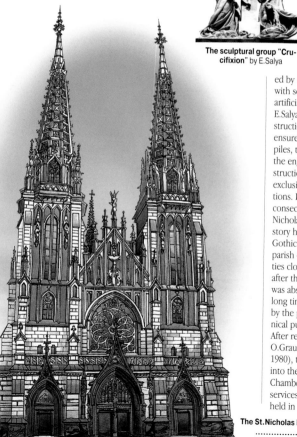

The sculpture on the facade of
Saint Nicholas' Cathedral

NATIONAL "OLIMPIYSKIY" SPORTS COMPLEX 5

55, Krasnoarmeyskaya St.

The biggest Ukrainian sports arena is located on Cherepanova Hill (where agricultural and industrial exhibitions were held in 1897 and 1913). At first the stadium had only one tier (the architect M.Grechina). The ceremonial opening was scheduled for 21 June 1941, but was disrupted by the Fascist bombing. The postwar achievements of Kyiv footballers and other sportsmen provided an incentive for rebuilding the stadium. The upper tier was added in 1967, increasing the stadium's capacity to 100 thousand spectators (now, as a result of improvements in seating, it accommodates 80 thousand). In July 1980 the football matches of the Group Tournament of the XXII Olympic Games were held here. Apart from the main arena, the Sports Complex includes covered swimming-pools, gymnasiums, a skating-rink, tennis courts and other struc-

The sculptural group "Crucifixion" by E.Salya

tures. The Sports Palace is situated nearby at the address 1, Kuybysheva St. (architects M.Grechina and A.Zavarov, engineer V.Repyakh, 1958 - 1960).

ST.NICHOLAS ROMAN CATHOLIC CHURCH 6

75, Krasnoarmeyskaya St.

A competition for designs for the construction of a Roman Catholic Church in Kyiv was held in 1898. The winning entry was student S.Volovskiy's design for a Gothic construction with two well-proportioned 60-meter towers. The architect V.Gorodetsky was assigned the final revision and management of the construction work. The Gothic structure successfully completed by the architect was enriched with sculptural decoration in artificial stone by the sculptor E.Salya. The stability of the construction on uneven ground is ensured by bore-and-stuffed piles, then a recent invention of the engineer A.Straus. The construction work was carried out exclusively from voluntary donations. In 1909 the Church was consecrated in the name of Saint Nicholas. To the left a three-story house in simple non-Gothic style was built for the parish clergy. The Soviet authorities closed the church in 1938 after the Roman Catholic priest was absent for two years. For a long time, the building was used by the punitive organs for technical purposes and as an archive. After restoration (the architect O.Grauzhis and others, 1979 - 1980), the Church was turned into the House of Organ and Chamber Music. Catholic divine services and concerts have been held in the church since 1992.

The St.Nicholas Roman Catholic Church

FORMER GYMNASIUM #4 **7**
96, Krasnoarmeyskaya St.

The building was built in 1898 in Renaissance style (architect N.Chekmaryov) in a place where horse-trading was formerly conducted. At first the Men's Gymnasium #4 was located here. Among its students were the poet-composer Alexander Vertinskiy and the Polish writer Yaroslav Ivaszkevicz.

UKRAINE PALACE **8**
103, Krasnoarmeyskaya St.

The opening of the republic's main auditorium in 1970 (architects E.Marinchenko, P.Zhylitskiy, I.Vayner) was set for the 100th anniversary of Lenin's birth. The palace is monumental without being excessively pompous. When you pass by, you can see the dynamic movement of its resilient front arch. The large hall, where the most important forums and concerts are held, seats about 4,000 spectators. The lobby is decorated with compositions from natural stone and wood. It took some time to find a place for building the palace. The Party leadership was going to put it in the place of the Mikhaylovskiy Cathedral, but Eugenia Marinchenko said: "Over my dead body!" The palace was finally built on

The Gymnasium # 4. From a beginning of 20 century postcard.

Krasnoarmeyskaya Street in the former market square. The reconstruction of 1998 renovated the interior and filled it with new equipment. From the outside, however, the palace has become "cold" and "aloof."

The House-Museum of Mariya Zankovetskaya

THE HOUSE-MUSEUM OF MARIYA ZANKOVETSKAYA **9**
121, Krasnoarmeyskaya St.
☎ 269–57–24
Ⓜ Ukraine Palace
Day off – Monday

The great Ukrainian dramatic actress Mariya Zankovetskaya (Adasovskaya) lived

her last years in a small house on Krasnoarmeyskaya Street. A memorial exposition of photographs, posters, documents and personal effects functions here. However, in 1980 this historic monument was demolished without a second thought. Nine years later it was recreated in almost the same place.

Y.PATON ELECTRIC WELDING INSTITUTE **10**
69, Gorkiy St.

The famous bridge engineer Yevgeniy Paton got interested in the problems of electric welding in old age (this technology, in particular, allowed more longer lasting and economic bridges to be built). The Electric Welding Institute he founded is now one of the most outstanding scientific and technical centers of Ukraine. Its developments are used in industry, building, defense and space programs. The oldest building of the institute at 69, Gorkiy St. (the architect A.Minkus, 1903-1904) was first designed as a technical school for Jewish boys, which was founded by the brothers Lazar and Leo Brodsky.

Mariya Zankovetskaya

Ukraine Palace

OUTSIDE THE
DOWNTOWN

OUTSIDE THE DOWNTOWN

At the end of the 19th century, the territory of the city covered only a small part of today's Kyiv. Many areas, which are now built-up with multi-story buildings and inhabited by tens of thousands of Kyivans, were formerly remote suburbs, with scattered hamlets and villages. As Kyiv gradually expanded, the former suburbs were absorbed. To the north the city limits took in Kurenevka and Priorka; to the northwest - Lukyanovka and Syrets; to the west - Shulyavka, Nivki, Svyatoshin; to the southwest - Solomenka; to the south - Demiyevka, Goloseyev and along the bank of the Dnieper - Zverinets. There are some interesting historic monuments in these areas. Many of them are very popular. Several modern buildings are also worthy of attention. Now thanks to the developed transport network, it will not take long to get acquainted with these suburban places of interest.

The former college at 164, Frunze St., built in Ukrainian Modern style (the architect V.Krychevskiy, 1911), was named after the pedagogue Sergey Grushevskiy. His son, the future head of Ukrainian Central Rada, founded this establishment with the money left by his father.

Sculptural decoration of the house at 23, Gogolevskaya St. (see 138)

The monument to Ivan Kotlyarevskiy in the square at the corner of Melnikova and Gertsena Streets (sculptor G.Kalchenko, architect A.Ignashenko, 1975). The bronze bust of the first classic of new Ukrainian literature stands on a column decorated with images of the heroes of his works "Eneida," "Natalka Poltavka" and "Moskal-Charodey."

The People's Actor of Ukraine **L.Bykov** at a subbotnik (in Communist times, this was a "voluntary" working day on a Saturday) at A.Dovzhenko film studio.

This **T-34 tank** was placed on Pobedy Avenue in 1964 as a monument to the members of the 3rd Guard Tank Army which took part in the liberation of Ky in November 1943.

A monument to police officers who were killed in the line of duty (sculptor V.Chepelik, 1998) in the shape of a granite mourning woman stands in Solomenskaya Square, in front of the National Academy of Internal Affairs of Ukraine (architect I.Barzylovych, 1952).

The Voznesenskiy Church is the parish church of Demiyevka, a former suburban village. There were several important industries in this area. The buildings of the biggest of these - a sugar refinery plant - are now occupied by the Karl Marx Confectionery. The church was originally built in 1883 from wood, but later it was rebuilt in brick and enlarged (architect E.Yermakov, 1900 and 1910). The Ukrainian poetess Lesia Ukrainka (Larissa Kosach) married the folklorist and musicologist Kliment Kvitka in the Vosnesenskiy church in 1907.

Ivan
Izhakevych
on Priorka.

The monument to Vladimir Vernadskiy at the junction of Pobedy Avenue and Vernadskiy Avenue (sculptor A.Skoblikov, 1981) is dedicated to the great natural scientist and philosopher and the first president of the Academy of Sciences of Ukraine.

Main entrance to the Exhibition Center of Ukraine.

The V.Vernadskiy National Library of Ukraine at 3, 40 Years of October Ave. (architects V.Gopkalo and V.Grechina, 1989) with its 27-floor book depository is the main block of the biggest book archive in Ukraine, numbering 13.5 million volumes.

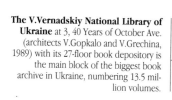

ST.CYRIL'S CHURCH

12, O.Teligi St.
☎ 468–11–26
Ⓜ Petrovka, Dorogozhichi
Day off – Friday

Prince Vsevolod (Kiril) Olgovich of Chernigov, who occupied Kyiv in 1139, founded a monastery in a northern suburb of the city named after his heavenly protector St.Cyril of Alexandria. In the second half of the 12th century Princess Maria, Vsevolod's widow, built here the stone Church of St.Cyril, which became the family chapel of the Olgoviches and housed the family sepulcher. About 800 sq. meters of fresco paintings from the 12th century have been preserved. Among the most interesting compositions are scenes from the life of St.Cyril of Alexandria, "The Angel Leading Young John into the Desert," the unique frescos on the topic of the Day of Judgment - "The Bosom of Abraham," "The March of the Princes", "The Angel Weaving the Sky," and others. Some of the paintings were done by Mikhail Vrubel to replace lost frescoes in the course of renovation. His works are "The Lamentation over the Grave," "Annunciation" and "The Entrance into Jerusalem." You can ascend a steep staircase to the gallery to get a view of Vrubel's composition "The Descent of the Holy Spirit" in the western arch. He also painted the faces of the prophets Moses and Solomon, and the symbolic fresco "Space." While working in Venice in 1884-1885, M.Vrubel created four icons for the icon case of the church: "The Blessed Virgin and Child," "Jesus Christ," "St.Cyril" and "St.Athanasius." The sketch for the face of the Blessed Virgin was made from the wife of Professor Prakhov, Emilia, with whom, as contemporaries reported, the artist was seriously in love. Part of the paintings date from the 17th-18th centuries. Among them is the portrait of Innokentiy Monastirskiy, the Father-Superior of Saint Cyril's Monastery, a diplomat and public figure. At that time, the ktitor of the monastery was the Cossack company commander Savva Tuptalo, who died at the age of 103 and

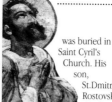

The Decent of the Holy Spirit.
Fragment. 1884.
M.Vrubel

was buried in Saint Cyril's Church. His son, St.Dmitri Rostovskiy, the future author of the classic life guide "Chetiy-Minei" took his monastic vows in the same church. Today Saint Cyril's Church is used as a museum, but religious services often take place here.

SAINT CYRIL'S HOSPITAL

The Monastery of Saint Cyril was closed in 1786 by the decree of Catherine II. In 1803 a sanitarium was transferred here from Podol. The architect I.Sharleman erected the brick buildings for a refuge for the handicapped (1823) and in between a one-story building with mezzanine, which became a laundry. Now this building contains the acting Orthodox Church of St.Basil. The hospital and the refuge made up the governor's charitable complex - the Saint Cyril Charitable Establishments. In the 19th-20th centuries numerous buildings were built here. Several of the sanitarium's buildings (not preserved) were erected by the engineer Fedor Geshvend. He was an inventor and in 1887 created a design for

St.Cyril's Church

a steam-powered jet airplane (steam plane). Although some details of the design of Geshvend's plane were very innovative, the model never flew. He went bankrupt and ended up in the refuge he built himself, where he died. Under the Soviets, Saint Cyril's Sanitarium was for unknown reasons named after Taras Shevchenko. It was subsequently renamed after Academician I.Pavlov, and it was only recently that its historic name was restored.

KURENEVKA

The former suburb of Kyiv - Kurenevka - extends from the foot of the hill on which stand Saint Cyril's Church and the hospital. Some historians attribute the origin of the name to the word "Kurens" meaning Cossack tents. The "Spartak" stadium is situated here at 105, Frunze St.

"THE HUT ON PRIORKA"

5, Vyshgorodskaya St.
☎ 432–76–27
Ⓜ Lukyanovskaya
Days off – Sunday, Monday

Priorka is situated behind Kurenevka, along Vyshgorodskaya Street. At the beginning of the 17th century, these lands were owned by a Dominican monastery and governed by a prior. In August 1859, Taras Shevchenko lived here in a small hut during his last tour of Ukraine. Today the hut has been rebuilt and houses a museum exhibition devoted to the

The Blessed Virgin with Child. 1884. M.Vrubel

Pokrovskaya Church

life of the ordinary Kyivans who were the contemporaries of Taras.

POKROVSKAYA (PRIORSKAYA) CHURCH
2, Mostitskiy Lane

This stone parish church was consecrated in 1906 (architects N.Kazanskiy, E.Yermakov). It once towered over Priorka, but now it is surrounded by big modern buildings. The famous artist Ivan Izhakevych took part in the decoration of the interior.

PUSHCHA-VODITSA

At the end of the 19th century, the former city forest with springs and lakes Pushcha-Voditsa was set aside as a place for the out-of-town cottages of the city dwellers. The picturesque nature, curative air and easy trip from the city all contributed to the success of this project. From 1900 to the present day, Kyivans can get to Pushcha-Voditsa by tram. In Soviet times, several health centers and resorts were built here. The Church of St.Seraphim Sarovskiy (42, N.Junkerova St.) was consecrated in 1910.

Fragment of the front of the
"Cat House"

THE FORMER "PEOPLE'S AUDITORIUM"
26, Vorovskogo St.

In an attempt to enlighten the poorest Kyivans in 1895 the local Society for the Support of Primary Education opened the "People's Auditorium," where free lectures and concerts were held in the vast hall. In 1909 the building was enlarged. The author of the design, the architect V.Rykov, would not accept any payment for his involvement in a good cause. After the revolution, the "People's Auditorium" was used as a theatre and club. Now it is occupied by a design institute.

"THE CAT HOUSE"
23, Gogolevskaya St.

This is the former apartment house of Colonel F.Yagimovskiy (architect V.Bessmertniy, 1909). It is decorated with elements of modernized gothic style. It is made especially distinctive by the lantern-tower at its right corner and the sculptures of cats and owls; unsleeping guards, on the front. This was the residence of the great

The "Cat House"

mechanical engineer, the KPI professor Stepan Tymoshenko, who worked for a long time in the USA. Opposite the "Cat House," the picturesque urban estate at #28 has been preserved. It formerly belonged to the artist Vladimir Orlovskiy (now it is a sanatorium for children). The owner lived in the house on the hill (the architect V.Nikolayev, 1892), the annex was the residence of his daugh-

ter and son-in-law - the famous painter Nikolay Pymonenko.

POKROVSKIY MONASTERY
(see 150)

46, ARTIOMA STREET

This detached house was rare for its time (architect A.Dobrovolskiy, 1948). It was assigned to the widow of General N.Vatutin, who liberated the city from the Nazis. But she refused to live in Kyiv, and the mansion was given to the literary couple A.Korneichuk and V.Vasilevskaya. Now the building is home to the American "Renaissance" Foundation, one of whose founders is the well-known philanthropist George Soros.

8, MELNIKOVA STREET

This expressive modern style building (architect V.Bessmertniy, 1910s) was built for the lawyer N.Grabar - the head of the charitable society that funded an educational "labor colony" for youth in Rubezhovka suburb. Perhaps the flowers of the field in the molded decor of the first floor symbolized Grabar's young pupils.

"KHRUSHCHEV'S SUMMER COTTAGE"
14, Gertsena St.

These two small elegant detached houses situated in a cozy park (architect N.Kazanskiy, 1890s), were once the property of a simple assistant pharmacist.

In Soviet times, they were used as a governmental villa. In the 1930s, the chief of the penal system of Ukraine V.Balitskiy lived here. After the war, its occupants were the Party leaders N.Khrushchev, N.Podgorniy, P.Shelest and others. This tradition was broken by

Lukyanovskiy penitentiary castle

V.Sherbitskiy, who gave "Khrushchev's Summer Cottage" (as it was called by the Kyivans) to the P. Buiko Institute of Pediatrics, Obstetrics and Gynecology.

LUKYANOVKA

This area was named after the local landowner Lukyan Alexandrovich - the head of a shoemakers guild in the 18th century. The front of the former Lukyanovskiy People's House at 5, Degtyariovskaya St. (architect M.Artynov, 1903) faces Lukyanovskaya Square. This was a club for the poor built by the local temperance society. To lure the people away from alcohol, the People's House offered a cheap canteen with a tea-room, library, educational courses and free plays starring known actors. Now this building, which resembles a fairy-tale house, contains the House of Culture of Electric Transportation Workers. Behind a high wall at 13, Degtyariovskaya St. stands the former Lukyanovskiy Penitentiary (architect M.Ikonnikov, 1863). Many famous public figures of different views served time in Lukyanovskiy prison. In 1881 S.Bogomolets, confined by the case of the "Southern Labor Union", gave birth to a boy, the future academician A.Bogomolets. In 1902, 11 distributors of the "Iskra" newspaper made a daring escape, among them the well-known revolutionaries N.Bauman, M.Lytvinov and O.Piatnitskiy. During the Stalin years, the jail was an important part of the repressive apparatus, and thousands of innocent people perished there. Now this it is a remand center. The Lukyanovskaya metro station appeared in Lukyanovskaya Square in 1997. The first McDonald's restaurant in Ukraine was opened nearby.

The hospital of water transport workers

HOSPITALS OF DIFFERENT RELIGIONS

At the turn of the 20th century, the low price of land lots and relatively clean air attracted many charitable institutions to Lukyanovka. The ensemble of buildings of the Jewish Hospital was built at 1 Baggovutskaya Street (architects V.Nikolayev, A.Minkus and others). The families of wealthy Jewish entrepreneurs - Brodsky, Zaks, Galperin, and Frenkel - thought it their duty to provide financial support. Now this territory is occupied by the Regional Hospital. The building at today's 32,

The TV-center building

Manuilskogo St. was formerly the Roman Catholic hospital named after the Polish public figure S.Siroczinski (architect K.Ivanitskiy, 1914). Now it houses the A.Romodanov Institute of Neurosurgery. Closer to the downtown area - at 9, Y.Kotsubinskogo St. - a fine building in Northern Modern Style has been preserved (architect E.Bradtman, 1913). This was initially the Lutheran Hospital, now it is the clinical hospital for marine-transport workers.

MAKARIEVSKAYA CHURCH
4–6, Staraya Poliana St.

The modest wooden church on the Yurkovitsa Hill was built in 1897 (architect E.Yermakov) in honour of the 400th anniversary of the tragic death of St.Makariy, the archbishop of Kyiv. The martyr Makariy was killed in a raid of Crimean Tatars on a Belarus village, where he was making a stop on his way from Vilnius to Kyiv. Some of the temple's icons were created by the painter I.Izhakevich, among them the lectern icon of St.Makariy with a portion of his relics.

THE INTERNATIONAL RELATIONS INSTITUTE
36/1, Mel'nikova St.

This is one of Kyiv's most prestigious higher educational establishments. Together with the Institute of Journalism it occupies a vast complex, which was originally designed for the

The International Relations Institute

Higher Party School of the Central Committee of the Communist Party of Ukraine (architects I.Shparo, Z.Chechik, 1980s).

LUKYANOVSKOYE CEMETERY (see 158-159)

THE TV CENTER AND TV-TOWER
42, Mel'nikova St.

The equipment and studio complex of the Kyiv TV center is a pencil-shaped skyscraper more than 90 meters high (the architect A.Komarovskiy and others). Construction started in the 1980s and is continuing up to now, although the majority of the buildings are already in operation. Across Mel'nikova Street stands the 380-meter high metal TV tower (1973). Its slim shape can be seen from all over

The TV tower

Kyiv. This is the highest construction in Ukraine. An original method of building up the tower from below was employed: every section was assembled on the ground and then powerful hydraulic jacks "raised" the construction for connection with the structure.

BABIY YAR (see 160)

POBEDY AVENUE

This is the longest avenue in Kyiv (11.2 kilometers). Previously it was the Brest-Litovsk highway leading out of the city to the west. When it came within the city limits, the highway became Brest-Litovsk Avenue, which starts from Vozdukhoflotskiy overpass and leads through the educational establishments and industrial enterprises of Shuliavka, the parks of the former hamlet of Nivki, to the old cottage area of Sviatoshin. In 1985, it was renamed Pobedy Avenue and extended to Pobedy Square. A wooden arch once stood at the crossing with today's Vozdukhoflotskiy Avenue, marking the entrance to Kyiv. Not far from there at 11, Pobedy Avenue stands the Wedding Palace (architects V.Gopkalo, V.Grechina, 1982), whose unusual shape gave rise to the nickname "the Bermuda Triangle."

The monument to V.Kirpichev.
Sculptor N.Deriguz

KYIV POLYTECHNICAL INSTITUTE
37, Pobedy Ave.

One of the biggest higher educational establishments of the capital, Kyiv Polytechnical Institute (KPI) was founded in 1898. One of those who initiated its opening was the well-known statesman, the Finance Minister Sergey Witte, whose life was closely connected to Kyiv. The institute trained specialists in the field of sugar industry, which then was thriving. There were 4 faculties: engineering, mechanical, chemical and agricultural. The core ensemble of the institute's buildings was formed by 1901 (Kyiv architects A.Kobelev, V.Obremskiy and others took part in executing a design by the St.Petersburg architect I.Kitner). The blocks are decorated in neo-Roman style. Later on modern educational buildings, a library, a concert hall were added. Sports facilities and dormitories were built nearby. The vast shady park of the KPI became one of the decorations of the avenue. By the entrance, a monument was put up to the professors and students of the institute who perished in WW II (sculptors A.Morozova, A.Suvorovtsev, 1967). A galaxy of outstanding scientists and engineers - professors and students of the institute - are bound up with its history. Monuments to V.Kirpichev, first rector of KPI, and professor S.Timoshenko (see 138) were placed before the main building in 1998. In front of the chemistry building stands a statue of the prominent scientist D.Mendeleyev (1995), who was the head of the examination board for its first finals. On the front of the main building there is a memorial sign to Professor E.Paton (see 132). His son B.Paton, president of the National Academy of Sciences of Ukraine, graduated from the institute. One of the bright pages in the history of KPI was the aviation hobby group organized by Professor N.Delone. The famous

On the territory of KPI

KPI main building

aircraft constructor I.Sikorski was a student of the institute. Prince A.Kudashev created the first domestic aircraft in 1910, while working at the institute. Aircraft building traditions were developed in the Soviet times, when the future spacecraft inventor S.Korolev worked here. Later the International University of Civil Aviation and a number of

The entrance to the Zoo

other higher educational establishments were organized on the basis of the institute. In 1995, KPI was given the status of a National University. Today 25,000 students study in 20 faculties.

THE ZOO
32, Pobedy Ave.

The biggest zoo in the former USSR (40 hectares of space), it was founded by the Kyiv Naturalists Society in 1908. After five years it was moved to opposite the KPI. 3.5 thousand animals and birds of more than 320 species live here now. Many pavilions and open-air cages were erected in 1960-1970s (the architect V.Mikhailov); at the entrance there are statues of a bison and lions (the sculptor Y.Ruban). See 216.

A.BOGOMOLETS MEDICAL UNIVERSITY
34, Pobedy Ave.

The year of foundation of this university is considered to be 1841, since it was then that the medical faculty of St.Vladimir's University started to work. It gained independent status in 1920. The medical university occupies several buildings in Kyiv, many of which are connected to working hospitals. The morphological faculty building (the architect L.Yurovskiy, 1954) is situated on the avenue. In front of it stands a bust of the physiologist A. Bogomolets, after whom the university was named in 1946. Here tens of thousands of doctors were trained in different specialities, including the astronaut Oleg Atkov.

PUSHKINSKIY PARK

When the 100th anniversary of Alexander Pushkin was celebrated in 1899, the city authorities decided to found a park in his honor. At the entrance to the park stands a monument to the poet with the following inscription on its pedestal: "To Pushkin from the Ukrainian people" (the sculptor A.Kovaliov, the architect V.Gnezdilov, 1962). Old-timers remember how an exhibition of captured fascist weaponry was held in the park in 1945.

A.DOVZHENKO FILM STUDIO
44, Pobedy Ave.

The construction of the buildings of the film studio - the biggest in the country

The monument to A.Pushkin

at the time - began in 1927 (the architect V.Rykov). A year later the pavilions were still clad in scaffolding, but the studio started to work. Some of the movies filmed in Kyiv became famous world-wide: "Earth" by Alexander Dovzhenko and "Shadows of Forgotten Ancestors" by Sergey Paradzhanov. There are memorial plates in memory of these film directors on the territory of the studio. Among the popular films shot here were: "Big Life" by L.Lukov; "The Tractor Drivers" by I.Pyr'yev; "Bogdan Khmel'nitsky" by I.Savchenko; "The Heroic Deed of a Scout" by B.Barnet; "After Two Hares" by V.Ivanov; "White Bird with a Black Mark" by Y.Il'yenko; and "Only the Old Go to Battle" by L.Bykov. One of the pavilions at the end of the ensemble is named "shchorsovskiy," because A.Dovzhenko shot his movie "Shchors" there. This is the museum of the studio. The apple orchard on the side of the avenue was

A.Dovzhenko

planted on the initiative of A.Dovzhenko. Since 1957, the Kyiv film studio has been named after him.

STATE ECONOMY UNIVERSITY
54/1, Pobedy Ave.

This is an offshoot of the Kyiv Institute of the National Economy, created in 1920 on the basis of the Kyiv Commercial Institute (see 124). The current building was erected in 1958 (architect L.Tyshkina). Under the current economic circumstances, the graduates of the university are in high demand.

THE "AVIANT" ENTERPRISE
100/1, Pobedy Ave.

This is the aircraft building union that executes the designs by the O.Antonov Design Bureau. It is organized on the basis of an aircraft construction plant founded in 1920. This is the place where the "An" airplanes are built, among them the world record holders for cargo capacity - the An-124 "Ruslan" and An-225 "Mriya". The enterprise buildings are on the site of the former Syrets military aerodrome, above which the pilot Piotr Nesterov "looped the loop" for the first time ever (in the avenue there is a memorial sign to mark this event - sculptor E.Karpov, architect A.Snitsarev, 1988).

Pobedy Avenue

A stamp with the portrait of P.Nesterov

Under the Soviet regime: concert in the Exhibition of the Achievements of National Economy

STADIUM "START"
Corner of Sholudenko St. and Marshal Rybalko St.

The stadium has been here since 1939. A memorial sign (sculptor A.Kharechko, architect A.Ignaschenko, 1981) was set here to commemorate the victory of Kyiv football-players over the German team "Flakelf" in August 1942. A legend was formed about the "Death Match," which said that four of our players were shot after the match because of their audacious victory. In actual fact, the men died six months later, and it was not connected to football. But the fact that the Kyivans recorded nine victories in nine games against different Nazi teams with a total score of 56:11 - this is undoubtedly a sporting and civil feat.

M.Ryl'sky

FORMER MILITARY SCHOOL
6, Vozdukhoflotskiy Ave.

One of the biggest buildings in old Kyiv was built in 1857 (architect I.Shtrom). Before the revolution this was the Vladimirsky Military School, which was named after the Grand Prince Vladimir Alexandrovich, whose birth coincided with the decision to organize the school. Among the former Kyiv cadets were: Lieutenant-General N.Dukhonin - Supreme Commander-in-Chief of the Russian Army under the Provisional Government; 1st Rank Army Commander S.Kamenev - commander-in-chief armed forces of the Soviet Republic; General-Cornet V.Salsky - commander-in-chief and military minister of the Ukrainian People's Republic; ace pilot E.Kruten; military diplomat A.Ignatiev; philosopher N.Berdiayev; painter N.Dubrovsky and others. In 1919 Red commanders were trained here. These included A.Golikov and the future writer A.Gaydar... Now the Ministry of Defense of Ukraine is located here. Vozdukhoflotskiy Avenue continues the direction of the former Cadet highway. It is called Vozdukhoflotskiy ("Air-Fleet") because it leads to the Zhuliany airport.

NATIONAL ACADEMY OF DEFENSE
28, Vozdukhoflot-skiy Ave.

This severe monumental building was built during the First World War for the Nikolayevsky artillery school (architect D.Zaytsev). In October 1918, the first Ukrainian national university was opened in the finished building. Now the National Academy of Defense of Ukraine is located here. The front of the building faces Solomenskaya Square (the name of the historic Solomenka district clearly comes from the thatched roofs of the former structures).

MUSEUM OF M.RYL'SKY IN GOLOSEYEVO
7, M.Ryl'skogo St.
☎ 265-85-72
Ⓜ Lybedskaya
Day off – Friday

The name of the locality is connected with the Goloseyevskaya hermitage - an out-of-town retreat of the Kyiv Pechersk Lavra founded in 1631 by the Metropolitan Piotr Mogila. In Soviet times the hermitage was ruined, and only the summer-house of the metropolitans survived (at 14, Colonel Zatevakhin St.). It is said that the monks planted the forest here on wasteland - this is where the word "Goloseyev" came from. The Ukrainian poet Maksim Ryl'sky spent the last years of his life in the picturesque forest park. A memorial museum was opened in his house, which keeps his personal effects, manuscripts, vast library, and recordings of the writer's voice.

EXPOCENTER OF UKRAINE
1, Academician Glushkov Ave.

The grandiose complex of the Exhibition of Advanced Experiments in the National Economy of the Ukrainian Soviet Socialist Republic was built on a territory of more than 300 hectares in 1952-1958. Part of the territory was taken up by elegant pavilions exhibiting the "fabulous prosperity of Ukraine under the Soviet regime." The center is now the National Exhibition Center (Expocenter) of Ukraine.

The monument Kyiv footballer

THE MUSEUM OF FOLK ARCHITECTURE AND WAY OF LIFE

Pirogov village
Krasnoznamennaya Street
☎ 266–24–16

The museum of people's architecture and way of life of Ukraine is located on a territory of about 150 hectares on the picturesque Kyiv outskirts near the Goloseyevsky forest. This is a remarkable ensemble of open-air exhibits. The museum is located near the village Pirogov not far from the city ring road. Construction began in 1969 on the initiative of the Ukrainian Society for Protection of Monuments of History and

On the territory the museum of the people's architecture and the way of life

Khata (house) from Podol

Culture. The museum has been open to visitors since 1976. S.Vergovsky, T.Dovzhenko, V.Orlov, L.Pribega, V.Sikorskiy, S.Smolinsky, B.Stamov, N.Khodakovsky and others took part in developing the conception and design of the museum. The museum structures (there are more than 300) are original examples of wooden architecture transported here from the different regions of Ukraine. The territory is divided into separate zones corresponding to the historical regions of the country. From the main entrance, the road leads across a large wheat field to the zone

Beehive

Middle Pridnieprovie with the great Church of the Great Martyr Saint Paraskeva Friday (Cherkassy region, 1742), the small Church of the Archangel Michael (1601), and the unique collection of windmills ("vitriaky"). Next on the hillside comes the zone Podolie where visitors can see the Church of Saint Nicholas and the bell tower from the beginning of the 19th century from near Gusiatin. A stone pot-house stands near the road. The complex Poltavshchina and Slobozhanshchina is situated in the centre of the museum territory. A little farther on, visitors can see the Polesiye zone with the Voskresenskaya Church (Rovenshchina, 17th-18th century) under its hipped roof. The exposition of village houses (khatas) here is unique for its age (1587 and 1687). In the northern part of the museum, the Carpathians zone is divided into small farms. The bell tower of the ancient Pokrovskaya Church rises above this zone. The museum collection contains different kinds of structures: watermills and forges, cattle-sheds ("shopa") and granary ("komora"), threshing floors and "stodola" for storing cereals, apiaries and hen houses, cellars and wells. The visitors can enter the buildings and

Pokrovskaya wooden Church from the Trans-Carpathian region

courtyards, see the details of old peasant life, household utensils, the stove, which was the centrepiece of any khata, since it was used for cooking, drying, heating and rest. Exhibits include objects used for housework, rest, wedding ceremonies, beautiful objects from wood and ceramics, examples of weaving and embroidery. The employees of the museum are dressed in national costumes that appear very natural here. Pirogovo museum is the biggest establishment of its kind in Eastern Europe. A visit to the museum allows you to get acquainted with the origins of the Ukrainian spirit and take an unforgettable walk through picturesque surroundings (see 206). Traditional fairs are organized on the territory of the museum in May and in September (at the beginning and the end of season), and holidays are celebrated according to folk traditions.

Potter

THE N.GRISHKO CENTRAL BOTANICAL GARDEN OF THE NATIONAL ACADEMY OF SCIENCES OF UKRAINE
1, Tymiryazevskaya St.

From ancient times this area was called Zverinets (Menagerie). Apparently Kyivan nobles used to hunt here (nearby was the princes' country residence known from the chronicles of the 11th-12th century as the Red Yard). In 1810-1812, a small Zverinets fortification was built (not preserved). In 1918, an ammunition depot here blew up affecting all Pechersk. It was decided to create the Botanical Garden of the National Academy of Sciences of Ukraine in Zverinets back in 1935, however full-scale construction work began only in post-war years. The scientific part of the plan was done by Academician N.Gryshko (the first director of the garden), and the planning was done by the architect A.Vlasov. The garden opened for the public in 1964. You can see interesting expositions in the areas: "The Forests of the Ukrainian Plains," "Ukrainian Carpathians," "The Ukrainian Steppe," "The Crimea" and "The Caucasus" etc. The garden has a superb rosarium, one of the best orchid collections in Europe, a rich collection of trees and bushes, as well as other plants. The lilacs are especially popular -

each spring people come to see them in bloom. But in other seasons too, the beautiful landscape and pure air attract thousands of visitors. The garden is situated on more than 130 hectares of land. The Troitskiy Monastery is also situated here (see 149).

An artist in the Botanical Garden

VYDUBITSKIY MONASTERY
(see 148)

THE INSTITUTE OF DURABILITY PROBLEMS
2, Tymiryazevskaya St.

This is a scientific institution that studies the endurance and durability of materials and constructions under extreme conditions. The place of the institute was occupied by the Bratskoye military cemetery in the years of World War I. In 1916 work began on a temple-monument to Russian soldiers and dedicated to St.Nicholas (architects P.Fetisov and V.Rykov). The Revolution prevented the construction from being completed. In the 1950s, the territory of the cemetery was transformed into a scientific center. The unfinished church that still overlooks Zverinets is used as a laboratory.

THE LYSAYA (BALD) MOUNTAIN
Trolley #15
Ⓜ Vydubichi

From ancient times the people held the Kyiv suburbs in ill repute - this was said to be where witches, werewolves and

other such creatures gathered on the Lysaya Mountain. There are actually several mountains with this name within the limits of the modern city. One of them is located between the railroad and the Stolichnoye highway. In 1871-1877, the Lysogorskiy Fort was built here - the only object to be built from the grandiose project for a semi-circle of fortresses around Kyiv designed by General E.Totleben. In the early 20th century, the Lysaya Mountain was used as a place of execution (D.Bogrov, the assassin of Stolypin, was hanged here). Now the Lysaya Mountain can be recognized

Vydubitskiy Monastery

from far off by the antennas of a radio complex that jammed "enemy broadcasts" in Brezhnev's times. The ramparts of Lysogorskiy Fort have been preserved along with several tunnels. You can see the names carved with bayonets in the brick walls by soldiers from different periods while standing on guard.

Troitskiy monastery. View from the Botanical Garden

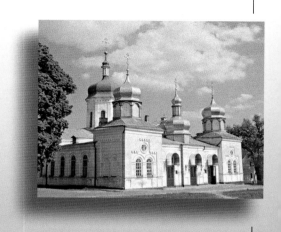

HOLY PLACES AND
NECROPOLISES

HOLY PLACES AND NECROPOLISES

There are many picturesque corners in the city, but some of them demand special treatment. Shouting and laughing sound inappropriate there, haste and bustle are undesirable. We are talking about the holy places of Kyiv, its necropolises - monastery and city cemeteries, the places of mass tragedies. Here you start to understand that earthly problems are transient. After communing with the ennobling sorrow of such places, visitors may depart with an enlightened soul.

Mikhailovskiy Gold-Domed Monastery

MIKHAILOVSKIY GOLD-DOMED MONASTERY
Mikhailovskaya Square

Back in the 11th century the Dmitriyevskiy Monastery stood here. It was founded by the Prince Isyaslav Yaroslavich of

The Economic Gate to Mikhailovskiy Gold-Domed Monastery

Kyiv (Christian name - Dmitri). In July 1108 his son Sviatopolk (Christian name - Mikhail) started to build the stone Mikhailovskaya church inside the monastery built by his father. The dome was plated with gold, and the new cathedral and later the

The refectory church

whole monastery became known as the Mikhailovskiy Gold-Domed. Over the next centuries, the Monastery was subsequently rebuilt. One of the reconstructions almost resulted in its destruction. In 1710 work began on construction of high side-chapels to the north and to the south. These started to sink and nearly tore the cathedral apart. The church was only saved by buttressing the side-chapels with inclined constructions.

By the middle of the 18th century and after numerous renovations, the Cathedral had seven domes, all of them gold-plated. The interior was decorated with frescos and mosaics. The southern chapel was dedicated to St.Catherine. They say that this was Tsar Peter the First's way of thanking his wife Catherine for her energetic actions to save the Tsar from Turkish captivity during the notorious Prutsk campaign. The northern side-chapel was named after St. Barbara, and the martyr's relics were placed here. A three-tier 49-meter column with a gold-plated top was erected in 1716-1719. The first money for

St.Zachary.
Cathedral fresco

its construction was donated by Iov Boretskiy - the former Father Superior of the monastery, and an outstanding figure of Orthodox enlightenment. The ensemble also included the refectory church of St.John the Divine (1713) to the south of the cathedral. The vast "Staropriimniy Yard" for pilgrims and guests of the monastery was built to the south of the refectory (now these are used as the buildings of the establishments at 4, Triokhsviatitel'skaya St.). There is information that it was in the yard of the Mikhailovskiy Monastery that Grigory Rasputin first met the relatives of the tsar, who opened his way to the state palaces. Along the northern border of the monastery extends the block of Barbara cells (architect E.Yermakov, 1898-1899). Other cells on the side of Triokhsviatitel'skaya Street (the architect P.Sparro, 1854-1856) are adjoining the bell tower.

ST.BARBARA

The principal relic of Mikhailovskiy Monastery, which used to attract thousands of pilgrims, is the remains of the

Martyr Barbara. Born at the end of the 3rd century in the family of a wealthy Roman nobleman in the eastern town Iliopol, St.Barbara became a follower of Christianity and openly renounced the pagan faith. She didn't give up her belief even under the inhuman tortures she was subjected to by the governor of Iliopol and her own father, and was executed. Her memory is honored all over the Christian world. In Raphael's famous painting the "Sistine Madonna," you can see St.Barbara at the side of the Blessed Virgin.

The fragment of "Eucharist" composition. Mosaic of the 12th century

THE TRAGEDY AND THE RESURRECTION

The history of the Gold-Domed Monastery goes back nine centuries. But the present generation of Kyivans still has problems getting used to seeing it as part of the city landscape. This was the result of the barbarism of the Bolshevik regime. In the 1930s the territory of the monastery was given over for construction of a building for the Soviet People's Committee, which was part of the design of a governmental area (see 42). The bell tower, a number of buildings and part of the wall were demolished. In 1937 detonators turned the

Memorial plate to N.Makarenko

Mikhailovskiy Monastery into a heap of stone. Local historians, archeologists and architects agreed to the demolition with heavy hearts. Only professor Nikolai Makarenko refused to sign the demolition act - and perished in a Novosibirsk jail. Now there is a memorial plate to him on the wall of the Cathedral. The projected building of the Soviet People's Committee of the Ukrainian Socialist Republic never materialized.

In 1997-2000, the holy place was restored with the support of the President of Ukraine and the city authorities (architect-restorer Y.Lositskiy and others). First to be restored were the western part of the stone walls round the monastery and the Economic Gate (from which a lane used to lead to the office of the monastery bursar). Then the bell tower was rebuilt, where instead of the former chiming clock

was placed a new electronic clock with hands and a set of chimes. Every hour the melodies

The Tomb of St.Barbara

of well-known Ukrainian compositions spread from Mikhailovskaya Square to the neighboring streets. There is an exhibition and an observation platform in the tower. At the turn of the 20th century the restored cathedral was consecrated. Its interior was decorated with a set of wooden baroque icons, copies of the former mosaics and frescos, which were kept in various museums, along with new works by Ukrainian monumental artists. The territory of the monastery has been tidied up and renovated. All the data from a thorough archeological study has been preserved. The monastery is home to the Ukrainian Orthodox Church of the Kyiv Patriarchite.

The kobzar at the main entrance to the monastery

VYDUBITSKIY MONASTERY

40, Vydubitskaya St.

The remarkable architectural and historic ensemble of the Vydubitskiy Monastery stands at the place known as Vydubichi. The name comes from the legend saying that it was here that the pagan idol Perun "vydybal," that is emerged from the waters of the Dnieper where it was thrown by Prince Vladimir. The monastery was widely known in the time of Kyiv Rus. The Igumen Sylvester edited the manuscript of the "Chronicle of Past Times" here. Originally the main temple of the monastery was the Cathedral of Saint Michael founded in 1070 by the prince Vsevolod Yaroslavich. Only part of it has survived. Rising above the Dnieper bank, it was protected from landslides by a supporting wall unprecedented for those times. The construction of the wall began in 1199 under the direction of the architect Piotr-Miloneg. But by the 16th century, when the monastery was in decline, the wall failed to protect the eastern part of the cathedral from collapse. Later a new church with elements of the Ukrainian

The bell tower of Vydubitskiy Monastery

baroque was constructed on the remains of Saint Michael's Cathedral (architect M.Yurasov, 1766-1769). Other buildings of the Vydubitskiy Monastery were constructed in the same style in 1696-1701 with funds of the

Cossack colonel Mikhail Miklashevsky from Starodubiye. These were Saint George's Cathedral and Refectory, and the Church of the Transfiguration of God. Saint George's Cathedral is an unsurpassed example of a five-domed Ukrainian church. Unfortunately, its five-tier icons were lost during the Soviet period. The walls of the refectory are decorated with ornamental patterns. Above the entry there is the symbol of Miklashevsky - a bow with crossed arrows. Here you can read from left to right in pairs the letters: "MMSCZA." These letters stand for: "Mikhail Miklashevsky, Starodubiye Colonel of the Zaporozhiye Army of his Majesty the Tsar." The bell tower provides a focal point in the composition of the Vydubitskiy Monastery. It was built up gradually: the two lower tiers were built at the time of the Ukrainian baroque, while the third tier with dome and spire was added on in classical style (architect A.Melensky, 1827-1833). The ensemble also includes blocks of cells built in the 18th-19th centuries. Now the monastery is occupied by the Ukrainian Orthodox Church (Kyiv Patriarchate). The poetic appearance of the Vydubitskiy Monastery retains its beauty and attractiveness to this day. You can spend a long time admiring its panoramas from the Dnieper or from the Central Botanical Garden.

Panorama of Vydubitskiy Monastery

The symbol of M.Miklashevsky

NECROPOLIS OF VYDUBITSKIY MONASTERY

For a long time there was a cemetery on the territory of the monastery. Under the Soviet regime most of the burial places were destroyed. But among those that survived, there are some precious historical relics. Here the remains of the great pedagogue Konstantin Ushinsky lie under a marble cross. In addition to his original epitaph, a new ideological one composed by P.Tychina was subsequently added. The cast iron gravestone with a lengthy inscription on the tomb of General of Artillery Lev Yashvill, a participant in the war

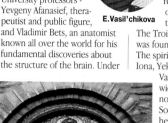
E.Vasil'chikova

with Napoleon, has also survived. The monastery also holds the tombs of the Kyiv University professors - Yevgeny Afanasief, therapeutist and public figure, and Vladimir Bets, an anatomist known all over the world for his fundamental discoveries about the structure of the brain. Under

monk of the Vydubitskiy Monastery, Ion created a hermit's retreat for himself on the hill above the monastery. The Troitsky Monastery was founded here in 1866. The spiritual daughter of Iona, Yekaterina Vasilchikova, the widow of the governor of the Southwest Territory, helped him. The monastery includes the Trinity Church (architect I.Antonov, 1871). Its pear-shaped dome is built in the baroque style of the Vydubitskiy monastery. Now the relics of Saint Iona are preserved in the church. An original page in the history of the monastery came at the beginning of 20th century, when there was an attempt to build a gigantic bell tower here, 10 meters taller than that of the Lavra (design by the architect V.Nikolayev, 1899). The idea was not realized due to the resistance of the metropolitan - a supporter of the interests of the Lavra. The wooden clock tower with the old mechanism has survived in the monastery. A Sunday school operates in the monastery.

Trinity (Ioninsky) Monastery

Vault of N.Leliavsky

to the caves was lost for a long period. Scientists were able to examine them for the first time only in 1910s. The scientists of those times (one of them, the historian and archaeologist I.Kamanin, was interred here near the entry in the caves) considered this underground monastery to be the oldest on the territory of Rus. However, contemporary specialists consider that it was created not earlier than the 12th century. In 1913, the Church of Birth of the Blessed Virgin was built above the caves (it was destroyed by an explosion in 1918). Now the Zverinetskiye caves are being studied by the specialists of the Museum of Kyiv History, and the Trinity Monastery regularly organizes visits by pilgrims.

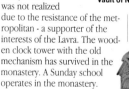

**Mosaic on the front of
Mikhaylovsky Church.**
K.Lobanovsky

a modest headstone lies the married couple Bogdan and Barbara Khanenko - famous patrons of the arts and founders of Museum of Arts (see 121). A classical mausoleum (architect V.Gorodetsky) contains the burial-vault of engineer hydrologist Nikolay Leliavsky. The painter and stage-designer Fedor Nirod, the descendant of a noble line, was recently interred in Vydubichi in the place where the lost family vault once stood. The headstone of Yakov Gandzuka, a fighter for the independence of Ukraine killed by Bol'sheviks in 1918, was recently restored.

TROITSKY (IONINSKY) MONASTERY
1, Timiriazevskaya St.
Entry from the territory of the N.Grishko Central Botanical Garden

The monastery was founded by Saint Iona (Miroshnichenko), a hermit and miracle worker, who lived more than 100 years. In his youth he was a monk in the Sarovskaya hermitage of Saint Seraphim. Later when he was a

ZVERINETSKIYE CAVES
17–22, Michurina St.

The caves are an underground corridor 150 meters long. Here there is an underground church with some niche burial-vaults like in the Lavra caves. The entry

**Headstone
of E.Afanasief**

FLOROVSKY CONVENT
5, Pritissko–Nikolskaya St.

The Kyivo-Florovsky Convent
has been mentioned in documents going back to the 15th
century. When the Voznesensky
Convent in Pechersk was dissolved in 1712 (for some time its
mother superior was the mother
of Ivan Mazepa - the hetman
hostile to Tsar Peter I), it was
joined to Kyivo-Florovsky convent. In 1722-1732, the
Voznesensky Church was built in
the Florovsky Convent. To the
west of it is the refectory church
in honour of the Tikhvinskaya
Blessed Virgin (previously - the
Church of Saint Flora and Saint
Laura). It was constructed on
the basis of a one-story building
built in 1695. The wall of the
refectory is decorated with the
painting "Saint Seraphim
Sarovskiy" from the beginning of
the 20th century. In 1811 the
convent was damaged by the
fire, which engulfed all Podol.
The renovation of the surviving
structures and construction of
new ones was carried out by the
architect Andrey Melensky. He
built the bell tower above the
gates of the convent (1821), the
picturesque one-story house of
the mother superior (1822) to
the south of the gates, and the
small Voskresenskaya Church is
attached to the convent hospital
(1824) on the heights to the
north of the
refectory. The
last temple of
the convent

Florovsky Convent

to be built was the Church of the
Kazan Icon of the Blessed Virgin
(architect P.Sparro, 1840-1844)
in Russian-Byzantine style. In
Soviet times, when an industrial

**The Grand Princess Alexandra
Petrovna**

enterprise operated on the territory of the convent, this church
was rebuilt as a factory workshop. But now the church is
reconstructed in its old appearance (architect Y.Lositsky,
E.Miroshnichenko). A functioning source of holy water has survived on the terri-
tory of the con-
vent, which
belongs to the

**Voskresenskaya
Church of the
Florovsky Convent**

Ukrainian Orthodox Church
(Moscow Patriarchate). In a little
glassed crypt in front of the
Voskresenskaya Church there is
the grave of the cenobite Helena
(Yekaterina Bakhteyeva, daughter of a general), which is honoured by the nuns and pilgrims.
She died in the convent at the
age of 78 years after a life filled
with distress and unjust persecu-
tions. Another remarkable destiny was that of the cenobite
Nectariya of Florovsky Convent,
in secular life Princess Nataliya
Dolgorukova (interred in Kyiv
Pechersk Lavra) - see 13. The
destiny of the princess inspired
the Russian poets K.Ryleyev,
I.Kozlov and N.Nekrasov.

POKROVSKY CONVENT
15, Bekhterievsky Lane

The convent was founded by the
Grand Princess Alexandra
Petrovna - the wife of the brother of Alexander II. A pilgrimage
to the Pechersk relics helped her
find relief after a severe illness.
The princess decided to provide
funds for founding a convent in
Kyiv and creating a charitable
medical foundation. In 1888 she
bought a plot of land in
Lukyanovka for the future convent. Previously there was a large
garden here that was visited by
the blessed celibate priest
Pheophil. Long before the creation of the convent he foretold

the holiness of this place. At the order of the grand princess, in 1889 the architect V.Nikolayev built the convent settlement in "Russian" style: the Pokrovskaya Church with cells, the hospital with its home church, and other residential and official buildings. In the same year, Alexandra settled in her cell for good. Later she secretly became a nun under the name Anastasia.

The main entry of the convent closes the prospect of Bekhteriovsky Lane. At the end of the 19th century, the Holy Gates were built here - an original arch resembling the head of a fairy-tale knight. Tsar Nikolay II, who visited the convent in 1896, funded the construction of the dispensary and therapeutical ward of the convent hospital (now this is the hospice in the north part of the convent with the church of Saint Agapit Pecherskiy). The charitable hospital attached to the convent was provided with modern equipment (here in 1896 an X-ray device was used for the first time in Kyiv). The convent was very popular thanks to its exemplary maintenance of the hospital. The nuns combined prayers with hard work for the good of the poor, and were a bright example of "living monasticism."

Nikolayevsky Cathedral of Pokrovskiy Convent

In 1896-1911 the Nikolaevskiy Cathedral was built in the convent. It became the biggest temple in Kyiv. The draft design was prepared by the Grand Prince Piotr Nikolayevich - the son of the founder of the convent. The blueprints were made by V.Nikolayev. The floor of the convent has a unique construction based on the intersection of two large brick arches. The interior paintings were done in the 1980s by artists from the Pochaevskaya Lavra.

In the socle there is another temple in honour of the Icon of the Blessed Virgin "Source of Life."

Pokrovskiy Convent. Central cells

Under the Soviet regime, the convent was dissolved, a working settlement was organized on its territory and the churches were disfigured. During the Nazi occupation, the religious life of the convent was restored. However, the nuns secretly sabotaged the Hitlerites, and helped many Kyivans avoid being sent to labour camps in Germany. After the war the convent continued to function. Now it belongs to the Ukrainian Orthodox church (Moscow Patriarchate). The Pokrovskaya church has been restored (architect Y.Lositsky, Y.Diahtiar, 1989-1990). Reconstruction of the Nikolayevsky Cathedral is also planned.

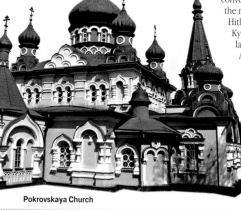

Pokrovskaya Church

KITAYEVSKAYA HERMITAGE
15, Kitayevskaya St.

The name of the Kitayevo district on the southern outskirts of Kyiv likely comes from the Turkic word "kitay" - meaning "fortification" (the remains of an Old Russian fortress were actually found here). Reliable information about the convent in Kitayevo goes back to 1716. The Kitayevskaya Hermitage came under the jurisdiction of Kyiv Pechersk Lavra. Here Saint Dosipheya, and the holy fools Pheophil and Paisy were celebrated for their spiritual feats. The monastery's main stone temple - the Church of the Holy Trinity - was built in Ukrainian baroque style (architect S.Kovnir, 1763-1767). Later the church was rebuilt. It was restored in the 1980s-1990s. The Church of Saint Seraphim Sarovskiy (1904), which is attached to the former hospice, has also survived. Since 1996 the hermitage has had the status of an independent monastery of the Ukrainian Orthodox Church. The Kitayevskaya Hermitage is located in picturesque surroundings near preserved forests and pools. Here an atmosphere of deep spirituality reigns.

Trinity Church

SAINT DOSIPHEYA

The hermit Decipher lived far outside Kyiv. He was known for his holiness, godliness and insight. He lived in a little cave near the Kitayevskaya Hermitage. In 1744 the Empress Elizabeth Petrovna visited his shelter. Later he taught and blessed the young

Prokhor Moshnina - the future Saint Seraphim Sarovskiy. When he died in 1776, the godly old man was buried in the wall of the Kitayevskaya Hermitage. Only then was it discovered that the hermit was the woman Dariya (Dosipheya) from the noble Ryazan family Tiapkin. Now the tomb of Saint Dosipheya is a holy place of the Kitayevskaya Hermitage, and her cave is opened for pilgrimage.

HERMITAGE OF PHEOPHAN
19, Academician Lebedev St.

The hermitage was formed on the territory of Lazarevschina - an out of town farm to the southeast of Kyiv not far from the Vasilkovsky road. In 1802 the farm was transferred to the

Saint Panteleimon's Cathedral

Mikhaylovsky Gold-Domed monastery as a summer residence for the higher orders of clergy. The monastery's superior, Father Pheophan (Shiyanov) built here the Church of the Miracle of the Archangel Michael (not survived) and a summerhouse. On the day of the consecration of the church, the church was renamed Pheophaniya in honor of Father Pheophan. In 1901 Pheophaniya was reorganized as a retreat. In 1915 it was reformed as an independent monastery. The monastery's main place of worship was Saint Panteleimon's Cathedral (architect E.Yermakov, 1904-1914). This monumental five-domed construction in "Russian" style became the biggest sacred construction on the outskirts of Kyiv. Under the Soviet regime the monastery was dissolved. Saint Panteleimon's Cathedral fell into decay and was ruined. But in the 1990s, the cathedral was restored and returned to the faithful. A woman's hermitage attached to the Pokrovskiy monastery was organized here (see 150).

Tomb of Saint Dosipheya

BAYKOVO CEMETERY

When the first municipal cemetery in Shchekavitsa (see 62) was full, it became necessary to create a new city necropolis. It was established in 1833 near the Baykovo farm. The cemetery contains sections for Orthodox, Catholic and Lutheran burials. Initially, the cemetery was located to the south of the present Baykovo Street. But later the cemetery was enlarged significantly to the north. The new area appeared opposite the old - behind a substantial brick wall. Many of the headstones became pieces of monumental art. In Soviet times it was traditional to bury the most famous and honoured figures at the Baykovo Cemetery.

Voznesenskaya Cemetery Church

**Alexander I rewards
Sergey Baykov**

OWNER OF BAYKOVO FARM

The name of Staff-Captain Sergey Baykov is written into the history of the Patriotic War of 1812. While the French Army was retreating from Russia, an advanced detachment led by Baykov captured the transport of Napoleon's Marshal Davout with valuable papers and the marshal's baton. Field-Marshal Kutuzov sent Baykov to Petersburg with a report. There the officer presented the unique trophy to Tsar Alexander I. The tsar rewarded Sergey Baykov with the Cross of Saint George. The hero later rose to the rank of Major General, took up residence in Kyiv, and bought a farm on the outskirts behind the Lybed River. This area was called Baykov's farm. This is the origin of the names of Baykova Hill, Baykova Street and Baykovo Cemetery.

VOZNESENSKAYA CHURCH

The cemetery's monumental Byzantine-style Voznesenskaya Church (architect V.Nikolayev, 1884-1889) was built on the proceeds from the sale of burial places. Under the Soviet regime, it escaped the fate of many Kyiv churches: it was preserved as a memorial hall for funeral ceremonies. Now divine services are once again held in the church.

CENTRAL ALLEY

The central alley of the Orthodox part of the New Baykovo Cemetery passes from the entrance with its "Russian" style bell tower (1909) to the Voznesenskaya Church. In order to make prestigious places available, many historic burial places were ruined. For example, the tomb of the Soviet academician and poet Pavlo Tychina (section #1) takes the place formerly occupied by the philanthropist G.Gladynuk. Some of the old tombs have survived however.

ROAD OF GRIEF

A crematorium was built at the end of Baykova Street (architect A.Miletsky, 1975). Along the road leading to the crematorium, the artists A.Rybachuk and V.Melnichenko created a Memorial Wall with an original sculptural composition of philosophic content. However, the ideological leaders of the Brezhnev epoch took this creation as an assault on the principles of socialist realism, and the composition was destroyed.

Crematorium

153

The headstone of the last all-powerful communist leader of Ukraine, **Vladimir Shcherbitskiy**. Section #6

Headstones of three geniuses of Ukrainian culture - the painter **Georgy Narbut**, the actress **Maria Zankovetskaya**, the actor and director **Nikolay Sadovsky**. Section #2

Old land lots

The monument over the grave of the great Ukrainian poet **Maksim Rylsky**. Section #1

Nikolay Roshchin-Insarov - an actor of the "Solovtsov" theater and the best Ukrainian interpreter of the role of Chatsky. He fell victim to the jealousy of the husband of an actress whom the unfortunate Roshchin started to woo. Section #1

The monument on the grave of the public figure and classic of Ukrainian music **Nikolay Lysenko**. Section #2

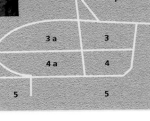

Ostap Vishnia (P.Gubenko) wrote feuilletons and satirical stories that made all Ukraine laugh. But there were difficult periods in his life, which was darkened by long exile. Section #2

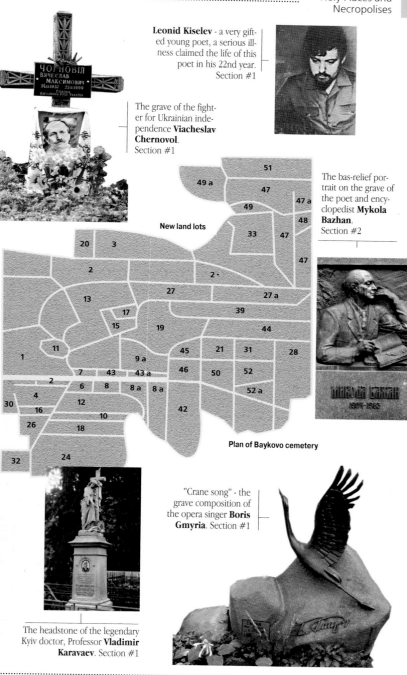

Leonid Kiselev - a very gifted young poet, a serious illness claimed the life of this poet in his 22nd year. Section #1

The grave of the fighter for Ukrainian independence **Viacheslav Chernovol**. Section #1

ЧОРНОВІЛ
ВЯЧЕСЛАВ
МАКСИМОВИЧ
24.12.1937   25.03.1999
ГОЛОВА
НАРОДНОГО РУХУ УКРАЇНИ

New land lots

51
49 a
47
47 a
49
48
33
47
47
20   3
2
2 ·
27
27 a
13
39
17
15   19
44
11
45   21   31   28
1
9 a
46   50   52
7   43   43 a
8 a   8 a
52 a
2
6   8
4
12
42
30
16
10
26
18
32   24

The bas-relief portrait on the grave of the poet and encyclopedist **Mykola Bazhan**. Section #2

МИКОЛА БАЖАН
1904-1983

Plan of Baykovo cemetery

"Crane song" - the grave composition of the opera singer **Boris Gmyria**. Section #1

The headstone of the legendary Kyiv doctor, Professor **Vladimir Karavaev**. Section #1

On the headstone of the "Ukrainian nightingale," the singer **Oksana Petrusenko**, it is written that she was a "National Artist of the USSR." Officially Oksana did not have this title. But nobody was more worthy of it than Petrusenko. Section #8

The unforgettable romantic band-master **Natan Rakhlin**. Section #33

This headstone in the form of an airplane wing is placed over the grave of the aircraft designer **Oleg Antonov**, creator of the famous An series of aircraft. Section #7

The grave monument of the historiographer and Ukrainian statesman **Mikhail Grushevsky**. Section #8

Grave statue of the great Ukrainian poetess **Lesia Ukrainka** (L.Kosach). Section #3 of the old cemetery

The fence and gates of the new Catholic part of the Baykovo cemetery

Gnat Yura - founder of the I.Franko theatre. Section #1

The grave of **Vadim Hetman** -
a prominent financier and the
"father" of the Ukrainian hryvnia. He was murdered.
Nearby rest the remains of the
Ukrainian poet and law advocate
Vasyl Stus, who perished in
the Ural camp. Section #52a

This marble cross marks
the grave of the favourite
of the Ukrainian people,
Ivan Mykolaychuk.
Section #33

The grave of the famous lawyer,
Professor **Alexander
Kistiakovski**. Section #5 of
the old cemetery

The headstone of the ballet dancer
Lidiya Gerasimchuk, "The Dying
Swan." Section #8a

157

LUKYANOVSKOYE CEMETERY

Founded in 1878 as the city's Orthodox cemetery, the Lukyanovskoye Cemetery worked until 1963. Here rest many social, scientific and creative figures whose names are worthy of respect. Victims of Stalin's repressions, including outstanding representatives of the "Shot Renaissance," were buried secretly in Lukyanovskoye Cemetery in unmarked graves. A symbolic cross stands by the cemetery entrance in honor of the new martyrs of the 20th century. In 1994 a decision of the Cabinet of Ministers of Ukraine gave the Lukyanovskoye Civil Cemetery the status of a state historic and memorial reserve. The territory and the tombs were renovated, and a museum exhibition was created. The researcher L.Protsenko contributed greatly to the study of the history of the cemetery.

The chapel over the tomb of **Stepan Solskiy**, Kyiv mayor 1887-1900 (architect E. Bradtman, 1902). Today this is the Church of the New Martyrs

The tombstone of the gynecologist and Corresponding Member of the Academy of Sciences of Ukrainian Soviet Socialist Republic **Alexander Lurie**. #13

The tombstone of the physician Academic **Nikolay Strazhesko**. #13

The tombs of the pilots **Piotr Nesterov** - the founder of aerobatics, who died ramming an enemy plane, and his pupil Yevgraph Kruten - "the Knight of the Skies," a World War I ace. #13

The tombstone of **Pavel Alioshin** - one of the most prominent architects of Kyiv in the 20th century. #15

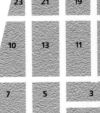

Plan Lukyanovsko cemete

The tombstone of the artist
Nikolay Pimonenko, master
of Ukrainian genre art. #20

The priest **Alexander
Glagolev** - a scientist,
teacher and righteous
man, who died in jail in
1937. A symbolic grave,
#45

New tombstone of the prominent artist
Alexander Murashko,
murdered in 1919. #20

Vladimir Pukhal'sky - outstanding musician and pedagogue, founder and first
director of the Kyiv
Conservatory, teacher of
V.Horowitz. #11

The tombstone of the
famous dramatic actress
Lubov Gakkebush. #20

The tomb of the general practitioner, academician and
humanist **Feofil Yanovskiy**.
#20

BABIY YAR

This is the name of a deep ravine in the northern part of Kyiv, which descends from the upland area of Syrets to the low-lying Kurenevka. Today the name is known to the world as a notorious symbol of the inhuman fascist genocide. When Hitler's troops occupied this city, the following announcement appeared on the walls of houses: "All the Jews of Kyiv and its suburbs should arrive at the corner of Mel'nikova and Dokterivska Streets (by the cemetery) on Monday, September 19, 1941 at 8:00 a.m. They are to have with them their documents, valuables and money, as well as warm clothes, underwear etc. Those Jews who fail to comply and are apprehended anywhere else shall be executed. Those citizens who enter the apartments left by the Jews and appropriate their belongings shall be executed." At that time there were tens of thousands of Jews in Kyiv (mostly old people, women, invalids and children). At dawn on September 25 almost all of them went to the place named in the announcement, at the corner of Mel'nikova and Degtyariovskaya Streets (as they are correctly called). The Jews hoped they would simply be evacuated to another location. They could hardly imagine that thousands of peaceful people were doomed to be executed by a firing squad. Not far from Babiy Yar stood German soldiers and local police. Those who passed the cordon were not allowed to

The German's announcement to all the Jews of Kyiv. 1941

come back. After that hell started. After their property was taken away, the people were led deep into the ravine, where they were battered with clubs and set upon by dogs. Then they were stripped and cut down by machinegun fire. The dead and the wounded fell into the ravine. In the report by the Einsatzgruppe "C" (a task force made up of police, SD and SS), it was noted that 33,771 people were massacred on September 29 and 30. This was how "the final solution of the Jewish problem" was carried out in Kyiv. The same fate awaited the Gypsies. Later this became a place for the execution of prisoners from the nearby Syrets concentration camp, members of the communist underground and Ukrainian patriots. The total number of victims was about 100 thousand. The Nazis forced prisoners of war to burn the corpses. But they failed to hide all the traces of their crimes. The few Jews who managed to escape from the Yar were hidden by Kyivans, although that was punishable by death. In 1943 a group of POWs responsible for burning the corpses managed to escape. Information about Babiy Yar was heard at the Nurenberg Trials. Meanwhile, in Kyiv a blasphemous attempt was made to fill up the ravine by dumping semi-liquid clay into it, in order to organize an amusement park in its place. But in 1961 the dike that was supposed to

The monument in memory of the murdered Soviet citizens

hold the clay gave way, and an avalanche of mud poured onto the houses of Kurenevka. The flood, known as the "Kurenevka Tragedy," took the lives of thousands of Kyivans. For a long time there was no memorial at Babiy Yar (the poet Y.Yevtushenko pointed that out in his poem). In 1976 an official monument in memory of the murdered Soviet citizens was built between the Yar and the site of the Syrets concentration camp (sculptor M.Lysenko and others). To mark the 50th anniversary of the Babiy Yar massacre, a new monument shaped like the Jewish symbol - the seven-candle Menorah - was set up much closer to the scene of the tragedy (architect Y.Paskevych, artist A.Levych and others, 1991). A path of sorrow leads to it from the office of the former Jewish cemetery (44 Mel'nikova St.). In 2001 another small monument dedicated to the children who perished in the Yar (sculptor V.Medvedev) was set up in the park by the Dorohozhichy metro station. Now every year on September 29 there is a march of mourning to Babiy Yar and a requiem mass takes place.

The "Menorah" monument

The monument to the perished children

THE BANKS OF THE
SLAVUTICH-DNIEPER

Nikolayev Kyiv Chain Bridge.
1857. From a drawing by A.Lang

THE BANKS OF
THE SLAVUTICH-DNIEPER

Our city was founded and grew on the right bank of a great river. The Dnieper is 2,285 km long (the third longest in Europe after the Volga and Danube). The Ancient Greeks gave it the name Borysthenes as the river flowing from the North. The Slavonians gave it the poetical name Slavutich. The present name of the river comes from the Scythian-Sarmatian "Danapras." From ancient times, people have sought to overcome this water frontier. As far back as 12th century in the times of Vladimir Monomakh, an attempt was made to cross the river with a pontoon bridge. From the end of 17th century pontoon bridges were regularly laid across the Dnieper. In 1853 the beautiful Chain Bridge (engineer C.Vignol) became the first permanent bridge in Kyiv. The metal chains based on 5 brick arches held the spans of the bridge. The bridge was destroyed by the Polish occupiers in 1920. In 1870 the Railroad Bridge was completed (engineer A.Struve). Over 1 kilometer in length, it became the longest bridge in Europe. It was destroyed during the World War II. Now that the city limits encompass a vast area on the left bank, there is a whole system of bridges over the Dnieper. If you wish, you can easily make a water trip on a passenger steamer (see 208) and see how down its whole length from the Moskovskiy Bridge to the Yuzhniy Bridge the river widens and at last attains a width of a kilometer.

The Moskovskiy Bridge (architect A.Dobrovol'skiy, engineer D.Fux, 1976) is the key structure of the northern road bridge passage. The beam of the main span is suspended by a bunch of steel ropes fixed to an A-pylon 115 meters in height.

The Podol'skiy Railroad Bridge (made of steel trusses during the First World War; it was rebuilt in 1929 and 1954 after being destroyed) closes the railway circle around Kyiv.

The Harbor Bridge (engineer V.Kiriyenko, 1963). Kyiv harbor was constructed back in 1897 - 1899 (engineer N.Maximovich). The bridge over it joins Podol with the industrial area of the Rybal'skiy Peninsula. This was

The Metro Bridge

the first time in the world a span was crossed with a ferroconcrete beam supported by shrouds.

The Foot-Bridge (engineer V.Kiriyenko, architect V.Suvorov, 1957) is a light elegant construction 400 meters in length that gives Kyivans easy access to the recreation area on Trukhanov Island.

The Metro Bridge (engineers G.Fux and Y.Inosov, 1965). An automobile road and a stretch of the metro railway draw a chain of arches in an expressive curve. At the start of the bridge, two statues rise over the platform of the Dnieper metro station: "XX century" and "Peace" (sculptors F.Kotsubinskiy, E.Kuntsevich and others).

The Rusanovskiy Bridge (1965). It continues the road from the Metro Bridge over the Rusanovskaya Canal. Instead of the present ferroconcrete road-

The Foot-Bridge

way, there used to be a beautiful bridge of tracery metal (engineer N.Belelubskiy, 1906), which was destroyed in the Second World War.

The Moskovskiy Bridge

The Paton Bridge

The Venetian Bridge (architect A.Ilyashenko, engineer V.Koval, 1966) is set over the Venetian Canal and joins the central part of Hydropark to the beaches of the Dolobetskiy Island.

The Paton Bridge (1953) is the longest (1543 meters) and most famous Kyiv bridge. It was the first wholly welded construction of such length in the world. It was the swan-song of the outstanding engineer Yevgeniy Paton. The 83-year old designer died shortly before the completion of construction, but his name is perpetuated in the name of the bridge.

The Darnitskiy Railway Bridge (engineers I.Barenboym, E.Radzevich and others, 1949). It took the place of the old bridge built by A.Struve.

The Yuzhniy Bridge (architect A.Gavrilov, the engineer G.Fux, 1990). Joint passage for automobiles and the metro. The shrouds holding the spans are supported by a two-column ferroconcrete construction 115 meters high.

THE TRUKHANOV ISLAND

An unlikely version widespread in popular literature connects the name of the island with the name of the Polovtsian Khan Tugorkan: allegedly the residence of his daughter, a wife of Prince Sviatopolk of Kyiv, was here. It is known for certain that from 17th century the island belonged to the city. At the turn of the 19th century there was a yard for repair of steam ships

here. A workers' village appeared on the island with the parish Church of Saint Elizabeth (1910, has not survived). The luxurious "Hermitage" restaurant and a biological station operated here. From 1887 the local yacht-club was based on "Trukhashka." In 1943 the village was burnt down by Nazi occupiers (a memorial is dedicated to it; sculptor V.Chepelik, 1989). Now the Trukhanov Island is used for recreation and

The Yuzhniy Bridge

water sports. The first beaches were arranged here by the Germans who occupied Kyiv in 1918.

THE HYDROPARK

It is situated in the place of the former Predmostnaya Slobodka, a settlement that appeared by the Chain Bridge and which was sometimes called the "Kyiv Venice." This settlement, like Trukhanov Island, was burnt down by the Nazis in 1943. Now it has a popular recreation and entertainment complex with beaches, sports grounds, attractions, cafes and restaurants. Thanks to the "Hydropark" metro station you can get here in minutes.

THE SHIP MONUMENTS

In the Sailors Park on the Rybalskiy Peninsula there is the

A memorial to the legendary founders of Kyiv

ironclad "Zhelezniakov" - a warship whose crew fought bravely with the Dunayskaya and Azovskaya military flotilla in the years of the Great Patriotic War. In 1967 the ironclad-memorial was set up near the Leninslaya Kuznitsa plant, where it was built. On the territory of the Shore Base for Underwater Technical Works on Zhukov Island, the diving boat "Aqualung" - a former mine sweeper, which neutralized a lot of mines in the Volga and the Dnieper - was set on a pedestal in 1984. In the park along the waterfront, between the Metro and Paton bridges, there stands a bronze boat. The four statues stand there - the great and wise Prince Kiy, the brave warrior Shchek with a bow in his hand, the inspired builder Khoriv, and their sister Lybed. This memorial to the epic founders of Kyiv (sculptor V.Boroday, architect N.Feschenko, 1982) has become one of the emblems of the city.

The ironclad "Zhelezniakov"

LEVOBEREZHIE (LEFT BANK) OF KYIV

Now it is difficult to believe that at the beginning of the 20th century all the present left-bank territory of Kyiv was not only outside the city limits, but actually belonged to another province (Chernigov Province). It was only in 1923 that it was included in Kyiv region. In 1927 the left-bank farms and villages were joined to our city. Previously the greater part of low-lying lands were under water during spring floods. The present Left Bank of Kyiv is a vast area of modern housing estates. Construction of such blocks was made possible after the level of the soil was raised by means of hydro-inwash. Hundreds of thousands of Kyivans live here.

ORIGIN OF HISTORIC NAMES OF HOUSING ESTATES

Many housing estates on the Left Bank inherited the old names of local villages:

Darnitsa - this toponym suggests that the land was once offered to somebody. But there are no established facts about it. Also the river Darnitsa runs here. The version stating that foreign ambassadors bearing gifts for the Kyiv princes stayed here is a fantasy.

Berezniaki, Osokorki - from the names of the plants.

Liski - from the neighboring little forest.

Kulikovo - from the name of birds that nested in the local

Panorama of Rusanovka district

bogs.

Bortnichi - from the local apiaries ("bort'" is a hollow tree where wild bees lived).

Raduzhny - from the old name of the lake called Radunka.

Vigurovshchina, Rusanovka, Pozniaki - from the names of ancient landowners.

Voskresenka, Nikol'skaya Slobodka, Troyeshchina - from the owners of the land: the Voskresenskaya Church in Podol, the Nikolsky Cloister in Pechersk and the Troitsky Hospital Cloister of the Kyiv Pechersk Lavra, respectively.

NOTABLE PLACES

The Nikol'skaya church in Nikol'skaya Slobodka district was built in 1880 on the territory of the present metro station "Levoberezhnaya." The poets Anna Akhmatova (Gorenko) and Nikolay Gumilev were married here in the parish church of the former village of the Ostersky district of Chernigov province in 1910. The church was demolished in 1961.

The monument to N.Gogol

The Sviato-Troitsky Cathedral in Vigurovschina-Troyeschina district (architect V.Grechina and others, 1997). It is a monumental construction. The design of this building follows the traditions of the Ukrainian baroque style.

A monument (sculptor V.Znoba, architects A.Malinovsky, Y.Moskal'tsov, 1968) is built on the site of the Darnitsa concentration camp, where in 1941-1943 the Nazis held Soviet prisoners of war in inhuman conditions.

The Rusanovka Canal appeared in 1960. Its bed was a bank for the hydro-inwash of the territory of the Rusanovka district. The line of floating fountains is the most spectacular sight of present Levoberezhie.

The monument to N.Gogol (sculptor A.Scoblikov, architects K.Sidorov, I.Ivanov, 1982). The monument is located on the Rusanovka waterfront. The bronze figure seems to be ascertaining how beautiful the Dnieper is in calm weather.

The Sviato-Troitsky cloister

HINTS FOR
THE TOURIST

HINTS FOR THE TOURIST

VISAS

Before entering Ukraine, you must obtain a visa at the Embassy, or Ukrainian Consulate abroad. Visas may be extended in Ukraine.

SOME CUSTOMS RULES

Information concerning goods and currencies passing through Ukrainian Customs must be inserted in your declaration form. You must indicate what and why you are importing and some other information on the request of the Customs officers.

One person can import into Ukraine:

- vodka - one litre
- wine - 2 litres
- tobacco goods - 200 cigarettes (or 200 grams of the goods)
- beer - 2 litres
- food - not exceeding 50 Euro (or equivalent) in value.

You will need a special permit to import or export:

- weapons of military type, specialized self-defence systems charged with the substances of tear-producing action - the permit of Ministry of Internal Affairs of Ukraine;
- animals - the veterinary certificate;
- medicine (not more than 5 packs of one type or the amount required by a patient for one course of medication according to a doctor's prescription) - the permit of Ministry of Health Care of Ukraine and so on.

If, during your stay in Ukraine, you purchase:

- original works of art, graphic or sculpture;
- works of applied art and traditional folk art;
- goods of museum significance;
- old books and so on, having artistic, historical, ethnographical and scientific value - State Service permit for the control over the transference of goods of cultural value through the Ukrainian State

Hello! Directory assistance?

Border.
State Service for the control over the transfer of goods of cultural value through the Ukrainian State Border at the Ministry of Culture of Ukraine
16, Lipskaya St., app 224
☎ 293-92-07

It is possible to export goods tax-free, providing their value in Ukrainian currency does not exceed the

At the reception desk

equivalent of 100.000 Euro, according to the exchange rate set by the National Bank of Ukraine on the date of filing the customs declaration.

WHERE TO GET INFORMATION

You can get the information you need at information desks, or from reference books and periodicals.
The telephone information service at 0-59 will give you all

How they strived against swinishness in Kyiv

Over one hundred years ago, when even the central streets of Kyiv were built up with low houses, many people kept pigs in their court yards. From time to time they released their animals from the narrow estates to the streets, which as it was, were none too clean. This was completely disastrous for Kyiv, and so the local authorities took radical measures. The police were empowered to confiscate the roaming pigs and take them to the police stations where they were to sell part of them in favour of the policemen. They started that business with enthusiasm, and soon neglected pigs disappeared from the Kyiv streets.

Historic anecdotes provided by M.Kal'nitski

answers to your questions in six languages or send information by fax free of charge. *The telephone of "Kyivgorspravka" is 0-61.* The telephone numbers of information services related to transportation, postal services and others can be found in their respective sections.

TIME

The clock in Ukraine is 2 hours ahead of Greenwich. From the end of March to October the summer time is in effect. *You can find out the time by calling 0-60.*

Alarm clock

ELECTRIC DEVICES

The voltage is 220 V, amplitude - 50 Hz. For devices made in Japan and the USA, an adapter would be required. European-standard sockets are usually used, but sometimes you can find a socket where the European plug would not fit in (in such a case a special adapter will come in handy).

LOST THINGS

"What fell from your cart is lost forever" is an old saying amongst Kyivans. It is quite difficult to find a lost thing in such a big city as Kyiv. But still, try to address the Lost and Found Office of the *Head Department of the Ministry of Internal Affairs at 229-78-44. If you loose something in the metro or forget something in the carriage, call 226-38-09. Information on things lost in trolleys and trams can be acquired at 291-04-06.* If the lost thing is insured, address

the militia immediately. The insurance company will demand an official letter of confirmation before refunding the value of the lost items.

YOUTH TOURISM

University students, postgraduates and students aged 12 and up, who have the international students ID ISIC, which is distributed in 90 countries of the world, can get discounts at some stores and pharmacies (5%), bars and restaurants (10-15%), night clubs and discos

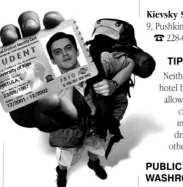

Traveling student

(10-50%), etc. The ISIC also authorizes 10% discounts for living quarters and transportation services.

In Ukraine the main distributor of ISIC is the tourist company "Kievskiy Sputnik". You can find detailed infor-

THE OFFICIAL HOLIDAYS

New Year - January 1
Christmas - January 7
International Women's Day - March 8
Easter - April 27
Labour Day - May 1-2
Victory Day - May 9
Pentecost - June 15
Constitution Day - June 28
Independence Day - August 24

Apart from the official holidays the Kyivans celebrate:

Old New Year - January 14
St.Valentine's Day - February 14
April Fool's Day - April 1
Kyiv Days - May 24-25
(the last weekend of May)
Youth Day - June 24

mation about discounts at sites www.sputnik.kiev.ua or www.isic.org

Kievsky Sputnik
9, Pushkinskaya St.
☎ 228-09-38, 228-89-01

TIPS

Neither restaurant bills nor hotel bills contain service allowances. Usually the clients give about 10% in tips to waiters, taxi-drivers, hairdressers and other service workers.

PUBLIC WASHROOMS

Public washrooms, paid as well as free, can be found in some underground passages (for example, in Maidan Nezalezhnosti, in Arsenalnaya Square, in L'va Tolstogo Square), in big shops, markets, stations. Paid public washrooms are cleaner and the fee is 40-50 kopeks.

SAFETY AND HEALTH

SAFETY

According to European standards Kyiv is quite safe. The criminal situation is stable, although as in any other big city, there are cases of theft and hooliganism. Crimes against foreigners are quite rare and usually consist of theft in public places, markets for example, overcrowded transport or mass festivities, when one's head is busy by looking around.

"Berkut" officer

So we recommend usual safety measures:

- always look after your luggage

- do not display precious belongings, do not carry your bag on your shoulder, but put it over your neck - in such a way it will not be torn out of your hands. Lately most hotels have installed safes for storing their client's precious belongings;

- do not store all your money in one place, take with you only the money you are planning to spent during the day. Hide your wallet in an inner pocket or in a "kangaroo-bag" to make the pickpocket's life harder;

- avoid dark unfamiliar streets at night, do not use private cars as cabs; in critical situations it's better to sacrifice your wallet, where we recommend you to put a symbolic sum of money;

- make several photocopies of your passport, driver's license, etc. Carry them on you and leave some at home. This will facilitate the renewal of those, if you loose them.

In case you still were absent-minded and as a result found out your wallet or some item of sentimental value was missing, immediately contact the militia by the number 02. Explain where you are and what happened. The operator will contact one of the mobile "Berkut" task force units,

Pharmacy sign

patrolling nearby. Chances are high, that the criminal will be apprehended "hot on the trail". There are four types of militia in Kyiv: patrol (responsible for order in the streets); state automobile inspection; mobile "Berkut" task force units and district officers. Any of them has the right to verify your ID (this does not have to be your passport, you can use your drivers license, work ID etc.) and in case you were judged suspicious, to invite you to follow him to the nearest militia station, where you can be detained "until the situation is cleared up".

If you have lost your passport, address the nearest militia station (you can find out the address in the "Yellow Pages" or use the 09 phone information service) and fill out a relevant statement. There you will be advised as to further action.

INSURANCE

To get free medical services, you have to get a policy of the State share insurance company of Ukraine for emergency medical assistance to foreign citizens. While the policy is valid, you can use the doctor's services as often as necessary. Of course, we hope you will never have to do this. Perhaps, your medical insurance company has an agreement with its Ukrainian counterpart on recognition of medical policies. Check it beforehand - in case it is so, the treatment will be paid by your company.

Ukraine has bilateral agreements with regards to free

Fireman   Doctor   Militiaman

emergency medical assistance with all the countries of the CIS, as well as with Bulgaria, Romania, Czech Republic, Great Britain and Mongolia. Certificates, which guarantee payment of emergency medical treatment in Ukraine, are sold in the countries of the EU by the company "AXA Colonia Krankerversiche-rung AG"; in Israel, Turkey and China - by "Mediton Invest LTD"; in Yugoslavia - "Mercur SV"; in Latvia - "Balva", Lithuania - "Sonoro-Guarantas"; Estonia - "Nordica".

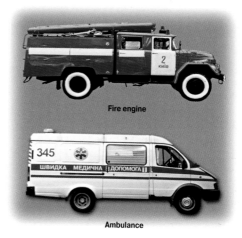

Fire engine

Ambulance

"UKRINMEDSTRAH"

You can also purchase an insurance policy in Ukraine. By buying a policy from "Ukrinmedstrah" company, you get access to help in the best hospitals, medical centres and clinics. If necessary, the company will arrange your transportation to the hospital by ambulance, airplane or helicopter. In the "Ukrinmedstrah" special dispatch centre work qualified doctors, who would diagnose the disease, organize and control medical assistance. When you contact the centre, please provide the following information:

- name and surname;
- series, number and date of expiration of the policy;
- complaints on the state of health;
- telephone number and location of the patient.

Depending on your state of health, the operator will send an emergency aid doctor, out to you.

PHARMACIES

You will easily find a pharmacy or a pharmacy kiosk in any district. Some chemist's shops are open after normal closing hours and on holidays. Kyiv pharmaceutists are highly qualified and will always advise you as to which medicine is best for you. *By dialling 0-67 you can find out which medications are available in any given pharmacy.* If you fall ill, *by dialling 0-83 you can call the "Health Service" for a free consultation.* In order to avoid spending money on medicine, be sure to bring those medicines you regularly use with you, especially if you suffer from a chronic diseases.

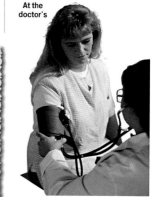

At the doctor's

I N   C A S E   O F   E M E R G E N C Y :

FIRE SERVICE	☎ 01
MILITIA	☎ 02
EMERGENCY	☎ 03
Rescue Service	☎ 295-24-47
"Ukrinmedstrah", 65, O.Gonchara St.	☎ 216-30-21
Chemist's shops, open after normal closing hours	
10, Artema St.	☎ 212-11-28
7, Besarabskaya Sq.	☎ 224-45-03
101, Krasnoarmeyskaya St.	☎ 269-11-75
Paid 24-hour medical assistance:	
"Boris"	☎ 213-03-03
"Medicom"	☎ 0-55, 234-03-03

POST AND TELEPHONE

Post office

POST

Around the city you can see yellow boxes with the blue emblem of "Ukrpost" - the company, which carries out postal services in Ukraine. District post offices are open from Monday to Friday from 9:00 to 19:00, on Saturdays - from 9:00 to 17:00. The central post office works with no days off from 8:00 to 21:00.

At any office you can:
- send a letter, telegram or book post;
- buy a postcard, fresh newspaper and lottery ticket;
- make a photocopy;
- buy a phone card for city phone or an Internet card;
- book international or intercity calls.

Post stamps are sold only at post offices or philatelist shops. The address of the sender and the receiver should be written according to European norms. In Kyiv your letter will arrive in 2 days, but it will take 7-10 days to get to Europe. It will cost you 30 kopeks to send a letter anywhere within Ukraine, 69 kopeks for the countries of the CIS, for the other countries - 3,49 UAH by air mail and 2,59 by ground transport. The Central and Levoberezhniy post offices are the best places for those who want to have all their mail-related questions answered immediately . There are usually no queues here, and inside the beautiful, vast and well-lit halls you will be able to concentrate on describing in a postcard, addressed to your beloved mother-in-law, what a good time you are having in far-away Kyiv. Post offices provide the following additional services:

n international urgent mail - up to 20 kg to 153 countries in the world (it is also possible from the post office #150);
n electronic mail (also available at post offices ##58, 150, 225);
n fax (also available at post offices ##21, 31, 53, 58, 150, 222).

TELEPHONE

In Kyiv 7-digit numbers are used, apart from emergency numbers, information services, etc.
The blue public telephones, which accept phone cards, can be found at metro stations, stores, hotels and on the street. Recently a new type of silver-coloured phones was introduced, they also accept coins. You can buy a phone card at the post office, in big stores, at stalls in the metro and at press kiosks.

Telephone, accepting cards

1. Insert the phone card this side away from you in the arrow's direction. Press the card until it stops.
2. Take off the receiver, wait for the dial tone. An inscription will appear on the tableau, indicating the quantity of time units left.
3. Dial your number and have your conversation.
4. Hang up the receiver and remove the card. If you forget to do so, you will be reminded by a special sound signal.
5. Emergency numbers 01, 02, 03, 04 are dialled without a card.

ADDRESSES AND TELEPHONE NUMBERS:

Central post office. 22, Kreshchatik St.	☎ 228-17-93
Levoberezhniy post office.	
16/4, Lunacharskogo St.	☎ 517-35-29
Information service of "Ukrpost"	☎ 0-65
Post offices	
#21 28/2, M.Grushevskogo St.	☎ 253-15-36
#31 1, Vokzal'naya Sq.	☎ 220-02-75
#53 59/65, Artema St.	☎ 211-30-91
#58 210, Borshchagovskaya St.	☎ 483-20-85
#150 102, Krasnoarmeyskaya St.	☎ 269-61-93
#222 45, Mayakovskogo Ave.	☎ 515-66-36
#225 15, Mayakovskogo Ave.	☎ 515-98-79

Postbox

10 kopeks

MONEY
CURRENCY EXCHANGE

You will have no problems exchanging money in Kyiv: a multitude of currency exchange booths is scattered throughout the capital. You can also find them in the airport, the railway station, hotels

Currency exchange tableau

and big shops. Working hours are 9:00 to 21:00. Russian rubles and American dollars, which are most popular in Kyiv, are accepted everywhere. But if you have guldens or tugriks - better go to a bank. And don't even think about trying to pay somewhere in foreign currency: from August 1995 by Decree of the President, all payments on the territory of Ukraine are to be effectuated in grivnas.
In places where there are high concentrations of tourists (airport, railway station, hotels) the exchange rate would be disadvantageous, as well as in some night clubs, expensive shops etc. But if you have to change money at night, better to do it there than to run down dark streets looking for an exchange booth which works at night.
Before you change your money, pay attention to the exchange rate displays. No commission is imposed for

1 grivnya
On the face is the picture of Vladimir the Great, on the back - Khersones Ruins

2 grivnyas
On the face is the picture of Yaroslav the Wise, on the back - St.Sofia Cathedral

50 kopeks

5 grivnyas
On the face is the picture of Bogdan Khmelnitsky, on the back - the church in Subbotovo village

25 kopeks

10 grivnyas
On the face is the picture of Ivan Mazepa, on the back - Kyiv-Pechersk Lavra

exchange. The cashier will give you a receipt, on which it will be indicated where, when and how much money you've changed.
We strongly advise you not to change money with accidental acquaintances or street money-changers: first - this is illegal; second - you are most likely to be cheated.

CREDIT CARDS

Many establishments, connected to tourism or recreation industries, accept credit cards for payment. The most common in Kyiv is "VISA". But when you go to a new place, it is better to find out, what means of payment are available for different services. You can

BANKS (CENTRAL OFFICES):

AVAL. 9, Leskova St.   ☎ 296-92-87
Pravex-bank. 9/2, Klovskiy Spusk   ☎ 573-92-78, 261-02-78
Privatbank. 12, Gogolevskaya St.   ☎ 216-87-76, 216-80-87
Prominvestbank. 7, Yaroslavov Val St.   ☎ 228-40-69
Nadra. 4, B.Khmel'nitskogo St.   ☎ 462-00-01, 462-00-05

20 grivnyas
On the face is the picture of Ivan Franko, on the back - Lviv Opera Theater

1 kopek

5 kopeks

2 kopeks

50 grivnyas
On the face is the picture of Mikhail Grushevsky, on the back - the building of the Verkhovnaya Rada of Ukraine

100 grivnyas
On the face is the picture of Taras Shevchenko, on the back - the National Reserve St.Sofia of Kyiv

200 grivnyas
On the face is the picture of Lesia Ukrainka, on the back - the gate tower to Lutsk Castle

- the notes are printed on special paper with water marks, seen against the light (portraits are situated in special places);

- inside every note there is a special protective metal strip; the portraits, inscriptions and separate decorative elements are done in relief printing, stand out and can be felt by fingers;

- the code drawing changes, if you hold the note at different angles;

- the merging drawing is placed in one and the same position on the face and on the back, when viewed against the light, they should correspond.

Cash dispenser

often see cash dispensers in the streets, which work in different languages.

TRAVELLER'S CHECKS

Traveller's checks can be converted to cash in some banks and at hotels which mostly cater to foreign tourists.

GRIVNYAS

The grivnya is the monetary unit of Ukraine. It is marked by the letters UAH, which are usually written on price-tags after the price. One grivnya consists of 100 kopeks.
The grivnya can never hope to get as much fakes as the

American dollar, but it is still faked, as any other currency. The Geneva Convention on the fight against faked money classifies such a crime as extraordinary. The most effective way to protect oneself from a fake is to use a special detector. In case you have no device of the sort, use the following advise:

- notes of 1, 2, 5, 10, 20, 50, 100 and 200 UAH are now current, each of them bears a relevant portrait of an outstanding figure of Ukrainian history and literature on the face, and historical monuments on the back;

There are many simple ways of protection, and even those listed will help you not to get into trouble.

COINS

In Ukraine there are coins of 1, 2, 5, 10, 25 and 50 kopeks.

TO KYIV BY CAR

"No nail, no bar" is a popular Kyiv auto wish. It means safety for the car and no problems for the driver. Knowing the traffic rules in Ukraine will save you the problems that may appear during the trip.

WHAT TO TAKE WITH YOU

According to Ukraine law, a driver should carry a registration document, a customs declaration for the car, and his driver's license. He must be able to produce these documents at the request of a State Automobile Inspection Official. In case the car is rented you must have a document verifying your right to keep and use the car.

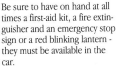

The badge of a parking ward

Be sure to have on hand at all times a first-aid kit, a fire extinguisher and an emergency stop sign or a red blinking lantern - they must be available in the car.

FUEL

Filling stations where you can feed your iron horse with petrol are everywhere. Most of them work around the clock. Gas filling stations are rare. Payments are made in cash by the litre. Credit cards are not usually acceptable.

The sign "Highway"

SOME RULES

The maximum speed for cars on Ukrainian roads is as follows:

- 60 km/h in populated areas;
- 80 km/h on the roads for cars;
- 130 km/h on the motorways (for example: the road to Borispol Airport).

Buckle up! Fastening seat-belts is mandatory for the driver and all passengers.

If your child is under 12 or his height is under 145 cm and the car has no special child seat, you'd better arrange the child on the back seat.

In Ukraine the presence of alcohol in the driver's blood is prohibited, so avoid consuming even low alcohol content beverages if you plan to drive a car shortly.

Breathalyzer tests are often conducted by traffic inspectors and transgressors are dealt with severely.

Kyiv's car owners have recently begun to pay for parking in many convenient places where earlier they were able to park free of charge. It appears, however, that such fees had a place in the history of Kyiv long before the days of the automobile.

In 1805, Kyiv governor Pyotr Pankratyev ordered the City Magistrate to collect "poberezhnoye" for the mooring of boats to the Dnieper banks from Obolon to the mouth of the Lybed. This hardly delighted the owners of the riverboats. But that measure had a specific aim: the collection of funds to strengthen the coastline and protect if from landslides.

State Automobile Inspection officials

PARKING

The rules of parking are more lenient than European ones. If you stop on a road section

The sign "Paid parking"

with a sign "Paid parking" the officer will record the length of your stay and when you are ready to leave will inform you of the amount you need to pay. In the downtown sector the cost of parking is about 1UAH/h. You can stay however long you wish; there is no time limitation. And at night the parking officers sleep peacefully, to the pleasure of the car drivers.

A ROAD ACCIDENT

If you are involved in an accident you will *need to call the State Automobile Inspection. You can reach them by dialling 02.* Never walk off the scene of an accident - this is a serious violation. Do not allow the other party to talk you into making a private settlement, as you can become the victim of swindle. If your car is insured, all the more reason to wait for the State Automobile Inspection officials to arrive, as your insurance company will require information of the traffic militia about the accident. According to Ukrainian laws the materials of traffic rule violations are put before court. Imposing a fine on the spot is abolished. Foreigners are as responsible to abide by the law as anyone else. If you violated the traffic rules the traffic militia officer makes out a report and passes it to a court of the district where the accident happened. You may appeal to the court against the official if you believe his actions incompetent.

A pedestrian crossing

"Student Driver" sign

ADVICE OF AN EXPERIENCED DRIVER

To protect your car from break-in or theft, we advise to install an alarm system and a mechanical antitheft device. Do not leave your car unattended. Do not leave any valuable things in the car; they attract thieves. Use fenced and guarded parking.

The drivers of transit vehicles would do well to stop for the night near a State Automobile Inspection post (Control Points). Apart from the official traffic rules there are traditional ones; you cannot find them in any book, though you should know them. A popular driver's

State Automobile Inspection Vehicle

rule "LFG" ("Let a fool go") means: however well you follow the rules, if someone outruns you or cuts your way in turning it is expensive to compete with him - let him go. A " Student Driver" sticker on the car window serves as a warning to keep off the car on the road: its owner first should learn to rule the car, not to sit in it. When oncoming cars signal with their lights, it may mean that you forgot to switch off your high beams, or warning of a dangerous section of the road, or most often of a State Automobile Inspection post with a speed control.

In the morning and the evening it is easy to get in a traffic jam in Kyiv. You can hear reports on traffic conditions broadcast from "Gala Radio" (100,0 FM) at 20 and 40 minutes of each hour. This will help you plan your route around the traffic jam.

A filling station

CAR RENTAL AGENCIES

Domino	☎ 235-62-69
Eurocar	☎ 238-26-91
Hertz Rent a Car	☎ 531-99-99

EVACUATION OF DAMAGED CARS

☎ 296-40-36
☎ 255-16-16
☎ 414-70-40

TRAVELING BY AIR

The most quickest, most convenient and romantic means of travel is air transport. There are two airports that serve the capital of Ukraine: "Boryspol" and "Kyiv" (Zhuliany).

"Boryspol" airport

BORYSPOL AIRPORT.
AIRLINES
FLIGHTS AND PRICES

"Boryspol" international airport is situated 40km away from downtown. It receives flights from throughout the world. Here work representative offices of a multitude of airlines. Among the lead-

Awaiting a flight

ing Ukrainian companies one can name "Ukrainian international airlines" which provides air communication with Western Europe,

and "Aerosvit" which specializes in flights in Europe and CIS. During the vacation season and on big holidays, Christmas, for example, the airport may be overloaded, so we advise you to book tickets well in advance. The most popular flights are to Moscow (Russia), Tel-Aviv (Israel), Antalia (Turkey).

There is a discount system for the handicapped, childrens' tickets, and discounts for those buying two way tickets and for tour groups. You can get information on prices and book tickets directly at the airlines or at tourist agencies.

SERVICES AND
PRICES

Lately the airport was renovated, its handling capacity has increased; faster services for passengers have been organized. Handy luggage carts are free of

charge. In the airport there is a post office, a medical emergency station and an interpreter's service firm. Friendly workers at the information desk will give you advise on any questions you may have.

In front of the desk there is a direct telephone to the "Boryspol" hotel, where you can visit the restaurant or kill some time in a cosy room in front of a TV set, if, for example, your flight is late. The hotel is near the airport: book a room and a special shuttle bus will drive you and your luggage to the hotel entrance free of charge.

In the airport there is a currency exchange booth, where they will change your money at a very low (unprofitable) exchange rate compared to Kyiv. So do it only if you absolutely can't wait to have a closer look at the Ukrainian hryvnia.

THE PLAN OF "BORYSPOL" AIRPORT

1. Entrance/exit
2. Information desk
3. Waiting hall
4. Information on arrival and departure
5. Customs (arrival)
6. Baggage hand out
7. Passport control (arrival)
8. Consular visa service
9. Passenger check-in
10. Customs (departure)
11. Post
12. Telephones
13. Moving staircase
14. Passport control (departure)
15. Security control
16. Boarding gates

You can have a snack in a cafe on the ground floor. The prices here are listed for 100 grams, so it is difficult to find out how much you'll finally have to pay, in case you are not an avid diet-lover and are used to weighing your food. Beer costs three times more than in Kyiv and the meals are also far from cheap. A small

Flights schedule

ing logic of prices: 1 hour - 20 UAH ($4, which is double the price of any Internet cafe in downtown Kyiv), half an hour - 15 UAH, a quarter of hour - 10 UAH.

Near the cafe there is a shop, where one can buy many guidebooks of different cities of the world, magazines and souvenirs - at double prices. So don't rush to spend your money - you can do it in Kyiv. On the first floor are situated a duty-free shop and a pub.

Information desk

GETTING TO 'BORISPOL'

The drive to "Boryspol" by taxi will cost you 65-75 UAH ($12-15). Drivers, awaiting clients at the airport, will charge you some more for the road to Kyiv - around 100 UAH

hotel. The "Poliot" shuttle bus goes to Pobedy Square through Leningradskaya Square. The trip takes about an hour. It is important to remember that the interval between bus departures is also approximately an hour long, so if you go to the airport, it is better to arrive at the bus terminal well in advance. Buses do not run from midnight to 4 a.m. The cost of a bus-ride is 8-10 UAH ($2).

"KYIV" (Zhuliany)

The airport "Kyiv" (Zhuliany) is within the city limits. It mostly handles domestic flights within the borders of the country. You can get there in 40 minutes by taking trolleybus #9 from St.Vladimir's Cathedral or Pobedy Square.

TELEPHONE NUMBERS:

Information desk in "Boryspol" airport	☎ 296-72-43
Search for luggage	☎ 296-74-98
Hotel "Boryspol"	☎ 296-71-05
Information service of the tickets desk	☎ 0-56
AIRLINES	
"Ukrainian International Airlines"	☎ 461-50-50
"Aerosweet"	☎ 220-52-67
"Center of Business Aviation"	☎ 247-17-90
"Kyiv" (Zhuliany) Airport	☎ 242-23-08

cup of coffee cost round $1, tea - $0.5.
An Internet cafe is hidden away in the corner, with an astound-

($18-20). So it is much more profitable to get to Kyiv by bus and then take a taxi, which will drive you to the

TO KYIV BY TRAIN

ROAD TO RAILWAY STATIONS

It is very easy to get to railway stations. The exit from the subway station "Vokzal'naya" will lead you to Privokzal'naya Square: to the Suburban and Central railway stations. To get to the Southern station, use the moving staircase to get to the 1st floor of the Central Station building and walk straight to the end of the gallery.

SERVICES

The information boards at the stations announce the time of arrival and departure of trains, the route, the platform and train numbers. At each platform there is also a tableau displaying information about the

Privokzal'naya Square. Central railroad station

train, which shortly arrives at this line. An announcer informs you about the arrival and departure of trains in Ukrainian, Russian and English. If you have arrived beforehand, better leave your luggage in the cloakroom. Do not be scared by announcements about change of shifts or lunch breaks: you will get your things when you come for them. At your services are a post office, public telephones, the Internet, snack bar, cafe and restaurant and several waiting rooms. In the small shops selling press and sou-

venirs you can buy a fresh newspaper, a detective story or some trifles.

Southern Station

ADDRESSES AND TELEPHONE NUMBERS

Central railway station
1, Privokzal'naya Sq.

Information service
of the Central Station
(arrival and departure of trains) ☎ 0-05

Booking railway tickets
with delivery
(6-45 days beforehand)
☎ 0-50

Railway ticket offices
38/40, T.Shevchenko Blvd.

We wish we had their problems…

About 100 years ago at the South-western railroad there were a lot of conflicts at ticket pay desks. As it is known, in Russia they used gold coins for payment. Apart from banknotes were current golden fivers and tenners ("half-imperials" and "imperials"), one gold ruble according to the official exchange rate equalled 1,5 in banknotes. Railroad cashiers refused to have "double book-keeping" and refused to accept gold from the passengers. This aroused indignation, so the head of the South-western railroad ordered them to accept the golden money at the official exchange rate, and also to pay the railroad workers part of their salary in the same coins.

If you need to change money, remember that the exchange rate here is calculated for those people, who are waiting their train and have no other option. In the Southern Station building a small hotel with very reasonable prices awaits travellers. To check-in you will need your passport and train ticket, confirming that of all means of transportation you would prefer a train to a submarine. Children up to 10 get a 50% discount. Vigilant porters will offer you their services if they see you carrying heavy bags.

There is a taxi stop in front of the train station. Prices, named by cabbies are aimed at those who are new to the city, and have nothing in common with the real tariffs.

Information tableau

TICKETS

To buy a ticket you will need your passport. Travelling by train is much cheaper than by air, so railroad tickets are in high demand. In summer, during the vacation season season, it is sometimes practically impossible to buy them. You can buy a ticket 45 days before the departure date. Tickets are available not only at the sta-

Awaiting the train

tions. *The advance ticket sale desks are located at 38/40, T.Shevchenko Blvd. You can book tickets by calling #0-50,* you will be charged a small fee to cover delivery costs.

The hall on the 1st floor of the Southern Station

TO KYIV BY BUS

The main bus station in Kyiv is the Central Coach Terminal at Moskovskaya Square. You can reach it in one stop going by trolley or shuttle-bus from "Lybedskaya" metro station. It is from here that buses depart for international voyages. Intercity bus transportation services are provided not only from the Central terminal, but also from "Darnitsa", "Dachnaya", "Podol", "Polesye" and "Yuzhnaya" terminals.

Central Coach Terminal

CENTRAL COACH TERMINAL

2/1, Nauki Ave.
Information service ☎ 265-04-30
Advance sale of tickets ☎ 265-02-54

COACH TERMINALS

"Darnitsa". 1, Gagarina Ave. ☎ 559-46-18
"Dachnaya". 142, Pobedy Ave. ☎ 444-14-03
"Podol". 15-a, Nizhniy Val St. ☎ 417-32-15
"Polesye". Shevchenko Sq. ☎ 430-35-54
"Yuzhnaya". 3, Glushkova Ave. ☎ 263-40-04

CITY TRANSPORT

THE CAPITAL METRO

The Kyiv Metro consists of the three lines: "Svyatoshino-Brovarskaya", "Kurenyovsko-Krasnoarmeyskaya" and "Syretsko-Pecherskaya", which join the housing areas on the right and left banks of the Dnieper to the city center. You can get from the final stations to the centre in 10 - 15 minutes. The Capital Metro is one of the most beautiful in Europe. Each of the metro stations has its own special features. The metro is mostly run underground and only partially overland (from "Lesnaya" to "Dnepr" stations in "Svyatoshino-Brovarskaya" line). From the windows of the carriages you can see Kiyv - Pechersk Lavra, picturesque green hills above the Dnieper and the modern housing areas on the left bank…

WORKING HOURS

The Metro is the quickest and most reliable and fast means of travelling around the city. It functions from 5:30 until 24:00. Approximate interval between trains: during rush hour (8:00 - 9:30 and 17:00 - 18:30) - 1-2 min-

It is easy to find a metro station - there is a big letter "M" above the entrance.

utes, in the day time - 5 minutes, but after 22:00 you may wait for a train on a platform for 15 - 20 minutes. You should take this into account when you plan to go by the last train (especially with changing lines), otherwise the doors of a carriage will shut in front of your face.

THE FARE

There is a single tariff for a metro trip - 50 kopeks. You must pay every time you pass through a turnstile, irrespective of how many stations you want to go and how many lines you want to change. From a cash-desk or a

A token machine

token machine (they are at the entrance of each station) a passenger buys a token and he can go around as long as he pleases, seeing the underground sights and studying the Ukrainian character, which is most obvious during rush-hour. For example, it is customary to give up ones seat for disabled and elderly people and for people with small children. If they don't give up their seat to a woman, then they will often offer to help her with a heavy bag. Don't be surprised when you are expected to follow these rules.

If you use the metro daily, we advise you to buy a monthly pass, it will save you the need to queue for tokens. Pay attention to the fact that the plastic monthly pass card has a magnetic strip and, in order not to spoil it, don't place it near metal or magnet things, for example keys or a player. After the 15th of each month, you can buy the monthly pass tickets for half price. If you have bulky luggage with you, you should buy an

A metro station. "Dorogozhichi"

additional ticket. There are a number of items prohibited to be taken on the Metro. Mainly, these consist of things either inconvenient or dangerous to other passengers.

THE RULES OF CONDUCT

In the carriages and vestibules you can learn the rules of conduct in the Metro. Apart from that each station has a scheme-board of the lines that enables you to get orientated. Even if you get lost, don't despair; address the assistant station-master, a militia officer in the station or just a passenger, and you will without fail be given the right directions.

Various shops and stands can be found in the vestibules and passages of the Metro, where you can buy a newspaper, a bunch of flowers, a greeting card, or

exchange the battery in your wrist-watch. We do not advise you to buy something from spontaneous salespeople. Although the Metro is the safest form of transportation as far as crime is concerned, unfortunately petty larcenies do

occur. So keep an eye on your things, put the wallet in the inside pocket, and think of your bag in the throng.

The metro counter is valid for one trip and unlimited number of line changes.

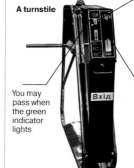

A turnstile

You may pass when the green indicator lights

Insert the card in the vertical slot of the turnstile with the magnet line on the right. Move the card down with a regular speed.

A month-ticket

THE SCHEME OF THE KYIV METRO

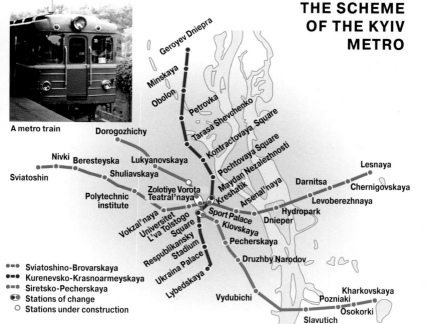

A metro train

Geroyev Dniepra
Minskaya
Obolon
Petrovka
Tarasa Shevchenko
Dorogozhichy
Kontractovaya Square
Pochtovaya Square
Nivki Beresteyska Lukyanovskaya
Sviatoshin Shuliavskaya
Maydan Nezalezhnosti
Lesnaya
Darnitsa Chernigovskaya
Zolotiye Vorota
Polytechnic Teatral'naya Kreshatik Arsenal'naya
institute Levoberezhnaya
Vokzal'naya Universitet Sport Palace Dnieper Hydropark
L'va Tolstogo Klovskaya
Square Pecherskaya
Respublikansky Stadium
Ukraina Palace Druzhby Narodov
Lybedskaya
Vydubichi Pozniaki Kharkovskaya
Osokorki
Slavutich

●■● Sviatoshino-Brovarskaya
●■● Kurenevsko-Krasnoarmeyskaya
●■● Siretsko-Pecherskaya
●● Stations of change
○ Stations under construction

181

CITY TRANSPORT

Buses, trolleybuses and tramways are more convenient than the metro for short distance travels. But the shortcoming of overland transport is that during rush-hour there is a high possibility of getting caught in a traffic jam. And in the summer, the stuffy air and cramped quarters are not conducive to producing pleasant feelings.

The passenger fare in urban transport is 50 kopeks. For children under 7 years the trip is free. Passengers can buy one-time tickets in kiosks at the stops. Or during the trip the conductor and sometimes the driver sell the tickets. This is even more convenient for the passengers. There are also tickets for a month, 15 days, 10 days, 7 days, 1 day. Even if you go only one station you should punch the ticket and keep it up to the end of your journey. The hefty young man standing nearby, can turn out to be a severe controller. And if you did not pay for your ticket in time, it could result in a 10 grivnya fine and a spoiled mood. The driver of overland transport does not

Shuttle-bus

Number of the route

Main stops on the way

524 (T-21) Маршрутне таксі
Контрактова площа
міст Патона, Ⓜ "Чернігівська"
ринок "Лісовий" (вул. Юності)
вул. Микитенка
вартість проїзду - 1 грн.

Tablet of shuttle bus

Passenger fare

always announce the names of the stops, so if you do not know the way, ask the conductor or passengers.

TAXIS

The sum to pay

The counter in taxi

The metropolitan taxis - these are cars of different models, different classes, of different firms. One can recognize them by the orange sign on the roof.

RADIO-TAXI

In Kyiv there are many firms of radio-

Metropolitan taxi

equipped taxis that work around the clock. One can order the car by phone and sometimes ask the price of the journey. We advise you to discuss your wishes with the dispatcher. Ask if there is an additional cost for luggage (this service is usually free), and if smoking is allowed in the car, if there is music... The drivers of some firms can help you with your baggage or accompany the client if the stairwell is dark, for example. Of course the taxi driver who renders you additional services has a right to expect a lavish tip that exceeds traditional 10 %.

FUNICULAR

In a few minutes it gets you from Pochtovaya Square (lower station) to Mikhaylovskaya Square (upper station). Working hours: from 6.30 to 23.00.

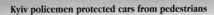

Kyiv policemen protected cars from pedestrians

Yes, just so: not the pedestrians from cars, but cars from pedestrians. In 1897-1907 (the first decade when the automobile transport was exploited in Kyiv) city policeman time and again received complaints about ill-mannered conduct towards the "self-moving carriage". After dark unknown persons threw stones at passing cars. The cabmen also behaved likewise because the horses were frightened of the noisy cars. So the policemen were ordered to protect the safety of the drivers, to catch the hooligans and take them to police stations.

The sign of Kyiv taxi

SHUTTLE BUSES

In Kyiv there are many microbuses which double and supplement the bus routes. These are shuttle buses. They are more reliable; running more often than the "big" transport and stopping any-where, at the request of the passengers, in addition to the regular stops. Try to hitch a lift and the driver will always stop near you if there are no inter-dictory traffic signs and there is a vacant seat in the bus. Waiting for the minivan on the terminal station, passengers form the queue.

The fare is 75 kopeks or 1 grivnya (sometimes on short routes - 50 kopeks). The pas-sengers should pay as they enter the van. Children under 7 years go for free but on the condition that they sit on their parents' knees and do not take up a separate place.

SERVICES AND PRICES

Not all cars are equipped with coun-ters. The price of the journey is paid by the number of kilometres (1kilo-metre - approximate-ly $0.18). But it is more convenient to discuss the price in advance. The Kyiv taxi service is relative-ly cheap in comparison with Europe prices. But one should take into consideration the dif-ferences in the work of firm: some want to be paid for giving of the car ordered by phone, for journeys and baggage; others - only for dis-tance. And others are paid according to fixed tariffs, counting the price based on the dis-tance. But practically all drivers will take into account if you are late by more than 5-10 minutes or if the driver needs to wait for you near the shop, for exam-ple. If you plan a lengthy trip around the city with sever-al stops, then you should hire a taxi by the hour, which accepts an hourly payment paying for the driver, rather than paying by the kilometre as well as waiting time. The most expensive starting-points are the airport and railway station. The drivers waiting for clients near the night-club, casinos, and luxurious hotels, often fix the price as they wish... We advise you not to deal with them, but to order a car by phone. This will save you a lot of money. For the journey to the Boryspol airport many firms have fixed prices: from the cen-tre of the city the price is $12-15. For the journey out of the city the driver will ask double price. New Year's Eve fares are also double price. The pay-ment is made only in cash. Not every driver will give you the ticket, so specify in advance if you need it. Many firms offer the service known as "autopilot" or "driver". If you arrived at the party in your own car and did not abstain from alcoholic bever-ages, then a driver can take you home in your car. It will cost $10 on average.

TAXI FIRMS:

AutoSvit	☎ 234-44-44
Elite-taxi	☎ 238-82-38
Radio-taxi	☎ 240-10-36
Taxi-blues	☎ 296-42-43
Taxies	☎ 295-95-08
Ukrprominvest	☎ 574-05-74
Express-taxi	☎ 239-15-15
Central dispatcher station	☎ 0-58

The sign of the bus stop

Поліклініка

A tick-et for the journey in over-land transport. It is meant for one journey and not valuable without punch.

ECONOMY AND SECURITY

In Kyiv hitch hiking is an accepted practice. And not only taxi drivers can slow down near you but also a driver who wants earn a little money. Getting a ride with a private driver will of course be cheap-er. But do not forget about security, especially at night. We do not recommend women to resort to the services of private drivers.

Trolleybus

183

DRINKS

The variety of alcoholic beverages in Kyiv is very wide; many recipes have been known by the Ukrainian people from ancient times. The Kyiv prince Vladimir said in the 10th century: "In Rus we like to drink for joy, and cannot live without it". Vodka, cognac, wine, juice - all of them are an integral part of every festive meal. From ancient times also came ethic norms, regulating the use of alcohol. Strong drinks were prohibited during fasts, important agricultural works etc.; the Zaporizhzhya Cossacks punished by death those who drank on war campaigns. The striving for diversification of tastes led to the creation of a multitude of new collections of wines and brands of strong drinks. It is common knowledge, that natural wines are good for health. Kyivans respect this medical prescription. Home-made wines from grapes, berries and fruit will always be the host's object of pride.

The bitter liqueur «Українська медова з перцем» ("Ukrains'ka medova z pertsem") from **«Nemmiroff»** - is exquisite and contradictory-natured vodka with an original and well-remembered taste. The bitter and pleasantly burning entry is succeeded by the taste of honey and finalized by the fragrant aroma of wild herbs. This vodka reflects all the beauty, versatility and unexpectedness of our life - from bitterness of separation to joy of new encounters…

Practically no festivity takes place without the legendary gorilka (vodka) and strong liqueur (bitter and sweet, which apart from original taste and aroma have tonic and even healing values). It is better to taste vodka in good company and with a lot of food.

It is difficult to imagine any solemn or romantic event without champagne: the first toast at birthdays, weddings, celebrations of New Year are always marked by a specific "salute" - the pop of the cork and sparkling drops.

Kyivans prefer **"Obolon'"** beer, which has a harmonious taste with characteristic hop bitterness and a pleasant aroma. Beer is served in bottles or tumblers. Traditional hors d'oeuvres are boiled crayfish, salted or stewed fish, dry bread and salted peanuts.

The fine wines **"Zolotiy Vil"** would impress the most refined connoisseur.

A glass of cognac will put a final touch to a successful business meeting…

The aroma of coffee will inspire you for new excursions.

Kyivans drink tea with lemon, cream, berries and herbs. **"Carpathian Tea"** (with St.-John's wort, camomile, mint, blackberries and others) is not only tasty, but also healthy.

Strolling in the city during the hot season, it is impossible not to stop at a stand selling refreshing drinks or to walk into a cafe to refresh oneself with a glass of juice or mineral water. Adults and kids just love **"Sandora"** juice.

Every nation has its own drinking traditions.
So when you are at a hospitable Kyivan table, remember the following:

■ On holidays Kyivans like to drink.

■ Some of them like to drink very much.

■ The feast usually begins with champagne, regardless of the food available. After the first solemn drink everybody shifts to what he likes, be it vodka, cognac, wine or mineral water (for those "unlucky", who have to drive back home).

■ At table the drinks are usually served by one and the same person (at home it will usually be the host). It is not accepted "to change the pouring hand".

■ Kyivans are very hospitable, and this is not only true for bread and salt. Do not accept any more drinks some more, if you think you've had enough. They may insist a lot, but if you give in to them, you risk getting drunk.

■ Do not be surprised, if you will be asked for a toast. A well-prepared greeting speech will help you to stand the eloquence exam with honour.

■ The most laconic Ukrainian toast: "Bud'mo!" This word means wishes of health, happiness, and everything one may wish.

NATIONAL CUISINE

Ukrainian national cookery numbers hundreds of recipes. Some dishes have a multi-century "seniority", as for example, the famous Ukrainian borshch - the forefather of many local soups. Today there are up to 30 ways of preparing borshch.

Diverse meat dishes occupy an honourable place in the Ukrainian menu. Pork is most commonly used, then - veal and chicken, usually fried and stewed. Such dishes as home stew, stuffed chicken, cold boiled pork stuffed with lard and garlic, home sausage, Ukrainian meat balls and pork, stewed with lard and cabbage. Meat, prepared in special clay bowls has a unique taste.

Among the favourite fish dishes of the Ukrainians one can name crucians baked in cream; pike stewed with horse-radish; pike perch stewed with mushrooms and crayfish…

It is impossible to stay in Kyiv and not to taste the legendary, praised in folk vareniks and halushkas.

Very popular are fried eggs with lard. Lard is one of the most popular Ukrainian dishes. It is eaten baked, fresh, salted, stewed, it is used to stuff meat to make it juicier.

Porridges from different cereals are eaten with milk, cream, sunflower oil or overfried onions and shkvarkas (small pieces of lard, fried to gold).

Ukrainian cuisine also provides a wide range of dishes, which would overjoy the fussiest gourmand. To prepare confectionery they use fruit, honey, poppy-seed, nuts etc.

Cossack meat dish from cold boiled pork, home sausage, head-cheese, meat loaf, balyk, bacon, fresh vegetables and Crimean onion.

Vareniks with potatoes, shkvarkas and onion - traditional Ukrainian dish.

Chicken loaf, stuffed with omelet and chicken liver.

Dishes of Ukrainian cuisine are represented by the restaurant "Cossack Mamay"

Stuffed tomatoes

Stuffed sweet pepper with tomato sauce.

Vinnitsa style paste from liver with fresh vegetables.

Fried home sausage with deep-fried onion.

Ukrainian borshch at chererinka style with pampushkas and garlic sauce.

Fried pork feet with potato salad.

Boiled sturgeon with lemon and vegetables.

Stuffed cabbage with veg-etable sauce.

Fried mushrooms with onion wrapped into pancakes.

Kyiv cutlets with potato cro-quettes, peas and vegetables.

Poppy cake with ice-cream

Ukrainian bread - symbol of hospitality

HOTELS AND ACCOMODATION

When planning a tour, every prudent tourist will make careful arrangements about where to rest after a day full of impressions. There are about 50 hotels to choose from in Kyiv which can satisfy any requirements concerning service, and provide comfort and safety.

CHOOSING A HOTEL

The Kyiv city administration puts much effort into the development of its hotel system. Among them are small, cosily homey ones as well as fashionable European-style hotels, and the old hotels of the "Soviet" type, which still only dream of the stars on their signs, and private apartments where very high quality service can sometimes be found. You can find Kyiv hotels information on the Internet at the site: **www.all-hotels.com.ua**

RESERVING A ROOM

In the summer, when the tourist season opens, as well as in the spring and the fall, when numerous exhibitions and conferences are held, it is quite difficult to get a room in a good class hotel (taking into account service quality, convenient location, service etc.). So we advise you to book a room. You can do this personally, by calling the hotel directly or by asking one of the travel agencies, which will provide you with an adequate lodging, taking into consideration all your requirements.

Impressa Hotel

CONVENIENCES

Hotel service is developing rapidly, doing its utmost to emulate the best world patterns. Some establishments have already been transformed into fine hotel complexes. *Dnieper Hotel* offers clients comfortable rooms with all possible conveniences: from air-conditioning to mini-bars. To the client's pleasure there is a conference-hall, a wellness centre, a beauty shop, a dry-cleaners etc. Room-service is round the clock. There is a restaurant, bars and casino in the hotel. *Kyivskiy President Hotel* invites you to visit a fitness-centre, a sauna, a swimming pool and a trainer hall.

Hall of the Hotel complex "President Hotel "Kyivskyi"

"Human zoo"

These days homeless people, either resting or sleeping, can be found even in the most unlikely places. But what members of the "bottom" of Kyiv's society thought up in July of 1899, is original even by today's standards. The police decided to investigate the state of the market at Troitskaya Square (now the square in front of the Olympic Stadium) at night. Amongst the shops and lockers, a travelling zoo, performing in Kyiv, was accommodated. Looking into the cages with predators, the policemen saw the forms of sleeping people in the spaces between the cages. They had to disturb the extemporaneous doss-house. When the policemen saw the awakened fellows in the light, they had good reason to congratulate one another. The fellows appeared to be a gang of professional thieves, which had been on the wanted list for a long time. They had bribed the zookeeper and in this very original way secured a shelter for themselves.

For businessmen, there is a business-centre and a congress-hall. For gambling fans there is a casino and for those who prefer more rowdy company, we recommend you visit a night-club.

The Impressa is one of the best private hotels. There are only 17 apartments there, but each has own its unique design.

A chambermaid

At the *Domus Hotel* you will find perfect conditions to working and resting. You will really feel at home there.

Premier Palace, a hotel in the city centre, is the first in Ukraine to earn the fifth star.

REDUCTIONS AND TIPS

An average cost of a double room is $70 - 150 a day. In many hotels discounts are available for permanent customers. Tips are not included, but if you are satisfied with service leave the chambermaid 5 -10 UAH.

HOTEL SERVICE

Private apartments are a good alternative to the hotels. You can usually find a decently decorated apartment with all the conveniences. The accommodation agencies render a lot of accompanying services: from meeting at the airport to providing the client with an interpreter. Due to the lower prices compared with the hotels (a double room is $40 - 80), such service is in popular demand. So you should reserve your accommodation beforehand and lay a good foundation for your vacation in Kyiv.

In the Premier Palace Hotel

These conventional signs will help you make the right decision when choosing your accommodations, taking into account the great variety of services offered by Kyiv hotels.

Personal safes
Laundry
Hairdressing salon
Car park
Around-the-clock service
Air-conditioner in the room
Gym
Sauna
Conveniences for businessmen
Conference hall
Cable TV
Restaurant
Conveniences for children
Payment by credit card
Services for disabled people
Currency exchange

PREDSLAVA
100 Gorkogo vul., #30 ☎ 268-6283
Ⓜ Palace Ukraine
www.predslava.com.ua
e-mail: predslava@nbi.com.ua

Cozy furnished apartments in the center of Kyiv by the day with a wide range of hotel services are offered to the convenience of clients. Services include cable TV and full-time security

Dnieper
1/2, Krestchatik St. ☎ 291-84-50
www.dnipro.kiev.ua Ⓜ Krestchatik

The hotel is located on Evropeyskaya Ploschad in front of Ukrainsky Dom and the National Philharmonic - in the centre of the business, political and cultural life of the capital. In the evenings there is live music in the restaurant. And those who want dancing can visit the disco-bar.

«SHERBORNE GUEST HOUSE»
4 Staronavodnytska Str., office 43
☎ 295-8832, 490-9693 Ⓜ Pecherskaya
www.sherbornehotel.com.ua
e-mail: reservation@sherbornehotel.com.ua

Sherborne Guest House is a privately-owned hotel offering furnished luxury class apartments in the centre of Kyiv. A combination of first class service and reasonable prices (40 % lower than in the state-run hotels) will guarantee an excellent stay in Kyiv. Sherborne Guest House is located in Pechersk, one of the historic and most prestigious parts of the city centre. Khreschatyk, the main street of the capital, as well as most museums, business centres, restaurants and night clubs are only minutes away from your apartment.

«RUS»
4 Hospitalnaya Str., ☎ 294-3020
Ⓜ Sport Palace
www.hotelrus.kiev.ua

Rus Hotel is situated in the center of Kyiv city in some steps from the famous Khreschatyk - a favorable place of businessmen, and tourists. Comfortable rooms, full range of the restaurant services, conference hall with audio- and video equipment with capacity up to 300 persons are to your services.

VOZDVIZHENSKY
60, Vozdvizhenskaya St.
☎ 531-99-31
Ⓜ Kontraktovaya Sq.

The hotel is placed in the heart of historic and cultural center of the city, a few steps of Andreyevsky Spusk. At your service there are comfortable rooms with mini bar, international and local phone, line, satellite broadcasting and air-conditioners. Every morning in cafe-bar smorgasbord is served. Its price is included in the cost of the room.

EATING OUT

Wandering in the streets and sightseeing, you will definitely become hungry, or as Ukrainians use to say, walk yourself into an appetite. There are many bars, cafes and restaurants in Kyiv to satisfy any taste. You can have a snack in a bistro or relax with a cup of coffee in the terrace of a small cafe. For those wishing to enjoy a nice evening out, there are many places where you can not only eat different succulent dishes, but also listen to live music and dance. If you need a business lunch or dinner - visit a quiet restaurant. And in case you are a fan of a certain cuisine - the best cooks are waiting for you.

In a bistro

WORKING HOURS

The restaurants are usually open from 11:00 a.m. until midnight, although many of them work on the last-client basis. Restaurants at night cubs and big hotels work round the clock. Only a reservation will guarantee you supper. In the hot season all tables out on the terraces may be occupied, while the inside will likely be empty.

MENU

Restaurants, which are frequently visited by foreign tourists, will have menus in English. Vegetarian dishes are not available everywhere, but can be done at your request.

DRESS

Official dress is a customary in only a few restaurants, although Kyivans traditionally tend to dress well, so wearing a skiing costume or SCUBA gear will not make you feel comfortable.

PRICES AND TIPS

Most restaurants accept the major credit cards, but it is better to determine in advance whether or not your credit card will be accepted. Although food is not expensive in Kyiv in comparison with European prices, the range of prices may by very wide. The cheapest dinner will cost you about $10, and connoisseurs of delicacy follow the motto "The price does not matter". It is common, and courteous, to leave a 10% tip for the waiter.

FAST FOOD RESTAURANTS

American pizza company   ☎ 228-48-85
Mak Smak.
■ 2, Besarabskaya Sq.   ☎ 234-84-84
■ 14, Kreshchatik St.
■ Pecherskaya" metro station
Rondo-pizza. 52 d, Artema St.   ☎ 246-92-20
Shvydko.
■ Underground passage at Maydan Nezalezhnosti
■ The Southern Railway Station
■ The "Square" book market under the Slava Square
Shelter. 15, Kreshchatik St.   ☎ 228-55-77

Cherry-cake with whipped cream and chocolate

INTERNATIONAL CUISINE

There are many national restaurants in Kyiv. You will find a big choice of traditional Japanese dishes in *Tokyo Restaurant*. The classical Italian "pasta" is waiting for you in *Apollo*. In the *Le Grand Cafe* the best of Ukrainian cuisine harmonizes with the best of the French. A gastronomic excursion around the world of Slavonic food is waiting for you at the restaurant *"Za Dvoma Zaytsyamy"*. It is impossible to visit Kyiv without meeting Ukrainian national food (see 186 - 187). In *Tsarskoye Selo Restaurant* all the dishes are prepared in a real Ukrainian oven after old recipes. *Cossack Mamay Restaurant* will treat you with the favorite dishes of Ukrainian hetmans.

CAFES

Real connoisseurs will certainly like the exotic atmosphere of the cosy *Caffa Cafe* and they will be pleasantly surprised by the wide choice of coffees, which aroma tickles nostrils from a half-a-block distance. In addition to coffee and coffee cocktails, the *Passage Coffee House* offers elegant little pastries and splendid cakes. *Bon-Bon Cafe* works 24 hours. You can have breakfast here and order a lovely delicacy to enjoy at home.

BARS

Alcoholic drinks are sold without restrictions and at any time of the day. Kyiv bars are places to meet and socialize. People come here to relax after work. The atmosphere in the bars is especially lively on Friday nights and on weekends. So we recommend booking seats in advance. The main course is a wide variety of reasonably priced beer; but the various appetizers may be quite expensive.

Tokyo Restaurant

FAST FOOD RESTAURANTS

The Ukrainian restaurant *"Shvydko"* (fast), which focuses on more traditional Ukrainian dishes, is proving to be competition for *McDonald's*. Included in the menu are salads, soups, vareniki and beer - all food is of domestic production, and the prices are unpretentious (dinner costs about 8 UAH - a little more then $1,5). Practically all the metropolitan pizza houses offer you the choice of take-out food, and many provide delivery service as well. The large variety of dishes and very reasonable prices (dinner - about $5) are attractive.

Little sweet tooth

The waiters' strike

Among the most influential trade unions of this city at the beginning of the 20th century was the union of waiters and valets. It would seem, that people of such a profession have no such problems with work conditions, as would have loaders or metalworkers. But they also had to fight for their rights. First of all, they had the longest workday, which reached 17-18 hours. Secondly, the owners demanded an unreasonably high share of the tips, which was far too high. Victualers also tried to get their piece of the cake, demanding deposits on dinnerware and fresh tablecloths. So in 1909 the union gave permission for the strike of the waiters of "Chateau de Fleur" - the most popular cafe in Kyiv. For the duration of the strike the strikers were supported by the union, getting 50 kopeks a day. The owners were taken aback. Losses grew with every passing day, and it was impossible to find decent substitutes for the professional and well-schooled waiters. And the strikers won. The owners had to reduce their appetites. .

These conventional signs will keep you from getting lost in Kyiv's gastronomic diversity. The variety of services, working hours, price categories, national cuisines, - all these will help you in choosing a restaurant, bar or cafe.

Price of a dinner of 3 dishes for one person

① - from $10 to $20
② - from $20 to $40
③ - from $40 and higher

Hours of work

⋈ Uniform		🍲 Set menu	
🦆 Live music		P Car park	
🛵 Delivery		🍸 Menu for children	
🍴 Order of a table		🍼 Conveniences for children	
🥃 Bar		💳 Payment by credit card	
🍶 Wine card		♿ Conveniences for disabled person	
⛩ Summer terrace		🌳 Calm restaurant	
V Vegetarian cuisine		$ Currency exchange	

TOKYO
10, Zoologicheskaya St.
☎ 490-06-04 12:00 - 24:00
Ⓜ Lukyanovskaya, Polytechnic Institute

 東京 TOKIO

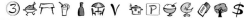 ③ 🛵🍴🥃 🍶⛩ V 🍲P🍸🍼💳🌳 $

The luxurious design of the restaurant creates Oriental mysterious spirit and makes you forget the rush of a big city.
The menu offers a wide choice of original Japanese cuisine: authentically prepared sushi, sashimi, chirashi, sushi-rolls, tempura, yakitori, teriyaki, exotic salads etc.

Enjoy your time at VIP room (with karaoke), share fresh atmosphere of the cozy summer terrace with your friends.

Business lunches, take-aways and deliveries by order are also at your convenience.

IRISH PUB "O'BRIENS"
17 a, Mikhaylovskaya St.
☎ 229-15-84
www.obriens.kiev.ua
 8:00 - 02:00 Ⓜ Zolotiye Vorota

 ③ 🦆🛵🍴🥃 🍶 V 🍲P💳 $

In a cosy Irish interior you can dine on traditional Irish and European dishes and the best of Ukrainian, Irish, German and Dutch beer... Also available are Satellite TV channels, big screen, darts. 8:00 - 12:00 - breakfast, 12:00 -15:00 - business lunch, 17:00 - 19:00 - "Happy hour" - 25% discount for beer.

Восток
11 Naberezhno-Khreschytikska Str.
☎ 416-53-75 Ⓜ Pochtovaya Square
 12:00 - up to the last client

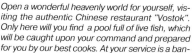 ② 🍶 V P🌳 $

Open a wonderful heavenly world for yourself, visiting the authentic Chinese restaurant "Vostok". Only here will you find a pool full of live fish, which will be caught upon your command and prepared for you by our best cooks. At your service is a banquet-hall with karaoke. Light music and a cosy atmosphere will help you to divert you from everyday problems.

Le Grand Café

4, Muzeyny Lane ☎ 228-72-08
www.legrandcafe.kiev.ua
🕐 Restaurant: Mon.-Sat. 12:00-24:00; Piano bar:
Mon.-Sun 11:30-2:00 Ⓜ Maydan Nezalezhnosti

Both halls captivate one with their excellent taste, the style of the interior made by well-known French designers L.Velfling and D.P. de Richmond, high level of service, and refined food turn the meal into gastronomic theatre. Wine card will satisfy the most demanding gourmets. Arrangement of presentations, parties, press-conferences, fourshets.

TENERIPHE

49, Gogolevskaya St. ☎ 216-75-71
🕐 12:00 - 02:00 Ⓜ Lukiyanovskaya

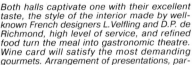

On Canary Islands there is an island of the same name. It is called "Canary Pearl". Restaurant-bar "Teneriphe" can be called "pearl of cookery art". If you decided to meet your friends in apleasant atmosphere, visit our restaurant. You will be pleasantly surprised by our choice of refined dishes, many of which are only available here.

SWING

11, Vladimirskaya St. ☎ 229-28-65
🕐 8:00 - 24:00 Ⓜ Maydan Nezalezhnosti

Restaurant - stylish interior, cozy decor. Every evening - live jazz from 20:00 to 23:00, the best jazz bands of Kyiv, cuisine in Fusion style, culinary masterpieces made by virtuoso cook. Pub - big screen for watching sport programs and news, range of dishes and drinks will satisfy the needs of the most fastidious gourmet.

AKAPULKO

112 a, Saksaganskogo St. ☎ 235-4097
🕐 11:00 - up to the last client
Ⓜ University, Vokzal'naya

A Latin American restaurant situated in the centre of Kyiv. The interior consists of two halls and a bar with cosy booths which facilitate relaxation and carry one away to the sunny south. The exotic dishes and seafood are the pride of the menu. You will enjoy soft tequila and fiery cocktails. In the evening we invite you to listen to live music. We organize banquets and fourshets.

KNIAZHIY GRAD

2, Bolshaya Zhitomirskaya St.
☎ 229-86-11, 228-37-29
🕐 12:00 - 24:00 Ⓜ Zolotiye Vorota

In the heart of the historic city, near Saint Sophiya and Mikhaylovsky Golden Domed Monasteries there is a cosy restaurant in Old Kyiv style. Here Ukrainian cuisine is combined with European standards of services. We also offer banquet and fourshet, service for special occasions and presentations.

GALLEON

55, Turgenevskaya St. ☎ 246-87-07
🕐 12:00 - up to the last clien
Ⓜ Lukiyanovskaya

In the romantic atmosphere of the Galleon bar, everyone will feel like a courageous captain. Magic cocktails will ignite your imagination. The experts will be able to appreciate the vine card at its true value. And dishes of world cuisine will satisfy the needs of the most fastidious gourmet.

RESTAURANTS AND CAFES:

Black Orange.
29-a, Sagaydachnogo St. ☎ 416-35-67
Chesky Lev-Pub. 3, Lysenko St. ☎ 234-46-37
O'Brian Irish Pub.
17-a, Mikhaylovskaya St. ☎ 229-15-84
Alligator. 1/1, Lukashevich St. ☎ 472-85-59
Alkatras. 67, Saksaganskogo St. ☎ 227-12-78
Uncle Sam. 37, Zhilyanskaya St. ☎ 227-20-00
Arizona Barbeque.
25, Naberezhno-Kreshchatitskaya St. ☎ 416-24-38
Arlekino pizza.
2, T.Shevchenko Blvd. ☎ 235-83-43
Azteka. 31-a, Vorovskogo St. ☎ 216-86-56
Bankir. 14, Institutskaya St. ☎ 293-28-91
Berliner Baren. 30-a, Artyoma St. ☎ 246-98-94
Stepan's Blinchiki. 36, Spasskaya St. ☎ 416-32-53
Bon-Bon. 15, Kreshchatic St. ☎ 228-27-82
Bon-Bon. 3, Leontovich St. ☎ 244-35-64
Venetia.
3-a, Rusanovskaya Naberezhnaya St. ☎ 555-17-30
Vinshtub. 9, Andreyevskaya St. ☎ 416-82-77
Vostok.
11, Naberezhno - Kreshchatitskaya St. ☎ 416-53-75
Vydubichi.
5, Naberezhno-Pecherskaya Road. ☎ 294-71-48
Gavrosh. 3/7, Mezhigorskaya St. ☎ 416-55-24
Galleon. 55, Turgenevskaya St. ☎ 246-87-07
Gold Cup. 22, Moskovskaya St. ☎ 254-22-04
Da Vinci. Europeyskaya Sq. ☎ 229-00-59
Da Mario. 52, Saksaganskogo St. ☎ 220-80-62
Dezha Vu. 30, B.Khmel'nitskogo St. ☎ 235-98-02
Desperados. 20, Artyoma St. ☎ 216-31-98
Dixieland.
14/2, Kirilo-Mefodiyevskaya St. ☎ 274-82-28
Center of tea art
7 Blvrd. Druzhby Narodiv
front door 4, Code 2 + 6, Apt. 60 ☎ 451-42-83
Coffee House. "Passage".
15, Kreshchatik St. ☎ 229-12-09
Za Dvoma Zaytsyamy.
34, Andreyevskiy Spusk. ☎ 416-35-16
Zaporozhye. 27, Sagaydachnogo St. ☎ 417-42-83
Cossack Mamay. 4, Proreznaya St. ☎ 228-42-73
Carmen. 7, Moskovskaya St. ☎ 291-48-77
Kioto. 2, Raisy Okipnoy St. ☎ 516-21-45
Kazachen'ki. 10, Sagaydachnogo St. ☎ 416-15-10
Kazachok. 118, Kirovogradskaya St. ☎ 250-93-48
Le Jardin (River Palace). Embankment,
near "Dnieper" metro station ☎ 416-82-04

Le Grand Cafe. 4, Muzeyny Line. ☎ 490-55-40
Long Fiong.
1-a, Naberezhno-Kreshchatitskaya St. ☎ 416-14-87
Miami Blues.
114, Krasnoarmeyskaya St. ☎ 252-87-21
Mimino. 10-a, Spasskaya St. ☎ 417-35-45
Monte Cristo.
27, T. Shevchenko Blvd. ☎ 224-61-63
Nobu. 12, Shota Rustaveli St. ☎ 246-77-34
Nox. 111/113, Krasnoarmeyskaya St. ☎ 269-59-56
Non-Stop. 6, Pobedy Ave. ☎ 216-40-73
Obolon. 32, Belorusskaya St. ☎ 219-31-43
Obolon na Podole.
71, Konstantinovskaya St. ☎ 417-33-59
Timeout. 50,Gorkogo St. ☎ 248-73-96
Pervak. 2, Rognedinskaya St. ☎ 235-09-52
Piano-Bar. 15/1, Frunze St. ☎ 463-76-37
Eric's Beer. 20, Krasnoarmeyskaya St. ☎ 235-94-72
Pivnoy Dvor. 49/51, Zhilyanskaya St. ☎ 246-64-44
Beer Club. 1/2, Simirenko St. ☎ 475-01-01
Pilzner Bar. 20, Pushkinskaya St. ☎ 234-31-11
Richelieu. 23, Krasnoarmeyskaya St. ☎ 235-88-62
Rostik's. 57/3, Krasnoarmeyskaya St. ☎ 227-37-75
Ryna. 44, Shchorsa St. ☎ 295-42-19
S Utra Do Nochi. 6, Sagaydachnogo St. ☎ 416-52-53
Stena. 2, Bessarabskaya square ☎ 235-80-45
San Tori. 41, Sagaydachnogo St. ☎ 462-49-94
Seoul. 160, Gorkogo St. ☎ 268-55-29
USSR. 42/1, Yanvarskogo Vosstaniya St. ☎ 290-30-66
Stary Podol. 19, Khoryva St. ☎ 416-05-30
Tequila House. 8, Spasskaya St. ☎ 417-03-58
Tenerife. 49, Gogolevskaya St. ☎ 216-75-71
Tokyo. 10, Zoologicheskaya St. ☎ 490-06-04
U Hetmana.
6, Yanvarskogo Vosstaniya St. ☎ 290-93-98
U Lukyana. 3, Degtyariovskaya St. ☎ 246-88-65
U Panikovskogo.
8, Prorizna St. ☎ 536-17-17
Haifa. 57, Konstantinovskaya St. ☎ 417-25-12
Hata Karasya. 139, Pobedy Av. ☎ 451-90-87
Khorivets. 23, Khoryva St. ☎ 416-02-38
Hutorok. 10-a, Naberezhno-
Kreshchatitskaya St. Berth #1 ☎ 416-80-39
Tsarskoye Selo.
42, Yanvarskogo Vosstaniya St. ☎ 573-97-75
Charm. 11, Mariny Raskovoy St. ☎ 517-17-97
Chateau de Fleur. 24, Kreshchatik St. ☎ 228-78-00
Shchekavitsa.
46/52, Konstantinovskaya St. ☎ 417-14-72
Egoist.
44, Moskovskaya St. ☎ 290-22-22

ENTERTAINMENT AND LEISURE

IN THE OPEN AIR

Romantic dates, unusual acquaintances, new encounters, vivid impressions… The most popular places of recreation of Kyivans in good weather are of course beautiful parks: elegant Kyivans and even more elegant guests of the capital with dignity walk in the alleys of Mariinsky (see 67) and Kreshchatiy (see 66) parks, or rest on benches in the shade of chestnuts and limes.

In the spring, when the lilacs are in bloom, every true Kyivan goes to the Gryshko Botanical Garden (see 144) to admire the tumult of colours.

In the last weekend of May, when the day of Kyiv is celebrated, a flood of people comes to Andreyevsky Spusk (see 46-50) to listen to street musicians, see a fancy-dress play in open air, buy a picture or some trifle from the craftsmen, selling their wares from stands.

On holidays in Maydan Nezalezhnosti (see 106) Ukrainian and foreign singers often give concerts. Here come all the youth of the city, and people of older generations do not object to dancing under the star-studded sky.

As Kyivans love to walk, the city authorities have decided to close traffic in Kreshchatik (see 100-106) on holidays and days off. Traffic is opened only late at night. Military parades, which are considered to be more a tribute to Soviet traditions and an interesting event, than a demonstration of military power, are held along the Kreshchatik on Victory Day (May 9) and Independence of Ukraine Day (August 24).

The playground

Firework displays are quite popular. On holidays, when it becomes dark, a multitude of people - families, friends, couples - come in the streets to marvel at the impressive fireballs, exploding in the night sky. It is better to see the salute from the banks of the Dnieper and from Maydan Nezalezhnosti. As a rule, the salute starts round 22:00, although it has never begun on time up to now. From half past ten all people are in excitement. When the salute starts, the people usually compete who shouts "Hooray!" louder - where else will you have the possibility to shout at the peak of your voice?

In general they like holidays in Kyiv, wait for them and try to make

The small horse-rider

the best of them: visit friends; invite friends and relatives, spent some time in the streets of the native city.

IN PIROGOVO

Save a separate day for this amazing trip. It is better to start off in the morning, to be able to see all the interesting places of the Museum of Folk Architecture and Way of Life (see 143), listen to folk musicians, ride a horse (do not miss the opportunity to become a real Cossack for awhile time). In the open air you are sure to get hungry, then you will have the opportunity to fully experience all the magnificence of Ukrainian national cuisine:

Fancy-worker

your mouth will water from the smell, coming from the shynok, and you will remember for the rest of your life that Cossack kulish is a dish of the gods. Visit the outdoor museum - and you will certainly wish to return here once more.

At the exhibition of flowers

Without irony we can say that choice of entertainment is an exclusively serious matter. In order to enjoy your leisure time to the fullest, you must make proper preparations. And thanks to these signs, your entertainment choices in Kyiv will be successful.

🎀	official clothes	P	parking
🐦	live music	🕺	strip show
🍴	restaurants	⚫	billiard
🪑	booking a table	🌐	roulette
🍸	bar	♤	playing cards
💳	credit card payment	🎰	slot machine
$	currency exchange	📼	disco

ALONG THE DNIEPER

A relaxing boat cruise will leave unforgettable impressions whether it be a romantic tour for two or a jubilee celebration with friends. In Podol, near "Pochtovaya Square" metro station, there is the River Boat Station (see 54). Motor ships of the touring class are equipped with bars and restaurants. Some owners of the ships arrange fireworks for the clients at night-time (on a prior order). But a simple hour or two watching from the deck a picturesque panorama of the Dnieper hills and drinking cold beer, isn't it a rest in a hot summer day?

RIVER BOAT STATION
3, Pochtovaya Sq.
Ⓜ Pochtovaya Square
Excursion-Passenger Agency
☎ 416-12-29
Tour services ☎ 462-50-19

At a berth

"PLAZMA" ENTERTINMENT COMPLEX
5-a V.Poryka Str. ☎ 433-67-78 Ⓜ Nyvky
Open twenty four rs.

Disco, restaurant, cocktail bar, striptease bar, billiard, games' hall. Original Club's concept makes it different from the others. The interior decoration's hot, bright colors, "leading" program, comfortable atmosphere - what else does one need to be relaxed? Come and make sure yourself.

BUDAPEST CLUB

The night club, casino, disco
3 Leontovycha Str ☎ 234-03-47 Ⓜ Teatralna
☑ Casino-open twenty four hours; night
club- from 22:00 till 5:00; striptease bar and
disco - from 23:00. Admission free
(Night club: UAH30.00 for men).

*American roulette, Caribbean poker with the
card change, dark boxing, possibility of a
high stakes game, Black Jack, game
machines.*

"JOSS"

NIGHT CLUB, CASINO, DISCO
2 Raisy Okypnoi Str. , Hotel "Tourist"
☎ 516-86-74, 552-50-91 Ⓜ Livoberezhna
☑ Open twenty four hours. Casino admission:
UAH50.00, on Wednesdays - UAH100.00.

*11 games tables, stakes from UAH2.00 till
UAH10 000.00. Roulette, poker, Black Jack.
Playing off of money prizes: 2 times/ week -
on Wednesdays and Fridays. Live jazz
evenings. Gratuitous bar for the players.*

"ILIUSIA" (ILLUSION) NIGHT CLUB

42/80 Saksaganskoho Str.,
☎ 246-62-76
☑ from 18:00 till 6:00
Ⓜ L'va Tolstogo
Admission free (Show - UAH50.00).

*The unforgettable rest and dainty cuisine.
Plunge into real wishes and realized dreams'
world. Magical show of the strip theater.*

"MAYAK" BILLIARD CLUB

13 Pr. Chervonykh Kozakiv
☎ 464-69-01
Ⓜ Petrivka ☑ Open twenty four hours.

*The excellent Club's equipment meets the
requirements of international Standards. You'll
see the high class play, to compete against worthy adversary, and the novice players shall obtain
a qualified marker's council. The rich wines' card,
excellent dishes of Ukrainian and European cuisine are waiting for you. One may organize a business meeting at the VIP-halls or family feasts.*

"ZAIR" CLUB

15 Griboedova Str., Irpin town
☎ (297) 62-248
☑ Open from Tuesday till Sunday: 21:00-6:00.

*In 15 minutes of drive from Kyiv. Two dance
grounds, staggering light and sound equipment. Disco, striptease bar, casino, billiard,
game machines, electronic roulette.
Restaurant is open every day from 12:00
and till the last client.*

CASINO "SALUTE INTERNATIONAL"

11-a Sichnevogo Povstannia Str.,
☎ 290-31-33
Ⓜ Arsenalna
☑ Open twenty four hours. Admission free.

*Amicable atmosphere, international class
personnel, comfortable interior, quiet ambience. Open twenty four hours: American
roulette, Black Jack, seven cards' poker,
game machines, gratuitous bar for permanent clients, VIP-Hall.*

"PORT" DISCO BAR

1 Blvrd. T.Shevchenka
☎ 235-37-51 Ⓜ Teatralna
☑ Open from 12:00 till the last client.

*A wide range of cocktails made by the profes-
sional barmen fascinates both by taste and
spectacle. Refined European culinary with
"Russian" accent shall dispose you to positive
emotions. A water pipe shall give you a possibility of relaxation after the intense day, and
the excellent music shall add a good mood.*

CORONA CLUB

4, Rognedinskaya St.
☎ 220-02-16 www.korona-club.kiev.ua
Ⓜ Sport Palace ☑ 0.00-24.00

*All the halls attract visitors due to their
extraordinary design. The convenient location in the city centre is one of the advan-
tages of the club. Corona will amaze you with
its originality. It is different in morning, after-
noon and at night, but you'll feel comfortable
at any time of the day.*

Venetian bridge

In summer, especially in July and August, it is very hot in Kyiv. The temperature often reaches 35 Celsius. A few years ago, escaping the heat, Kyivans rushed outside city limits - in the forest or summer cottages. Now people go to the Hydropark - carrying a book, a crossword or a tennis racket. And they are not disappointed. Here one can find recreation for any taste. You can make your hands sore rowing a rented boat or rush along on a scooter, imagining yourself the hero of "Police Academy - 6". In the big amusement park kids will have fun riding electromobiles - small replicas of real cars, while their parents can test their vestibular apparatus on an extreme merry-go-round. A sports ground with courts for badminton, gorodki, table tennis and tennis awaits those who love active recreation. And for those who like to shoot, there is a shooting gallery and a ground for

paintball. You can renew your strengths by a copious lunch in one of the numerous cafes and restaurants.

Those who prefer to spend the day lounging in the sun can go to one of the well-groomed beaches. Umbrellas, trestlebeds, cloakrooms, chaise lounges, pure sand... You can enjoy all this in "Oasis" (to the left of the walkbridge) or in "Sun City" (to the right). There are also grounds for volleyball, a swimming pool and a slide, which will take you directly into the water.

In the evening you will be whirled in dance and gamble. Professional tables for billiards will give players the opportunity to feel the excitement of a

well-marked ball. In the casino "Vasilek" you will forget about time: roulette, poker and even... cockroach races for those, who love exotics. In Hydropark you can dance anywhere you like (you only need the desire to do so), for music comes from everywhere. But those who really love dancing

At the athletic field

prefer the night disco "Dance Club 28".

So, 10 minutes away from downtown - and you are in the world of sun and pleasure.

Pleasure boat

"Sun City" beach

Entertainment and leisure

AT NIGHT

Industry of night entertainment in Kyiv is developed practically as in any large European city. The choice is so large that it is hard to choose really. A lot of cafes and bars are open through the night, offering entertaining programs. About 80 discos and night-clubs are available. Casinos wait for hazardous and venture-some people to taste Fortuna. To take delight of the night Kyiv in full, plan everything before-hand: where to eat, where to dance, where to listen music, and where to play roulette or black-jack. A few of night-clubs are open for customary clients. As a rule everybody can have a good time there. However, when a show of a star occurs a good class club, to get in there is not easy, so in such days you should to book tickets in advance. The prices to enter depend on the content of the program and may vary from 30 to 100 UAH. Women are allowed with price reduction or free. Sometimes a drink is included in the price. Majority of the enter-tainments offer strip shows of different grade of openness and sight. Concerts, thematic parties with contests and awards are

Artists of a night show

Roulette

NIGHT CLUBS, CASINOS

First. 12, Gospitalnaya St.	☎ 220-19-78
Billiard Darts. 38/1, Polevaya St., bldg 24	☎ 441-17-14
Bingo. 112, Pobedy Ave.	☎ 444-25-55
Brakes. English Billiard Club. 23-b, Perova Blvd.	☎ 512-97-73
Budapest Club. 3, Leontovicha St.	☎ 228-28-84
Gabriela. 1/2, Kreshchatic St.	☎ 228-88-21
Zaporozhye. 27-a, Sagaydachnogo St.	☎ 416-45-08
Cabaret. 12, Gospitalnaya St.	☎ 294-30-06
Karambol. 10/1, Gorodetskogo St.	☎ 228-29-70
Caribbean Club. 4, Kominterna St.	☎ 244-42-90
Kletka. 3, Kutuzova Line	☎ 573-88-48
Corona-Club. 4, Rognedenskaya St.	☎ 220-02-16
Red and Black. 24, Pobedy Ave.	☎ 274-09-53
Nica. 16, Dovzhenko St.	☎ 455-56-44
Night Mask. 19, Shota Rustaveli St.	☎ 246-78-29
New York. 2, Perova Blvd.	☎ 558-25-45
Opera. 51/53, Vladimirskaya St.	☎ 228-28-36
Restown Club. 3, Zheleznyaka St.	☎ 444-81-50
River Palace. Naberezhnoye Highway	☎ 416-82-04
Rumors. 51-a, Garmatnaya St.	☎ 484-98-64
Rumta. 10/37, Industrialnaya St., 3 floor	☎ 446-64-48
Red Lion. 27-a, Kreshchatic St.	☎ 228-67-46
Salute. 11-a, Yanvarskogo Vosstaniya St.	☎ 290-31-33
Sokol. 20, Garmatnaya St.	☎ 458-44-77
Split. 6, Proreznaya St.	☎ 228-58-77
Tea Club 7 Blvrd. Druzhby Narodiv front door 4, Code 2 + 6, Apt. 60	☎ 451-42-83
Strike Bowling Club. 84, Pobedy Ave.	☎ 442-64-64
Fiesta. 115, Gorkogo St.	☎ 269-40-29
Chicago. 3, Raisy Okipnoy St.	☎ 517-41-48
Storm. 8/4, Zhelyabova St.	☎ 459-65-11
Evrica. 30-a, Lesia Ukrainka Blvd.	☎ 295-90-81
Eldorado. 34, Lesia Ukrainka Blvd.	☎ 295-49-97
Eltorito. 16, Vladimiro-Lybidskaya St.	☎ 269-31-80
Etual. 2, Grinchenko St.	☎ 228-37-03

In Joss Night Club

held in the clubs. Discos wait for dancers, and the doors of nice and cozy little restaurants, which menus contain "musical dishes", are open for live music livers. For billiard admirers, specialized clubs offer amateur and professional tables.

CINEMA

These days Kyivans go to the cinema less often than 10 years ago. But lately some modern cinemas with the latest technical equipment have opened: big screen, stereo sound and so on. The most popular are "Kinopalats" and " Ukraina". The most fashionable films, mainly American ones, are shown there. "Orbita" shows stereo pictures.

TICKETS AND PRICES

Phone a cinema in order to determine the repertoire and time of performance. You can buy tickets directly from the ticket-office or book them by phone (voice records are in Ukrainian but you can book the tickets in Russian too). If the film is new you should reserve the ticket a few days earlier, especially for the night show or at weekend. In the modern cinemas a ticket costs 20 - 50 UAH.

But in a week or two you can see the same films for 6 - 18 UAH in the halls remaining from the Soviet times ("Kinopanorama", "Zhovten" and others).

REPERTOIRE

To know the repertoires of the cinemas, theatres and concert halls, you can look through "Delovaya Stolitsa" weekly newspaper. Every Monday they issue "Afisha" magazine, which will not only tell you "what" and "where", but also whether or not it is worth watching.

**The auditorium
of Ukraina Cinema**

CINEMA

Zhovten	26, Konstantinovskaya St.
	☎ 417-2702 (advertising), 417-3004 (booking)
Kiev	19 Chervonoarmiyska Str.,
	☎ 221-08-81 (advertising)
Kievskaya Rus	93, Artyoma St.
	☎ 213-2309 (advertising), 216-7474 (booking)
Kinopalats	1, Institutskaya St. ☎ 228-72-23 (advertising)
Kinopanorama	19, Shota Rustaveli St.
	☎ 227-11-35 (advertiing)
Orbita	29, Kreshchatic St.
	☎ 228-18-49 (advertising), 234-13-86 (booking)
Ukraina	5, Gorodetskogo St.
	☎ 229-63-01 (advertising), 229-67-50 (booking)

Zhovten Cinema

TO THE THEATRE

There are about 30 theatres in Kyiv. The assortment of performances is quite large - from opera and ballet to puppet show, from classical to avant-garde. Concerts of orchestral and chamber music are essential parts of the theatre repertoire of the capital. The plays start at 19:00, and at weekends some stages give morning shows (at 12:00 or 13:00).

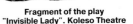

Fragment of the play "Invisible Lady". Koleso Theatre

PRICES AND TICKETS

You can buy tickets directly from the theatre box offices, at the ticket stands and stalls in the metro or from theatre agents. The prices depend on the demand of the play and may range from 2 UAH for a children's show to 1000 UAH for a concert of a foreign star.

CLASSICAL MUSIC

T.Shevchenko Ukraine National Opera
5, Lysenko St.
Ⓜ Teatral'naya
☎ 229-11-69

The main theatre stage of the land (see 110). The repertoire numbers over 50 plays. The popular opera shows are given in the original languages. One of the latest ballet productions is "Vienna Waltz" on Straus music.

The Conservatory

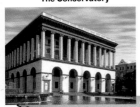

N.Lysenko Ukraine National Philharmonic
2, Vladimirskiy Spusk St.
Ⓜ Kreshchatic
☎ 228-16-97

Due to the exclusive acoustics the audience have a unique opportunity to dive into the world of classical music (see 66).

National Organ and Chamber Music House
77, Krasnoarmeyskaya St.
Ⓜ Ukraine Palace
☎ 268-31-86

It is situated in the building of the St Nikolay Catholic Church, which is known with its unique architecture. This is a place of pilgrimage for intellectual chamber music lovers (see 131).

CONCERT HALLS

Ukraina Palace
103, Krasnoarmeyskaya St.
Ⓜ Ukraina Palace
☎ 247-24-76

Not only concerts of the world stars or the Russian performers desperately loved by the Philistines are held here but pre-sentations of the state awards. In the days of the winter school vacation children come here to see the "Main Christmas Tree" of the land (see 132).

International Culture and Art Center
1, Institutskaya St.
Ⓜ Kreshchatik
☎ 228-74-82

Many people still call it "October Palace". Concerts and recitals are held here (see 72).

OPERETTA

Kyiv State Operetta Theatre
53/3, Krasnoarmeyskaya St.
Ⓜ Respublikanskiy Stadium
☎ 227-26-30

The repertoire includes the operettas and musicals of Ukrainian and foreign composers, performed by talented actors (see 130).

Let's make Sara Bernard for the five

Over a hundred years ago Sara Bernard visited Kyiv on a concert tour. Everybody wanted to see the famous French actress but the tickets were expensive. Still the quick witted Kyivites found the solution. In those days the plays were held with little intervals. If a play with Sara Bernard consisted of five acts, five people shared the ticket. The first one watched the first act; in the interval the second one exchanged with the first, and so on. And then all five of them could boast of seeing the great Sara Bernard.

DRAMATIC THEATRES
I.Franko Ukraine Drama Theatre
3, I.Franko Sq.
Ⓜ Kreshchatik
☎ 229-59-91

It is famous for its rich repertoire of dramatic plays by classic and modern authors as well as the troupe of the popular actors (see 105).

Lesya Ukrainka Russian Drama Theatre
5, B.Khmel'nit-skogo St.
Ⓜ Teatral'naya
☎ 224-90-63

The "Russian Drama" troupe does not only give successful performances throughout the world, but often receive well-known theatre collec-tives from different countries on its own stage (see 112).

Left Bank Drama and Comedy Theatre
25, Brovarskaya St.
Ⓜ Levoberezhnaya
☎ 517-19-55

THEATRE TICKET BOXES
Verkhniy Val St.
(the underground passage)
☎ 416-52-88
51/53, Vladimirskaya St.
☎ 224-75-93
16, Krasnoarmeyskaya St.
☎ 224-82-34
21, Kreshchatik St.
☎ 228-76-42
Maydan Nazalezhnosti
(the underground passage)
☎ 229-28-00
19, Pobedy Ave.
☎ 274-09-80

A playbill stand

Its plays are of a stable success lately; the theatre administra-tion did not make a mistake to stake on the comedy.

Suzirya Theatre Art Studio
14a, Yaroslavov Val St.
Ⓜ Zolotiye Vorota
☎ 212-41-88

The original plays combining different genres of the art: classical drama, author song, modern choreography etc.

Koleso Theatre
8, Andreyevskiy Spusk St.
Ⓜ Kontractovaya Square
☎ 416-04-22

In the warm chamber atmos-phere of the theatre the spec-tator will feel a participant of the performance.

Fragment of the play "Red Riding Hood". Puppet theatre

THEATRE FOR CHILDREN

The Theatre for the Junior Spectator on Lipki
15/17, Lipskaya St.
Ⓜ Arsenalnaya
☎ 295-54-83

Beautiful plays after the works of the best child authors of the world are aimed at children of different ages (see 64).

The puppet theatre
29/3, Sagaydachnogo St.
Ⓜ Pochtovaya Square
☎ 416-58-58

The welcoming atmosphere will leave nobody untouched. Everything is bound to the faith of the children in fairy tales. The kids sit separately from the parents and are able to feel like experienced theatre-goers, but

The joyful clown will make adults and children laugh

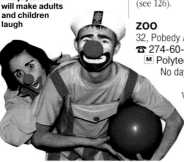

the adults also gradually become absorbed in the puppets and leave the play enlightened.

Music Theatre for children and youth
2, Mezhigorskaya St.
Ⓜ Kontraktovaya Square
☎ 416-34-24

Plays for little lovers of opera and ballet.

V.Shevchenko with his pet

CIRCUS
2, Pobedy Sq.
☎ 216-60-08
Ⓜ Vokzalnaya, University

The program is often changed. Predators and gymnasts, illusionists and clowns - you will find here anything you can think of when you hear the word "circus" (see 126).

ZOO
32, Pobedy Ave.
☎ 274-60-54
Ⓜ Polytechnic Institute"
No days off

What child will refuse a visit to the zoo (see 140)? This is also a good

At Zoo

opportunity for adults to remember their childhood. Here you will see funny monkeys, predators lazily basking in the sun, admire the exotic tapir and watch the bird life. In the zoo there are several playgrounds with swings and attractions. A "live corner" has recently opened where kids can communicate with animals: pet a goat, hold a turtle, have a closer acquaintance with brother-rabbit. Here you can buy food for animals (only 30 kopeks per pack), so you can treat a guinea pig you liked without being afraid to harm it. The worker of the zoo will advice you as to how to treat the animal and see

- Maybe they are alive?
Stone figures of mammoths in the zoo court

to it that nobody harms a small goose, lost in the grass...
The entry ticket costs 5 UAH for an adult and 1,5 UAH for a child.

GOING SHOPPING

S hopping is always pleasant, especially if you combine it with sightseeing, not forgetting to rest along the way in a summer cafe or picturesque park. There are many different shops in Kyiv. Small private boutiques selling souvenirs and foodstuff and big supermarkets, where you can find anything you need. The diversity of prices can be quite big - from moderate and reasonable to almost skyrocketing, aimed at snobs and thick wallets.

WORKING HOURS

The shops work from 10:00 to 20:00. The foodstuff shops open a little earlier - at 8:00 or 9:00. Some work until 23:00. In any district you will find shops working 24 hours a day. Their selection of wares is not very rich, but it will not let you starve in the middle of the night. Most shops do not have days off and lunch breaks.

GOING SHOPPING

If credit cards are accepted in the shop, you will see corresponding signs on the entrance door of at the cashier's office. But it would be a good idea to have some

Bread shop displays

cash on hand. In supermarkets, which recall Soviet times

("*Central Department Store*", "*Ukraina*", "*Childrens World*"), you can buy clothes, utensils, toys and many other things. Kyivans like to buy groceries in modern supermarkets, which have been recently built ("*Billa*", "*Velyka Kyshenia*" - translated as "big pocket", "*Fourshet*"). Souvenir shops are mostly located downtown. Here you can buy ceramics, original wood crafted utensils, unique handmade embroidery in the national tradition and different jewelry. We also suggest you should go to Andreyevsky Spusk (see 46), where you can find souvenirs at any taste - from a *clay dzvinochok* (bell) to a modern landscape of Kyiv.

Expensive boutiques are located in the area of Kreshchatik, Vladimirskaya, Artema, L'va Tolstogo and Krasnoarmeyskaya streets. If you are looking for an elegant coat or a stylish swimsuit, this is the place to go.

Salons and antique shops are also

located downtown. Their exquisite displays attract one's attention, causing one to first stop and look, and then go in and buy something as a memory of Kyiv.

Tray at the book market

BOOKS

The most popular bookshops are located not far from Kreshchatik Street. "*Znannya*" ("Knowledge") specializes in manuals, "*Naukova Dumka*" - in scientific literature, the name of the shop "*Mystetstvo*" (art) speaks for itself. A seven-minute walk away is situated "*Medical Book*". In front of Kreshchatik metro station is situated the shop for books in foreign languages "*Planet*".

Mechanic shopkeepers in the 19th century?

Today it seems fantastic, but around 100 years ago there was a possibility to install vending machines in Kyiv. In February 1899 the representative of the firm "Automat" from Liege came to this city to get a monopoly for supplies of vending machines, shaped as boxes for selling different wares: tobacco, stationary goods, post stamps. The same machines would polish the clients' shoes and hats for a coin. As it was written in the newspaper "Word of Kyiv", - "On every box there will be inscriptions under respective slots, so anybody will be able to claim the goods he wants from the mechanic trader". But the novelty did not settle down in Kyiv. People, not machines, continued to sell tobacco and polish shoes.

In Kyiv there are two book markets: one in open air (near Petrovka metro) and one underground (in the subterranean passageway under the Slava Square). Here you will find practically anything: from a modern detective story to a well-illustrated children's encyclopedia.

A soft toy - gift for the kids

Newspapers and magazines can be bought in big shops, "Press" kiosks, at trays in the streets and in the metro.

MARKETS AND FAIRS

Ukrainian and, especially Kyiv's, food markets (they are situated in every district) - are a unique world, functioning independently, not comparable to any thing else in life. Colourfulness and diversity of foodstuff stuns your imagination. Here you can buy home-bred eggs with miraculous orange yolks, fragrant *oliya* (vegetable oil); cottage cheese, so fat that it is cut by knife and golden *tsybulia* (onion), tied into garlands.

The further from downtown - the cheaper. The most expensive, but also the most picturesque is the Bessarabka market in the heart of the city. It is a custom to bargain with the traders. Sometimes it turns into real action: a cold beauty frantically bargains to buy some lard; an old woman, selling vegetables from her garden, generously lowers the price for a bundle of

carrots by 10 kopeks… If you come here not only for shopping, but also to get acquainted to the habits of the Kyivans, we advise you to do it in the morning of a day off: from 10 to 11 the trade is at its peak. Markets are closed on Mondays.

Seasonal and festive fairs - on Christmas, Day of Kyiv and Independence Day, take place in Kyiv. Here Ukrainian manufacturers display their products (usually the fairs are quite crowded, as the selection of goods is big, and the prices are moderate).

Fruit stand at the Bessarabka Market

ADDRESSES:

Supermarkets
Velyka Kyshenia.
57, Zheleznodorozhnoye Shosse ☎ 461-99-21
Tico-market. 96, Gonchara St. ☎ 216-26-86
Furshet. 165, Gorkiy St. ☎ 252-80-28

Department stores
Pecherskiy. 4, Suvorova St. ☎ 290-81-00
Central Universal Shop. 2, B.Khmel'nitskogo St. ☎ 224-95-05
Ukraine. 3, Pobedy Sq. ☎ 274-50-22
Children's World. 3, Malyshko St. ☎ 559-21-70

Boutiques
Image studio. 8, Bratskaya St., floor 2 ☎ 416-85-88
Anna Babenko. 9, Bolshaya Zhitomirskaya St. ☎ 228-02-74
Olga&Symonov. 2-a, Chekistov Lane ☎ 253-74-01
Sergey Byzov. 25, Sofievskaya St. ☎ 228-81-90

Souvenirs and jewelry
Antique. 36-b B.Khmel'nitskogo St. ☎ 224-12-53
Jindo. 1/2, Kreshchatik St. ☎ 229-87-41
Perlyna. 21, Kreshchatik St. ☎ 228-17-73
Ukrainian Souvenirs. 23, Krasnoarmeyskaya St. ☎ 224-85-16
Art salon. 27/1, B.Khmel'nitskogo St. ☎ 235-63-25

Flowers
Christine. 2, Pirogova St. ☎ 224-09-90
Roksolana. 3-b, B.Khmel'nitskogo St. ☎ 462-01-33
Kvity. 23, Shota Rustaveli St. ☎ 244-33-35
Kvity-Ukraine. 49, Artema St. ☎ 216-42-90

Books
Books supermarket "Bukva".
21/61 L'va Tolstogo Str. ☎ 224-81-97
Znannya. 44, Kreshchatik St. ☎ 229-10-45
Mystetstvo. 24, Kreshchatik St. ☎ 228-36-68
Planet. 30, Kreshchatik St. ☎ 224-03-73

Kyiv florist

PHRASEBOOK

My name is ...	Меня зовут ...	Menia zovut ...
I live in ...	Я живу в ...	Ya zhivu v ...
I like Kyiv	Мне нравится в Киеве	Mne nravitsa v Kieve
I need an interpreter	Мне нужен переводчик	Mne nuzhen perevodchik
How are things going?	Как дела?	Kak dela?
Great!	Прекрасно!	Prekrasno!
I like to travel	Я люблю путешествовать	Ya l'ubl'u puteshestvovat'

Good day	Добрый день	Dobriy den'
Welcome	Добро пожаловать	Dobro pozhalovat'
Glad to see you	Очень рад(а) вас видеть	Ochen' rad(a) vas videt'
Thank you	Спасибо	Spasibo
You are welcome	Пожалуйста	Pozhaluysta
Sorry	Извините	Izvinite
I agree	Я согласен (согласна)	Ya soglasen (soglasna)
Unfortunately I can't	К сожалению, я не могу	K sozhaleniu, ya ne mogu
See you	До встречи	Do vstrechi
Goodbye	До свидания	Do svidania
Have a nice day	Всего хорошего	Vsego horoshego
Come again	Приходите к нам еще	Prihodite k nam eshcho
I want to invite you to ...	Я хочу пригласить вас к...	Ya hochu priglasit' vas k ...
Give my greetings to ...	Передайте от меня привет господже (господину)...	Peredaite ot menia privet gospoje (gospodinu)
Farewell	Счастливого пути	Schastlivogo puti
Good night	Спокойной ночи!	Spokoynoy nochi!
Happy holiday	Поздравляю с праздником	Pozdravliayu s prazdnikom
I wish you happiness	Желаю счастья	Jelayu schastia

City	Город	Gorod
Street	Улица	Ulitsa
Next stop	Следующая остановка	Sleduyushchaia ostanovka
Hotel	Гостиница	Gostinitsa
I need to make a call	Мне нужно позвонить	Mne nuzhno pozvonit'
Take me to this address	Отвезите меня по этому адресу	Otvezite menia po etomu adresu
Show me on the map the road to ...	Покажите мне на карте дорогу к ...	Pokajite mne na karte dorogu k ...
I am lost	Я заблудился (заблудилась)	Ya zabludilsia (zabludilas')
Write me the address	Напишите мне адрес	Napishite mne adres
What is the name of this avenue?	Как называется этот проспект?	Kak nazivaetsia etot prospekt?
What direction should I take to get to ...?	В каком направлении мне идти к...?	V kakom napravlenii mne idti k ...?
On the left (To the left)	Слева (налево)	Sleva (nalevo)
On the right (To the right)	Справа (направо)	Sprava (napravo)
Bon appetite!	Приятного аппетита!	Priyatnogo apetita!
Coffee with cream	Кофе со сливками	Kofe so slivkami
Ice-cream	Мороженое	Morojenoe
Cheers! (toast)	За здравие! (тост)	Za zdravie (tost)

I'm not feeling well	Я плохо себя чувствую	Ya ploho sebia chustvuyu
Do you have this medicine?	У вас есть это лекарство?	U vas est' eto lekarstvo?
Call a doctor (the police)	Срочно вызовите врача (милицию)	Srochno vizovite vracha (militsiyu)
Hospital	Больница	Bol'nitsa

Wet paint	Осторожно, окрашено!	Ostorozhno, okrasheno!
No smoking!	Курить воспрещается!	Kurit' vospreshchaetsia!